JUS'
GOOD THING

A **Faith** Inspired Recipe for **Optimism**

Nancy Pelander Johnson

PUBLISHERS

Chattanooga, TN

CONTENTS

INTRODUCTION

Did you once sit at the table of optimism but lately notice your spiritual plate is empty? And when you peer into the cupboard of your soul, is it bare and in need of restocking?

You shake your head. Life has cooked up another big pot of negativity. You'd been through challenges before—and survived. But now, you're living in the *in-between* times. You know those times when commonality sets in—but life is still as rough around the edges as a spoon caught in the disposal?

Negativity boils over. Optimism sours. It can happen to even the most devoted Christ follower. It's a helpless feeling when the Master's recipe for living slips from your hands. Then, sadness and discouragement replace hope and joy on your daily life menu. And the *good things* God intended for you no longer seem to be within reach.

Something has to change.

I know the feeling; it happened to me. I wasn't following God's recipe. My faith—and the spiritual nourishment that had fed my soul—dissipated as I stirred the dark mix of negativity.

Finally, out of desperation, I prayed.

Nine words changed my life:

"What about *one good thing* that happens each day?"

As a defeatist, I was skeptical. I'd have to submit to God. It wouldn't be easy, but I took the challenge. Trusting God's lead, I scrapped negativity and found optimism through His goodness and Word. You can do the same!

God will supply the ingredients you will need for spiritual nourishment. (He did for me.) It comes together in a beautiful mix, wonderfully served. Sitting at the table of optimism, you will look forward to savoring God's peace, hope, and joy—the *good things* He intends for you.

Be prepared to enter the Lord's proverbial "kitchen." It's a great feeling! Reach up and don the apron set aside for you—the one labeled "Purveyor of God's Goodness." You'll wear it proudly!

I want to share with you how this book originated. I reflected on past battles with negative thinking and unfavorable circumstances, then realized that I (and a few others close to me) had experiences to share. Armed with an answer to prayer, I was confident others would benefit from the lessons we learned. This book, *Just One Good Thing: A Faith-Inspired Recipe for Optimism,* was born from those trials—and triumphs.

The "Daily Morsels" are based on true stories and include Bible verses about "good things." The stories show how God's people—today and in Jesus' time—turned from negative thoughts or circumstances and found optimism through God's goodness and Word.

The book is divided into four themes of seven stories each, with each theme based on a characteristic of God's goodness. Part One is God as Master Caretaker; Part Two is God as Master Provider; Part Three is God as Master Teacher; and Part Four is God as Master Counselor.

Easy to follow, the stories can be read daily or customized to suit your schedule. The stories and lessons also work well in a group setting. Another option is to divide the stories and studies into four sections and complete one section of seven stories at a time.

Self-assessment worksheets with thought-provoking questions for study and self-reflection are located at the end of each story. In addition, a "One Good Thing" Journal application will help you build a positive outlook.

With perseverance and faith, you can scrap negative thinking and fill your spiritual plate with *good things*. Be prepared to sit at God's table of optimism, where abundant servings of peace, hope, and joy await!

God is good all the time. His "Good Book" serves as our recipe for living.

CHAPTER ONE

INGREDIENTS, THE "ONE GOOD THING"

The alarm sounds. You wake up. *This will be a good day. Right?*

Oops. Did you hesitate for a moment—or need to think about your answer?

If so, you're not alone. Join the club—the one that millions of others belong to who worry or harbor negative thoughts. (As you probably know, it's not a fun club, so you might want to consider canceling your membership!)

Here's a bit of research for you about worried thinking. According to a study by Dr. Robert L. Leahy, 85% of worries have a neutral or positive outcome meaning that 17 out of every 20 worries you have turn out okay. As for the other 15%, Dr. Leahy reported that they believed the other 15% had handled the situation much better than they thought they would."[1]

The truth about us comes to light: we tend to worry and think negatively rather than maintain a positive outlook. The negative thoughts override the positive ones. Since most of our concerns don't result in the potential disaster we had anticipated, it means that most of our worrisome thoughts are needless!

No one purposely worries or harbors negative thoughts, but

1. Leahy, Dr. Robert L. "Feeling Like You're Drowning in Worry?" Avail Content posted 4 years ago.

Retrieved from https://avail.app/public/articles/stop-worrying#:~:text-t−Robert%20L.,than%20they%20thought%20they%20would.

the tendency to focus on negative things thwarts our best intentions to look at the bright side.

Negativity. It lurks at every corner with a waiting snare. It can rob you of the *good things* God wants for you—such as peace, hope, and joy. It will taunt you to sit at the table of worry, sadness, and fear. It can brew up a strong cup of destructive thoughts, catching you at the first sip.

The word "negativity" sounds as distasteful as a rubbery, overcooked egg.

Are you seeking a way to clean out the negativity from your mind's pantry and fill your spiritual plate with something good?

If so, I found a way to do just that, and I'd like to share it with you.

Born Pessimist. You've heard the phrase. It could have been the headline of my birth announcement if it had revealed my true nature:

Female child, born prematurely on a gloomy spring day. Weighed no more than a can of Folger's coffee. Presented with a fearful, fussy temperament and wrapped in a blanket of pessimism.

The idea of a "born pessimist" is absurd, but for me, the title fit. When I was five, my mother noticed I didn't possess the same happy, optimistic outlook as her. She'd shake her head and say, "Sweetie, you can't see the light of day."

Mom was right. I'd turn a sunny, blue-sky morning into a rainy tempest with one frown. My melancholy attitude affected everything. In grade school, I hugged the walls of the hallway corridor. In junior high, I feared speaking out loud when a teacher asked me a question. In high school, I didn't believe I had a chance to make the gymnastics team. In college, I talked myself out of a nursing degree when I failed math.

How might things have turned out if I had faced these situations with an affirmative outlook?

Later, when I became a wife and mother, the destructive attitude followed. I adored my husband and our daughters but was hard on myself. I'd become an expert at negative self-talk. I was convincing—*I believed everything I thought.*

Negative thoughts are like potato chips—you can't have just one. One bite leads to another. When does it end? If there was such a thing as "emotional indigestion," I had it.

Additional stressors poured into my already simmering pot of daily struggles. Our daughter, son-in-law, and newly born grandson moved away, my husband had to retire early, and my mother was diagnosed with Alzheimer's.

I confided in a co-worker. "You're just experiencing *life,* Nancy," she responded flatly.

"Maybe so," I replied, "but I'm not handling it well."

Every morning, I grumbled. *"What could be good about today?"* Gloom became a steady diet on my daily menu.

My spiritual health suffered, too. I'd regularly attended church but began to make excuses: "I'm too tired," "I don't feel good," or, "I overslept." But skipping out on my faith only worsened my state of hopelessness.

Fast forward three months to the Thursday after Christmas. I sat alone that afternoon at a café table at the Barnes and Noble bookshop. It was my favorite place to sip coffee, write in my journal, and explore the state of my soul.

The flood came without warning. The dam let loose; the gush of unwanted emotion unleashed its torrent. I reached into my front jeans pocket for a tissue. It ripped. A half sheet was not enough to dry my eyes. Tears kept coming.

Every café table was taken; mine was the only one with a vacant chair. I rested my head in my hands. Maybe it would look like I was reading instead of having a meltdown. A teardrop splattered onto my journal page. What did it matter? The journal was old—like me.

Were the tears triggered by the soft Christmas music playing in the background or the empty chair at the table? Or was it a combination of recent emotional hits?

I'd been through tough times before—and survived. But this was different. I was living in the "in-between times." Life events had sandwiched themselves, one layer after the next, on top of me. Weighted down, every day had become a struggle.

The Christmas music in the café grated on my nerves. I didn't want to hear lyrics about feeling happy—especially not jolly.

I squinted as the sun poked through the café window. My emotional barometer contradicted the sunny 70-degree weather. Unpredictable tempest: heart cloudy, chilly, with occasional gusts of bitterness calling for an extended forecast of gloom.

I clutched my pen, the journal open to a blank page. I used to find solace in this type of writing, but not anymore. The blue corduroy cover was as stained as the contents within. The spine had unraveled. Some pages were dog-eared, some rumpled in frustration. It added up to one long-winded, melancholy story.

I flipped through the pages, landing on an entry from six weeks earlier:

November 11th – Mom's Diagnosis

Dear Mom, we had many good years together. Your memory isn't what it used to be, but I was unprepared when the doctor said, "She has Alzheimer's."

I stare at the empty chair across the table. I miss you, Mom. I miss our coffee and Danish roll conversations. I miss your sparkling eyes, smile, and sage advice: "Life is what you make it" and "Expect change." But I didn't expect the type of change that took away your memory.

Mom always told me to expect change. She was right. Change came. It moved in when I least expected, bringing a suitcase of unwanted things.

I unpacked the gloomy suitcase of melancholy baggage. Buttoning the wrinkled shirt of mediocrity, I adjusted its uneven collar, then put on the ragged pants of despair. Over my shoulders, I draped a cloak of sadness and slipped on the shoes of pessimism. How poorly dressed I was!

Change took up residence. What had happened to my life? I used to have faith—and joy. But not now.

I shifted uneasily in the café chair and looked up from my dog-eared journal. I'd stepped away from God. I'd only started praying again in the past two months out of desperation.

I closed my eyes, taking in the clink of utensils, the *whoosh* of steam from the espresso machine, and the soft chatter of people in the café. I took in a ragged breath. *Inhale. Exhale.* Muscles in my shoulders began to relax as my arms dropped to my side. My cheeks softened as the tension in my jaw released. *Inhale. Exhale.* The bustling sounds that surrounded me did not penetrate the quietness inside.

A small, still voice spoke to my heart in the stillness with a clear, succinct message. *What about one good thing that happens each day?*

Stunned, I sat with my mouth agape. These were not *my* words.

A wave of calm enveloped me as an immense sense of peace and love surrounded me. I felt as if the wisp of a gentle breeze had instantaneously swept away my burdens.

A streak of joy coursed through me. *One good thing.* Was this the nudge I needed to change my thinking, the answer to the prayer I was waiting for?

I stared at the heartache-filled pages of my journal. But now, I had found Jesus outside of these margins of sorrow. I knew what I had to do. *Close the journal. Put it away.* I stuffed it into my purse. This was the last time I would use it.

That night, I knelt beside my bed as I had done every night for weeks. My prayers had been desperate—until now:

Thank You, God, for answering my prayers. From now on, things are going to be different.

I stood up, walked to my desk, and took out a fresh piece of notebook paper. I ran my hand over its smooth surface and retrieved a new pen from its package. It felt sleek between my fingers.

Putting pen to paper, I hesitated. The corduroy journal had been a catharsis for many things, but rarely for *good* ones. Now, the challenge would be to focus on the positive instead of the negative—*God's* way.

At the top of my paper, I penned *"One Good Thing."* As I did so, I noticed the letters "G-o-d" were contained within the word "good." *Yes, God is good!* He is the source of all things good. He had me in mind—even in my lowest moments.

The ink flowed smoothly onto the paper as I described my *one good thing.* I was thankful the message had come to my heart—and changed my life. (Sometimes change can be a good thing.) I was on my journey toward a new way of thinking.

I slipped the journal page inside my Bible on the nightstand but couldn't sleep. The melancholy addiction to "Old Corduroy" tugged at my heart. It had been my steady companion for a long time. My past protested. I got up, went to my bedroom closet, and switched on the light. I'd stashed the journal on the top shelf.

I reached up.

No, don't.

In a bittersweet gesture, I lowered my arm.

I lay back down in bed. I was relieved I'd resisted the temptation to fall back into my old habits. Instead, I'd succeeded by completing my first *One Good Thing* journal entry. It was something positive—something good.

Snuggling beneath warm covers, I folded my hands. *Thank You, God, for your goodness.* Then, I pondered this thought: *What might His Word say about goodness—or good things?*

I didn't know what tomorrow would bring or what the *Good Shepherd* had in store for me. But one thing was sure: I felt a glimmer of hope.

CHAPTER TWO
HOW TO USE THIS BOOK

The twenty-eight "Daily Morsel" stories in this book are meant to inspire and encourage you toward a faith-inspired (spiritual) optimism.

A simple three-part plan will help you reach your goal of building a positive mindset. The essential ingredients of the plan are outlined for you below:

1) Begin by reading each biblically centered *"Daily Morsel"* story.
2) At the end of each story, complete the worksheet with the questions for study and self-reflection:

a). "Personal Insight" offers a challenge for thinking and faith.

b). "Reflection: My *"One Good Thing"* reminder will encourage you to think of something good related to the story.

c). "Today's Serving" summarizes the story.

d). "A Cupful of Reality" poses thought-provoking questions or statements about your experiences.

e). "A Taste of Spiritual Nourishment" is a one-word "tidbit" (or snack) for your soul's refreshment.

f). "The "Table of Optimism" prompts you to ponder your hope for today.

g). The "Prayer for Today" provides "food for thought" through requests for common spiritual needs.

3) The *"One Good Thing"* Journal page: This is your personal journal page, where you will briefly describe, in a few words or sentences, the "one good thing" that takes place for you each day. The journal page has a blank space for you to fill in entries for each day of the week. A reproducible journal page is provided for you.

Putting the journal to good use will help you build a habit of thinking with a positive mindset. It will also make you aware of the *good things* that might have otherwise gone unnoticed.

Bible Verses: Here is a brief note of instruction as you study the Bible verse for each Daily Morsel story. As you read the verse that mentions a "good thing" or "good things," ask yourself the following four questions as you ponder the meaning—or "ingredients"—of each verse:

1. How is the Lord using these words for my instruction?
2. How does this verse lead me to trust Him?
3. How does this scripture advocate living by His Word?
4. And, how does the "good thing" (or "good things") mentioned in this verse apply to my life?

These steps can be helpful as you follow the "Master's Recipe" to discover the *good things* God intends for His people—that's you!

Completing the "One Good Thing" journal entries is integral to defeating negative thoughts and reinforcing a positive outlook. Don't worry about having to write a lot in your journal entry. Jot down a few words, a phrase, or a sentence or two to describe your "one good thing" for each day.

For best results, keep up with the journal entries (even if you take a break from reading the Daily Morsel stories every day). Consistency is the key.

The goal of this book is to help you defeat negative thinking and replace it with an optimistic spiritual outlook. The "Master's Recipe" is God's Word—the Bible, or as we could say, the "Good Book." We are fortunate to have the Lord's Word and instruction to guide us. It's a go-to source for our needs and is filled with God's unique blend of spiritual nourishment to feed our hungry, faith-yearning appetites.

As you work through *Just One Good Thing (A Faith-Inspired Recipe for Optimism)*, I'd be happy to answer any questions you have, and I look forward to hearing about your progress. (For more information, see "A Personal Note" at the end of this chapter.)

This book provides a simple method to boost your faith outlook and discover the *good things* God desires for you!

Before you begin reading the stories, please take a moment to rate your optimism. Using the scale below, from zero to ten, with zero being none and ten as the highest, how would you rate your level of optimism now?

Circle your answer:

        0 1 2 3 4 5 6 7 8 9 10

(Keep this answer in mind. You will refer to it later.)

Getting Started With "One Good Thing"

I was determined to make a change—and you can do the same!

How it started: After writing my first journal entry on Day One (feeling a glimmer of hope that the answered prayer would work), I was determined to keep up the habit each day. However, I faced an obstacle: I was accustomed to writing sad things. To think about something *good* was the opposite of what I'd ever done. But, determined to break a bad habit, I devised a rule for writing in my journal: *Choose the positive. No day is perfect. If you have a rough day, it doesn't have to keep you from discovering something positive that can come from it.*

Choosing "the positive" as you write your journal entries is an important step toward building optimism.

If negativity is a familiar bedfellow for you as it was for me, be forewarned. It can be challenging to write about positive things.

Pessimism can rear its ugly head and taunt you with untruths, such as, *"You'll never come up with anything good."*

You might have to fight self-doubt as I did. But with effort, you can do it.

Following is the entry I wrote on Day Two in my journal:

Journal entry: Friday, December 28:

After dinner, we watched a comedy. It felt good to laugh again.

Positive words. A tiny success.

It took time for me to get accustomed to writing something upbeat. It felt foreign and might feel that way for you, too.

However, after completing journal entries for the first couple of weeks, I felt as if I was learning a new language—*the language of optimism.* So, there is hope. I found it—and I think you will, too!

But, to backtrack, let me tell you about the stumbling block I hit at the end of my first week of journal entries. On Day Seven, I woke up feeling awful and had to call in sick at work. A dreary and sarcastic thought intruded.

Oh, great. Nothing can be good about a sick day!

Feeling terrible, I couldn't imagine what I could write in my journal that night. But as I reached for my "One Good Thing" journal page, I was surprised. I had positive aspects—even more than one "good thing"—to write about:

Hot tea and honey soothing to throat. Slept all afternoon. Watched a favorite TV show.

I marveled at the thought. My *sick* day had produced something positive.

My first week of keeping my journal entries was complete. As I looked back at the journal entries for the week, I realized good things *were* taking place in my life. They were small things—but they gave me hope that I could change.

As a few weeks passed, positive thoughts began to interrupt my habit of negative thoughts. It was a good sign—little things made a difference:

I watched with wonder as silent snowflakes dusted the ground of our desert home.

Following a thunderstorm, a double rainbow spread bright rays of color across the sky.

When least expected, an old friend stopped by to visit.

Let's face it. Only a tiny percentage of our life events—weddings, graduations, births, promotions, or retirements—are milestones. The "small events"—living in the *in-between times*—account for most of our days.

Sometimes, the "little things are the big things." Like the phrase, "I Love You." These small words carry a significant impact, don't they?

A friend once asked me if I remembered what I received for Christmas the previous year. I was surprised I'd forgotten the "big" gifts. Instead, I fondly recalled the ballpoint pens and dark chocolates my husband put in my stocking and the mouth-watering pumpkin and pecan pies our daughters baked for our Christmas Eve dessert.

Little things make a difference. That's how *Just One Good Thing (A Faith-Inspired Recipe for Optimism)* was born. Following God's lead, a simple answer to prayer put me on the right track to turn my thinking from gloom to joy.

Finding Balance in the Journey

When seeking optimism, be prepared! You're about to embark on a journey of self-discovery—the *good things* in your world that may have previously gone unnoticed. As you fill up on the positives, there will be less room for the negatives.

The "Seesaw" Principle:

Remember the old-time pharmacy scales? They looked like a balance—or a child's see-saw on the playground.

Imagine sitting on the end of that seesaw, but no one is seated opposite you. You're stuck on the ground, unable to rise from where you are. It would be best to have someone—or something—to balance you on the other side.

Add "positive" weight to the other end of the seesaw, and you'll rise. You're no longer stuck.

The idea relates to positive and negative thinking. If you thrive in a reassuring environment, it will help keep you balanced in mind, body, and spirit. Conversely, a negative atmosphere will squelch or depress these efforts, creating imbalance.

Your body and brain require proper nutrients to function well, and your heart and mind should be balanced to maintain spiritual health.

You don't want to sit on that uneven seesaw. Weighted down. Stuck. There is no one—or no one thing—to counterbalance you. The negative weight pins you down, depriving you of the "positive" end of the board.

Hope is found in a positive state of balance and spiritual wellness. I found it, and I believe you will, too!

Seeking God's Goodness
God is great, and He is good. Perhaps these words remind you of a childhood mealtime prayer. The words are simple but speak volumes.

God's goodness is all-encompassing. He loves us, provides for us, and wants *good things* for us. When we pray, He listens. When we seek repentance, He forgives us. And through our faith, we trust in Him to supply our needs.

But sometimes, we take good things for granted. Without the right attitude, we might fail to notice the good things in our lives each day. But if we follow the "Master's Recipe" for living—following God's lead, trusting Him, and living according to His Word, we will more readily embrace gratefulness.

The "Daily Morsels," based on true stories, will offer encouragement, and show you how God's goodness can shine through even in difficult circumstances.

The four themes of the book, based on characteristics of God's goodness, consist of seven stories each and show God's care for us even when we are wrestling with negativity.

God is patient. He waits for us to seek Him so we may attain the fullness of the *good things* He desires for us.

Frequently Asked Questions: Keeping Your "One Good Thing" Journal

1. When is the best time to record my "One Good Thing" journal entry?
Think of a time of day you can most easily commit to. Your journal entry only needs to be a few words or a sentence or two, so it shouldn't take long. Keep your journal page in a convenient place in the kitchen, next to your phone or computer, or anywhere you will quickly see it.

A night owl, I wrote my journal entries before going to bed late at night. A friend who likes to get up early fills in her journal when she sits down for her morning coffee.

Whatever works best for you, commit to setting aside that time of day to write your "One Good Thing."

2. What happens if I forget?
Forgive yourself. You're only human. Try to recall what you wanted to write that day, but if you don't remember, go on to the next day. The important thing is to do your best to be consistent.

3. What do you suggest if I dislike writing on a journal page?
Consider using a calendar page on your phone or computer or a printed calendar on your refrigerator or workspace—somewhere you will access it easily. Another option is to use a digital recording.

Initially, I used the journal pages to record my daily entries. Later, I began writing them on a large calendar on the refrigerator. Just a few words were enough to jot down the good things taking place. This served as a convenient way to record the good things happening for our family, both big and small: graduations, birthdays, accomplishments at work or school, memorable trips, vacations, or even a child's lost tooth or a friend's visit.

Saving your journal pages or calendars is an excellent way to create a record of the "good things" that take place in your life and can become personal or family keepsakes.

4. How long should I keep up the journal?
Keep up with the journal until you finish the book. Then, you can decide if you would like to continue. If it becomes an ingrained habit for you, as it did for me, you may feel prompted to keep up with the journaling. It is fun to record good things and look back at them.

You can also use the journal pages as needed. If you notice a slump in your thinking, return to journaling to get yourself back on track. I did this occasionally and found it helpful, so I wanted to pass this on to you.

Additional tips:
*If you're not sure what to write, pray about it!
*Re-reading your previous journal entries can be mood-lifting
*Your journal entries are like little rewards—positive and good

If you keep up with your journal, you'll be pleasantly surprised at all the good things that take place by the year's end.

5. Can you guarantee the "One Good Thing" method will work for me?
There is no guarantee it will work for everyone, but if you have the determination and willpower to change and trust that God will help you, you will likely succeed.

6. How long will it take before I see results?
There isn't a simple answer to this question. How you think and perceive ideas—and your expectations—will differ from someone else's. However, here are four things to keep in mind to help you achieve the best results:

1. Be consistent in doing the readings, workbook pages, and journal entries.
2. Work through the book as suggested.

3. Set goals for yourself.

4. Lastly, *expect* good results. Optimism is the goal, so a little faith can go a long way!

A Personal Note

It is my hope that *Just One Good Thing (A Faith-Inspired Recipe for Optimism)* will be as helpful to you as it was to me. A renewed perspective will brighten your day. The banquet table is set. Take a seat at God's table of optimism, where plentiful servings of His joy, peace, and hope await.

As you embark on this journey of discovery, I gladly welcome your feedback or comments. Connect with me at my website, OneGoodThingGod.com.

I am excited for you. May God richly bless you as you discover the *good things* He has in store for you!

In Christ,
Nancy Pelander Johnson

PART ONE
GOD AS MASTER CARETAKER

GOD AS MASTER CARETAKER

Where would we be without caretakers? They are companions, guardians, protectors, overseers, custodians, and compassionate beings who care about us and make us feel important—and *loved*.

There was someone who took care of you when you were born. They fed, clothed, and nurtured you as you grew.

Some have a mother and father who cared for them; others might have a family member, foster family, or guardian. But not everyone's childhood experiences are good. If that is the case, think of the person—or persons—in your life who have provided the most nurturing care for you, even if outside of the family circle.

Knowing you had someone to watch over and love you is comforting.

As years pass, you may no longer have that special person—or persons—in your life. But no matter what happens, there will always be One who cares for you without ceasing. God—the author of life and creator of heaven and earth is the master caretaker of everything—and everyone. He has known you—and loved you—from the beginning.

Each "Daily Morsel" in Part One of this book shows how God, the Master Caretaker, cares for His children, including you, no matter their age.

As you read these stories, know how much God desires *good things* for you. Be encouraged, for you are loved and cherished by the Creator—the Master Caretaker.

Recipe

My Daily Morsel #1

Prep Time _____

Cook Time _____

Oven Temp _____

Serves _____

Topic: **Wisdom**

_____

_____

_____

_____

_____

Bible Verse for Study

"Wisdom, like an inheritance, is a **good thing** and benefits those who see the sun."

Ecclesiastes 7:11

_____

_____

_____

_____

GRANDMOTHER OLAFSSON'S GIFT

Wisdom—the word brings back memories of Grandmother Olafsson during my visit to the family farm in Pennsylvania, the summer I was twelve. She looked how I'd remembered since we'd moved away a few years earlier. She wore the same faded housecoat with blue flowers, white snaps, and a torn pocket. She brushed the same long white hair every morning while sitting in her rocker on the porch. Then, her knotted fingers pushed in a hairpin to form the same tight bun against the nape of her neck.

Her habit of humming continuously bothered almost everyone but me. Today was no different. It was a tune I did not recognize. I surmised it was probably a song from Sweden, the "old country," as my father put it.

"Elizabeth, be careful," my great-aunt chided. She watched as her elderly sister placed the cane too close to the table leg as she prepared to sit. Her movements were slow and deliberate, and her hand shook as she let go of the cane.

My father used to say his mother was a stubborn woman. A delivery man once showed up at her door with a wheelchair my aunt had ordered for her. As the story goes, my grandmother tried to poke the delivery man with her cane, yelling, "Do away with dat!" Finally, she swatted at the wheelchair, hollering, "My bones vill not lie still!"

My aunt felt terrible for the poor delivery man, who hightailed it down the steps and to his truck with the wheelchair. She said

Grandma had puckered her lips, ready to spit at the man, but the only sound coming from her mouth was *Pfftt*.

My father said his aunt was embarrassed. After that, she never attempted to get Grandmother Olafsson to use a wheelchair.

On the first morning of my stay at the farmhouse, Grandmother sat at her usual place at the table next to the large picture window overlooking the field. Her head swayed gently as she hummed. She did this until she was ready to speak. To her, words were not a frivolous affair. She did not waste them.

Grandmother motioned to me with her bent, crooked finger.

"Come. Sit, Nonny."

I shyly approached the table, looking down at the smooth, worn lines of the chair's arm. *Nonny*. It was not my real name, but the closest my grandmother could get with her thick accent. She tapped her cane on the floor twice to announce she had something to say. Then, Grandmother looked straight at me.

"What you do vhen you grow up tall, Nonny?"

I felt my face turn warm, then hot. I shrugged, pretending not to know. But Grandmother was waiting for my answer. Would I tell her my heartfelt secret? I took a deep breath. "I'd like to become a nurse or a teacher," I said. Self-conscious, I bit my lip. "But I don't know if I can do it," I replied wistfully.

Grandmother's soft gaze turned to a glare. Her small round spectacles made her eyes look much bigger than they were. She had my attention.

"Vere der is a vill, der is a vay," she said. Grandmother grasped the finely meshed chain tucked beneath the collar of her housecoat and slid it off. I didn't see what was at the end of the chain until she opened her palm. A tarnished cross lay in the center of her wrinkled hand, the chain coiled beneath it.

She pointed to the cross.

"Dis is the vay, Nonny."

I shivered as Grandmother's crippled digits placed the necklace into my hands. My finger traced over a word on the back of the cross, but it didn't look like English. Whatever it said, it was important to my grandmother. Her eyes looked loving yet serious.

Conversation over. Grandmother Olafsson got up slowly, propping herself with the cane. She gained her balance and turned into the hallway. The humming resumed.

"Wait," I said, standing. "Your cross . . ."

Grandmother Olafsson stopped humming only long enough to utter these words: "Dat is for you, child."

"Thank you, Grandmother," I murmured. I was happy to receive the necklace. I knew it was special and felt honored she'd given it to me.

She replied with a phrase in Swedish I didn't understand, but she said it lovingly. I put the chain around my neck and felt the cross touch the skin above my summer shirt. Grandmother said something else in Swedish, then smiled a toothless grin.

The thump of her cane quieted as she disappeared around the corner to her bedroom.

I wasn't sure I understood Grandmother's wisdom about the "vill and the vay," but my heart would later recapture those words.

I had no idea the summer I was twelve would be the last time I'd see my grandmother. My father got the phone call on Christmas Eve. His eyes turned watery, and his voice quieted. "She died tonight, Honey," he said, his gaze downward.

"Why on Christmas Eve?" I cried. I ran to my room, sobbing until no more tears would come.

Fast forward six years. I entered college and declared my major in nursing. Math and Chemistry weren't going well. I had a sinking feeling it wouldn't be an easy career path. I was terrible at math, and my grades reflected the struggle.

What if I fail? My self-esteem plummeted, I couldn't focus, and hours of studying got me nowhere.

To escape the pressure, I let my studies slide. My roommates were having much more fun than I was, so I joined in with reckless abandon. I went to late-night parties and hung around people my parents would not have liked.

Wrapped up in my new social life, I wasn't communicating with Mom and Dad very often. Sometimes, I ignored my mother's phone calls or made excuses for not being available when I was out with my friends.

I no longer wore the cross my grandmother had given me, and to tell you the truth, I didn't know where it was. I wasn't taking it to heart like I had when I was twelve. I convinced myself it didn't matter; I wasn't attending church anyway.

On a dreary December day, my mood matched the weather. I wasn't studying because I'd given up trying to remedy my failing grades. I walked to get out of the dorm and headed to Varsity Pond, one of my favorite places on campus. As a child, my father brought us here to ice skate. The frozen pond was once again covered in layers of ice. Cottonwood trees and willows surrounding the lake were dressed in winter white, which brought back memories of my wobbly skating over the uneven ridges in the ice and my father cheering us on.

I stopped at a bench and brushed off a layer of snow. It was the same cast iron bench I sat on when my father used to bring us to the pond.

Mom and Dad. So many memories of growing up. I knew they loved me very much and always had. A wave of guilt coursed through me. I hadn't been thinking of them, and it was disrespectful of me not to answer Mom's phone calls.

Christmas break was only one week away.

This year marked seven years since Grandmother Olafsson had passed away. I thought about the necklace. How negligent I'd been, not knowing where it was.

As tiny snowflakes began to fall, salty tears ran down my cold, nearly numb cheeks.

By early afternoon, I made a tearful decision. I packed a suitcase, left campus, and drove home. I didn't know what kind of reaction to expect from my parents. Would they be angry? Would my recent poor behavior change their attitude toward me?

When I showed up at the house, Mom and Dad were surprised, but shocked that I'd left campus before taking my final exams. But they warmly embraced me as I released a stream of tears. I apologized for the heartache I'd caused and thanked them for their support despite my recent lack of communication.

Mom and I had a long talk. She encouraged me to attempt the final exams and not throw away the opportunity to do my best. I had to agree she had a point.

I told her I'd been thinking about Grandma Olafsson and felt ashamed I didn't know where the necklace was. Mom told me to have hope, but we searched until dinner with no luck.

As I unpacked my suitcase, Mom called to me from downstairs. She'd found the necklace! It was in a small decorative tin imprinted with holly and ivy. I remembered wearing it at Christmas, but that was long ago. Somehow, it had gotten mixed up with other holiday gift boxes Mom hadn't used in a long time.

Finding the necklace in a Christmas box. How ironic. Grandmother Olafsson had passed away on Christmas Eve, and this year's Christmas Eve was only one week away.

Mom and I were so happy we stood at the bottom of the stairs and hugged, as happy tears escaped. I was again celebrating the special gift Grandmother Olafsson had given me.

Just as I did when I was twelve, I placed the chain around my neck. I felt the cross touch the skin on my chest. The chain was a little shorter now, but the necklace rested just above my heart. I closed my eyes. I felt as if Grandmother Olafsson was speaking to me, saying, *"Nonny, dis is the vay."*

I said a prayer of thanks. Mom and I had found the cross, and

I'd found my faith again. My grandmother's words came alive for me that day. From then on, I wore the necklace.

With support from my parents and my college counselor, I enrolled in tutoring for math and chemistry, then retook the classes I'd failed.

Grandmother Olafsson's words of wisdom pulled at my heartstrings. She was right. I had the will to work hard so that I would succeed. And the "way?" It came about through my renewed faith in God.

I bowed my head and held the Cross in my palm that hung below my shirt collar.

Thank You, God. And thank you, Grandmother Olafsson.

⎯⎯

Wisdom! What I admired most about my grandmother was her acquired knowledge of a lifetime of learning and personal experience. She'd shared the best she had with me: love, life experience, and faith.

For many of us, wisdom comes from remarkable people, whether a grandparent, mother, father, friend, or another significant person we admire and respect.

Our verse for today, from Ecclesiastes 7:11, describes wisdom in this way: *"Wisdom, like an inheritance, is a good thing and benefits those who see the sun."*

But then, how are wisdom and inheritance alike, you may ask? To clarify the meaning of each, we turn to definitions from *Webster's Dictionary*:

Webster's defines wisdom as *"A wise attitude or course of action; the teachings of the ancient wise men."*[1] Wise action and the teaching and experience of those before us are sobering thoughts. We can learn much from the ancient people.

Webster's defines inheritance as: *"the acquisition of a possession,*

---

1. *Merriam-Webster Online*, s.v.v. "Wisdom." Accessed August 28, 2023 https://www.merriam-webster.com

condition, or trait from past generations.[2]

Inheritance can be a physical object but also a condition or trait.

The Bible encourages seeking wisdom over possessions as the material things we own will eventually deteriorate.

———

Wisdom, once acquired, for most, usually remains and is not subdued, destroyed, or taken away. King Solomon was an exception. He'd prayed to God for wisdom instead of wealth, and God granted him great wisdom. As a result, he became wealthy; however, later, his prideful behavior displeased God. As a result, he was no longer considered wise, for a wise man would not have chosen to step away from God's provision.

Wisdom and inheritance are *good things* from the passing of many generations of the Lord's people. God works in many ways. Who better to learn from than those who have gone on before us in His name? Unfortunately for Solomon, he was no longer a good example of a wise leader.

As a young person, I'd looked up to my grandmother as a person of faith, even though I'd neglected to appreciate all she'd done for me. Sadly, she died before knowing her influence would lead me back to the cross. I will never forget her words: "*Dis is the vay, Nonny.*"

Following the Word of the Lord leads to wisdom, an inheritance God gives us. The words of Ecclesiastes ring true. Wisdom benefits those who see life through the light of Christ, as expressed in Ecclesiastes 7:11. It benefits *"those who see the sun."*

And that's *one good thing.*

———

---

2. *Merriam-Webster Online*, s.v.v. "Inheritance." Accessed August 28, 2023. https://www.merriam-webster.com

Worksheet for My Daily Morsel #1

Test your interpretation skills:
"Wisdom, like an inheritance, is a good thing and *benefits those who see the sun*." What is your interpretation of wisdom benefitting those who "*see the sun*"?

_____

_____

_____

_____

Personal Insight:
Has gaining an inheritance impacted your life? If so, did it come from possessions, conditions, or traits?

_____

_____

_____

_____

Reflection: My "One Good Thing"
What *good thing* has come from the wisdom accumulated in your life, and how has it benefited you? Was there a wise person who influenced and guided you? If so, share about them.

_____

_____

_____

_____

Today's Serving: The Wisdom of Caring
Nonny slipped away from God. She dismissed the importance of her relationships. She asked for forgiveness when she realized the negative effect of her poor behavior and attitude. Finding the cross rekindled her love for her grandmother and the wisdom she had imparted. The gift of wisdom greatly benefitted King Solomon—until he abused his power and turned to sinful ways. Not turning from sin, he passed up on the opportunity to receive the good things God had in store for him and lost his reputation as a great and wise man.

A Cupful of Reality: Have you—or someone you know—ever had an experience like Nonny's? If so, describe:

_____

_____

_____

_____

Was there a resolution, turning point, or positive turnout?

_____

_____

_____

_____

A Taste of Spiritual Nourishment:
From today's Bible verse in Ecclesiastes comes a key word, *sun*. God's light is a necessary ingredient for your life. It is bright, illuminating, and warm and brings with it a feeling of hope!

The Table of Optimism:
Hope resides at the Table of Optimism. What is your hope for today?

_____

_____

_____

_____

Prayer for Today:
Lord, help me to look to You for wisdom through Your Word. Let me recognize those who have gone before me and the knowledge they have imparted. May I also share the good things I have been given to serve others. In Jesus's name, Amen.

Recipe

My Daily Morsel #2

Prep Time

Cook Time

Oven Temp

Serves

Topic: **God's Compassion and Kindness**

Bible Verse for Study

"I will tell of the kindnesses of the LORD, the deeds for which
he is to be praised, according to all the LORD has done for us—
yes, the many **good things** he has done for Israel, according
to his compassion and many kindnesses."

Ecclesiastes 7:11

Let Me
Count the Ways

"Let me count the ways I love you," my mother would say softly, stroking my hair. This early memory of my mother's kindness and compassion made me feel safe and loved. I'd been afraid of the dark and scared to be alone. I could not see her face in the shadows, but I could hear the smile in her voice.

Even with a nightlight and my bedroom door left ajar, I wouldn't sleep unless my mother was beside me. She'd stay by my side until I could sleep on my own.

My mother's love was rich—richer than her homemade Golden Pound Cake—the most heavenly dessert I'd ever tasted. Likewise, her faith in God was rich. She took my brother and me to church every Sunday. She brought us up with an appetite for faith, teaching us right from wrong and impressing the importance of kindness to others.

I wanted to please my mother but often didn't measure up. At age six, one evening, as my parents watched television, I played nearby, running my toy cars in circles around the base of a floor lamp.

"Stop, or you'll knock the lamp over," Mom said.

In my six-year-old thinking, I decided if I moved over an inch or two, I would have done as she had asked and could still reach my cars.

Her response caught me off guard. She stormed over and stood me up by the collar.

"You're not listening!" *Swat* came her hand to my behind.

I ran to my room crying, humiliated by the spanking.

Fuming inside, I opened my desk drawer and took out a sheet of notebook paper. I folded it in half and, with a blue crayon, wrote, "*I hate Mommy,*"and then taped the note to my door.

Minutes later, I heard a knock. I reluctantly turned the door-knob and peered out. There stood my mother. She had tears in her eyes. I was better at spelling than I thought. She did not say anything but removed the sign and shut my door. I heard her footsteps trail off down the hallway. Sadness welled up inside me as I popped my door open.

"I'm sorry, Mommy," I cried. "I don't hate you!"

There was no response. Didn't she hear me? Or maybe she didn't want to answer. Either way, it was too late to take back the unkind words.

Plopping face-down onto my bed, tears soaked my pink-striped pillowcase as I wiped the moisture from my face. What would I do now? I'd behaved terribly.

Taking another piece of paper, I folded it to make a card, then drew a flower on the front using the same blue crayon. On the inside, in my best penmanship, I wrote, "*Mommy, Sorry for being mean. I love you more than pound cake.*"

At bedtime, my mother returned to my room. I was too ashamed to look into her eyes, so I stared at my feet, wiggling my toes be-tween the gray carpet fibers. Mom came over. We hugged—and cried. I think our hearts needed a band-aid; tears were leaking out.

When I gave her the card, her eyes filled with tears. I felt terri-ble, but she said they were happy tears, not sad ones.

I promised my mother I would never repeat unkind things. She smiled, tucked me into bed, and we said night-time prayers. I wondered how she could still love me when I'd been so mean. But that was my mother. She loved me, no matter what.

A few years passed, and I began junior high school. On a Friday afternoon in seventh-grade English, our teacher, white-haired Mrs. "W," scraped the chalkboard with her nails to get our attention. I thought her sweet voice would reveal a kind and compassionate nature. I was wrong. In addition to her habit of scraping her nails on the chalkboard to get our attention, she refused to listen to our complaints about the amount of homework she assigned every Friday. It ruined every weekend.

No one liked her, not even I.

One afternoon, when Mrs. W. stepped out of the classroom, a boy in a flannel shirt with stringy hair piped up. "She's going to give us another (expletive) load of homework. So, let's have a sit-down strike!"

"Yeah!" others shouted.

I looked around the room. Some of my classmates seemed as shocked as I was. Still, this was a mean thing to do to a teacher— even if we didn't like her. Comments and complaints escalated into a circus of unkind verbiage.

Flannel Shirt was first to sit on the floor next to his desk, and others followed suit. I debated nervously but succumbed and sat on the floor as the rest.

As she rounded the corner of the classroom, Mrs. W's pink complexion paled. Her eyes wide, she scanned the room as Flannel Shirt initiated the chorus, "Strike! Strike!"

Mrs. W. bolted from the room. Laughter and snickers ensued. The gleeful moment, however, was sabotaged when the principal walked in. I swallowed hard, as a shiver ran through me.

In a deep, baritone voice, Mr. Haney cleared his throat and immediately commanded us to return to our seats. We sat down, although Flannel Shirt was the last to comply.

A short man, the principal's piercing glare commanded attention. He pressed his lips together tightly. I thought he would yell at us, but he didn't. Instead, he matter-of-factly explained our fate. "Your parents will be notified, and you will each have one week of detention."

No one said a word. Not even *Flannel Shirt*. We sat in silence until the principal dismissed us.

The following Monday, Mrs. W. returned to the classroom. She was quieter than usual, but her sharp-edged demeanor hadn't changed. She assigned a lengthy research paper with a two-page list of requirements. Additional punishment. Thank you, Mrs. W.

I shook my head and pressed down with angst upon my notebook paper as I scribbled the notes on the board.

Not fair! The assignment should belong to *Flannel Shirt* and the other guy who started the sit-down strike—not to the rest of us.

Angry, I decided not to write the paper.

Mrs. W. noticed I didn't submit my paper by the deadline. "You have twenty-four hours," she said. I thought she was giving me a break. But no. "You'll be docked fifteen points for late work," she added. *Such charity.*

The next day, when I got home from school, Mom waited at the door, her hands on her hips.

Something's up. I set my backpack on the floor.

"Your teacher phoned. She said you didn't turn in your research paper."

My mind raced as I fumbled for words. *I can't tell her the truth.*

"I...turned it in at the main office before catching the bus," I said swiftly.

"Oh...all right, that's good," she said, half smiling. She kissed my cheek and was off to the kitchen.

Off the hook. I sighed with relief.

While making taffy in Home Economics the next afternoon, I heard my name called over the loudspeaker to report to the main office. I was surprised and a little nervous. Why? Was it because I wasn't wearing the new glasses Mom bought me? She'd made a big fuss about it to my homeroom teacher. But, if this were the case, why hadn't my teacher said something?

I sucked in a deep breath as I approached the office where my mother and the principal waited. My knees felt like rubber. Mom glared at me, her jaw set.

Haney looked at me with steely gray eyes. "No one was able to locate the paper you turned in, Nancy," he said.

In a shaky voice, I confessed I hadn't written the paper. I'd lied.

Haney gave me an ultimatum. "Write the paper—or fail the class," he said.

I agreed to write the paper. I wasn't about to repeat *that* class.

When the meeting ended, I'd missed the bus and rode home with my mother. She was reticent, but it didn't matter. I didn't feel like talking to her, anyway. She was mad at me.

After dinner, Mom, Dad, and I sat at the dinner table to talk. Dad was stern, but after I acknowledged my mistake and apologized, he excused himself from the table. Then, Mom took over. She was upset but listened.

"I don't condone your behavior," she said. "But next time, will you ask for help when needed?

"Yes, Mom."

"You know I love you and only want what is best for you."

I nodded. Thank goodness my mother was a forgiving person.

I completed the research paper. My grade would have been better if Mrs. W. hadn't deducted points for lateness, but that was my fault.

It wasn't until later that I understood Mrs. W. was only trying to do what was best for us. She had a tough exterior but was committed to teaching. My mother had a tough exterior, too, but her kindness eventually shined through.

In high school, I worked hard to make good grades to get into college. However, my quest for freedom grew more assertive, as did my insistence I was right. I wanted to stay out later with friends and travel by myself during the summer. When my mother said no, I got mad.

"You could have adopted someone better than me!" I scoffed. Mom bolted from the room in tears.

Oh, no. Why did I say that? I made her cry and had broken my promise not to say hurtful things.

I'd failed. Adding insult to injury, earlier in the week, I informed my mother that I didn't want to go to church with her anymore. That didn't go over well.

Later, I overheard my mother confide in a friend, telling her how much she'd been praying for me.

Despite all the hurt I caused, Mom still loved me.

The following September, I went away to college, happy to be away from my overprotective parents. I was independent and wanted to do things my way. I stayed out late and went to parties. I gained freedom, but it came at a price when my grades slipped.

I also conveniently chose to abandon God and slept in on Sundays.

Then, a few months later, one of the girls I'd gotten to know in my art class was absent for a while. I thought of her but hadn't reached out to befriend her outside of the classroom. Our instructor gave us the solemn news the following Monday when I came to class. Our classmate—the girl I could have gotten to know—died after contracting encephalitis.

A memorial service was held at the chapel on campus. Every seat was filled. I sat in a back pew to have quick access to a bathroom. I couldn't stop crying. It was at this moment I silently cried out to God.

Sitting in a large crowd of people, I felt alone. Thoughts of my parents came to mind and how much they loved me. If only they could be at my side. I longed for their hugs. My heart had roamed far away from their help and guidance, and from God's help and guidance, too.

My guilt overwhelmed me, as did the thought that my class-mate's mother and father were grieving the loss of their precious daughter. Why hadn't I reached out to her? We'd talked during class, and sometimes we sat together. And now she was gone. I leaned forward, my head in my hands, and sobbed.

There were so many times my mother had tried to convince me to go back to church, but I was stubborn and wouldn't listen. But now, I understood she only wanted what was best for me.

Not long after the memorial service, I met the man I wanted to spend the rest of my life with. He asked me out for coffee after English class. We were immediately drawn to each other. I didn't tell my mother about him right away because we were getting serious, and I didn't want her to find out.

But Mom knew I was hiding something. She feared I was getting in over my head in the relationship, and she didn't want me to get hurt.

The following morning, while I was getting dressed, my mother called. I picked up the receiver, stalling.

Mom's voice was abrupt. "You're not telling me the truth," she said, "and I'm worried about what you are doing."

"I know, Mom, but..."

"Will you come home this weekend?" she pleaded. "I'll pay for your plane ticket."

She knew I didn't have enough money for the flight. I couldn't blame her or my dad for wanting to talk to me. They knew nothing about the young man who had stolen their daughter's heart.

I accepted Mom's offer and took the flight home. We had a good talk. Because of their love for me, they only wanted to be sure I was confident about what I was doing, that I was happy, and that my boyfriend would be responsible, caring, and respectful.

My parents' fears were relieved when I told them we had start-ed attending church together. Two weeks later, I brought my boyfriend home to meet my parents. We announced our engagement and were married six months later.

I asked God for forgiveness for the unkind things I'd done or said and for the times I hadn't listened. Mom forgave me. I realized how deep her love was for me. I could count her love and many kindnesses—the kindnesses and love my Father in heaven also bestowed on me.

God has dealt with many stubborn people through the ages, and the Israelites were no exception (half of the book of Isaiah is about rebellion). When I became a parent, the Bible passages describing their behavior tugged at my heartstrings. It seemed incomprehensible that an entire *nation* rebelled against God and refused to listen to Him.

A subheading of the New International Version, beginning with Isaiah 48, says it all: "Stubborn Israel." The people were stubborn, all right. Perhaps this was a facade for rebellion, just like the teenage girl in today's story.

Examples from the book of Isaiah showing God's view of Israel's rebellion:

1:2(b): *"I reared children and brought them up, but they have rebelled against me."*

1:3(b) *"...but Israel does not know, my people do not understand."*

1:4(a) *"Woe to the sinful nation, a people whose guilt is great..."*

1:4(b) *"...a brood of evildoers, children given to corruption!"*

1:4(b) *"They have forsaken the Lord; they have spurned the Holy One of Israel and turned their backs on him."*

1:17 *"Learn to do right; seek justice..."*

Numerous judgments appear in the Book of Isaiah. Yet, Chapter 9 reveals good news regarding Isaiah's prophecy of the coming Savior. Chapter 11 offers good news, too, pointing to the Branch from Jesse, the lineage of which Jesus would come.

God chose Isaiah to be His spokesperson to remind the people of His Covenant, reveal their sins, and warn them of God's judgment. Isaiah tried his best, but the people turned their backs on the Lord. Did they pretend not to hear (as a certain 6-year-old in our story)? Did they think they could manage independently (as a certain college student thought she could do?)

Following many writings of judgment and doom, the second half of the book of Isaiah offers recompense: God offers redemption to those who were sorry for their sins.

The latter chapters of Isaiah show a return to goodness. People once again praise God. The redeemed are joyful. God's people are comforted, and invitations for the thirsty in spirit are welcomed. The Lord offers hope for the future and calls Israel a chosen nation.

God shows kindness and compassion for His people who return to faith (Isaiah 63:7).

God does the same for us as He did for the people of Israel. I know He did for me. When I called Him for help, He brought me back into His fold. I felt His kindness, His compassion, His love. I wanted the freedom to make my own decisions, but what I needed was His direction.

When I started to pay attention to God's Word, whether at church or reading my Bible, I felt God's love for me. It was His voice that spoke to my heart when He answered my prayers. His nurturing and healing Spirit made me feel safe, warm and loved.

I often wondered how God could love me for all the wrong things I did, but His love for me never changed. I thought of the love my mother showed me as a small child, lying by my side and holding me when I was afraid of the dark. Later, she waited for me, confronted me, challenged me, called me out on my mistakes, listened to me, wiped my tears when I cried and forgave me. My mother was a beautiful example of the kind of love that I think God desires that we will show to one another.

Looking back at Isaiah's life, he likely recognized that difficult circumstances (a nation in rebellion) could bring about change that could be turned into something good. He spread the news of God's kindness and compassion and leaned on the Lord's promises.

I learned to lean on God's promises, too, knowing they'd never be broken. If I could write God a thank you note and hand it to heaven, I'd do it. But I can thank Him, give Him glory, and show gratitude for His great kindness and compassion.

If the Lord could forgive a nation of some of the most disobedient sinners in biblical history, I knew He could forgive me, too.

And that's *one good thing.*

Worksheet for My Daily Morsel #2
Personal Insight:
How has God's kindness and compassion impacted your life?

_____
_____
_____
_____

Reflection: My "One Good Thing:"
God is forgiving. What "one good thing" has come from God's forgiveness for you?

_____
_____
_____
_____
_____

Today's Serving:
It's hard enough for young people to listen and abide by rules given by parents, teachers, or authority figures. Unfortunately, many adults don't listen, either. The Israelites certainly didn't, but they finally turned from their shameful ways. They realized what they'd been missing when they restored their faith in God and were thankful for all the *good things* He had promised them.

A Cupful of Reality:
Have you had an experience like the young person in today's story or a tale of not listening like the Israelites? If so, what happened? How did this turn into something positive? If it did not work out positively, how might it have worked out differently with more obedience?

_____

_____

_____

_____

_____

A Taste of Spiritual Nourishment:
From our verse in Isaiah comes a key word, *praise*. When you begin your day by praising God for His kindness and compassion, you are one step ahead of letting negative thoughts intrude.

The Table of Optimism:
Hope resides at the Table of Optimism. What is your hope for today?

_____

_____

_____

_____

Prayer for Today:
Dear Father in heaven,

Let me count the ways I love You. Let my mouth be filled with praise for Your great love, kindness, and compassion. Sometimes, I don't feel I deserve what is good because of all I lack. But I know You forgive me, and I am grateful You love me—just as I am. In Jesus's name, amen.

Recipe

Prep Time

Cook Time

Oven Temp

Serves

Topic: **God's Promises**

Bible Verse for Study

"You, LORD, are God! You have promised these **good things** to your servant."

1 Chronicles 17:26

Mayhem for Thanksgiving

I have fond memories of Thanksgiving while growing up. Mom would greet me in the kitchen with sink-wet hands. I knew she loved me, but the wet hug sent a chill down my neck.

Mom was too busy to dry her hands. While cooking, she'd triple-step between the pantry, refrigerator, sink, stove, and oven like a crazy dance.

Mom didn't miss a beat. She'd stir gravy with one hand and mix ingredients for green bean casserole with the other, all while keeping the sweet potatoes from over-caramelizing and basting the turkey in the oven. She always said she had eyes in the back of her head. I believed it. She'd catch my brother and cousin sneaking olives from the condiment tray while facing away from the dining room.

"*Tsk-tsk*, boys!" Mom called out as they scampered down the stairs to the basement. Their mouths filled with olives; they looked like greedy squirrels with overstuffed cheeks. Mom knew best and had a hiding place in the cupboard with extra cans of olives.

Later, as the timer buzzed, I ran to the kitchen to watch Mom pull a perfectly golden bird from the oven. *Ahh.* I breathed in the aroma, imagining the taste of turkey slathered in gravy, the combination of sage, celery, and onion in the stuffing. My stomach rumbled. I longed for a bite.

Mom's glare told me, "Not yet."

Next came the tradition of every Thanksgiving. First, Mom would climb the stepstool to retrieve Great Grandma's serving platter from the hutch's top shelf. Then, holding the plate against her chest with both hands, she'd carefully climb down.

"Did you know this is nearly 150 years old?" she'd say, carefully setting the tray on the padded tablecloth.

"Yes, Mom." I nodded. The plate was special to her. She reminded me of this every Thanksgiving. But it was becoming special to me, too. I loved the brightly colored yellow and orange tulip pattern in the center. Running my finger around the edge, I traced the part resembling a textured basket weave.

Mom gave me a squinty-eyed look. I raised my hand from the plate. I wasn't supposed to touch it, but it was hard to resist. The colorful pattern reminded me of my favorite candy.

Dad sharpened the cleaver and sliced the turkey. Then, Mom layered the slices of meat on the platter. When she finished, a little bit of the flower pattern peaked through. It was so pretty.

A hand-crocheted tablecloth, silverware, and china from two generations made our plain dining room table look like a setting in an elegant restaurant. At least, I imagined it that way. I'd only seen pictures of such things in magazines.

Mom worried the delicate plates might chip, so she placed them on the table herself. My job was to fold napkins and set out the silverware.

"It's real silver, you know."

"Okay, Mom," I'd sigh. She always reminded me of this at Thanksgiving. I suppose there were some things she wanted to impress upon me; this was one of them. I held up a spoon in my hand. It felt sleek and lighter than our regular tableware. It was so shiny I could see my reflection: blue horn-rimmed glasses, blonde bob, blue eyes.

Mom said we were lucky to inherit my great-grandmother's serving tray, china, and silverware. They would have been too expensive to purchase at today's prices.

The subject of money came up often. I'd overheard Mom and Dad talk about the budget. They would have to be frugal. I knew the meaning of the word. Mom would have to spend less on everything—including groceries.

Thanksgiving was the exception. We had *real* milk on the table, a welcome relief from the usual powdered, foamy mixture that wasn't my favorite.

After Thanksgiving, Mom's kitchen work was more manageable. She made turkey soup, turkey casserole, turkey sandwiches, and omelets with turkey. My favorite meal was turkey with mashed potatoes and gravy, even though I got tired of the turkey.

It didn't do any good to complain. "We don't waste food," Mom would remind me. One day, she wrapped a single leftover hamburger in freezer paper.

"Aren't we going to eat the hamburger?" I asked. Mom shook her head as she slid it into the freezer. "No," she said. "I'll use it in the next batch of spaghetti sauce."

I was glad Mom didn't have to stretch *today's* meal as it was Thanksgiving.

We took our place at the table. I couldn't wait to eat.

"Let's bow our heads." Mom said.

Dad cleared his throat. He always said the blessing at Thanksgiving. His words were exact, well-thought-out, and purposeful. He said he was thankful to God for each of us, for all we had, and for the blessing of the food at our Thanksgiving table. I knew he meant what he said. He'd told me stories about growing up poor.

After dinner, we gathered around the fireplace. The warm, cozy feeling was topped off with Mom's steaming hot apple pie from the oven. As we indulged in dessert, the adults chatted. My face turned warm to hot when Mom bragged about me before the company. I felt embarrassed, but I knew it was Mom's way of showing her love for me.

The pleasant memories made me smile.

—

Years passed. Thanksgiving changed. Dad was diagnosed with Pulmonary Fibrosis and died at age 71. Later, after a nine-year battle with Alzheimer's, Mom passed away.

Mom and Dad were the foundation of our growing-up years. Now they were gone. Holidays would never be the same. They were the holders of the family traditions passed down by grandparents, great-grandparents, and those before them. Something else was missing at Thanksgiving, too, but I couldn't figure out what it was.

Maybe it was our lifestyle? My husband and I weren't rich, but we could buy things my parents could never have afforded. Growing up during the Great Depression, they learned to be content with what they had. Depression-era thinking affected everything they did, including hanging on to old furniture. Some of it was outdated, and I couldn't see keeping it.

I hesitated about getting rid of Mom's Duncan-Phyfe drop-leaf table. It was the extra table she used in the den. I didn't know how old it was, but she'd had it since she and Dad married. The aging was apparent—it had a cracked claw foot, and the wooden brace supporting the hinged table part was broken. It had a few dings in the finish, too. I couldn't imagine trying to repair it.

The thought of new furniture beckoned, and I sold the table. Later, I regretted my decision. An acquaintance with knowledge of antiques told me the repair would have been affordable. "It wouldn't have cost as much as the table you bought," she said. I should have learned from Mom and Dad to be content with what I had.

The purposeful Thanksgiving of the past gave way to a new era. Now, my husband was the one who would take a moment to say the Thanksgiving Blessing. But it was just that—a *moment*—not taken seriously. Prayer used to be the focus of our Thanksgiving meal. But not now.

Instead, noisy chaos ensued. Food was passed to the right and left as utensils clinked against dishware. For some, the unspoken goal was to fill their plate with as much food as possible in the least amount of time. We were having total mayhem for Thanksgiving.

"Pass the turkey!" "Butter over here!" "Send the rolls!" "Gimme' the gravy!" The cacophony of voices sounded across the table as plates of food were handed to whoever barked their request first.

Faces leaned over plates while jaws chewing accompanied the disharmonic ting of forks scraping on china. Open mouths awaited morsels like starving baby birds. *Gluttony.* How did we get like this?

I looked around the table and shook my head. I felt ashamed. This wouldn't have happened if Mom and Dad had been here. Like Mom's old Duncan Phyfe table, our family traditions had given way to cracks and breakage. Along with that, add in a fractured faith.

Times had changed. Faces looked at cell phones instead of at each other. Personal video games took the place of kids playing in the yard. And addiction to sports on television kept some from interacting with the family.

A lot of things were different from when I was growing up. However, one truth was evident: We had almost everything we wanted, but what we *needed* wasn't for sale. Reverence and thankfulness were not available on store shelves. Would I be able to place it in our hearts again?

—

The Wednesday before Thanksgiving, I stood in a line extending one aisle from the grocery checkout. Most carts, as well as mine, were filled to the brim.

Can't I pay for my groceries and go home? I had too much to do to be stuck here on Thanksgiving Eve.

The man in front of me let out a slew of unacceptable expressions. I had to admit his words matched the grumbling I felt inside.

Miserable, no-good day! Long lines. Rush-hour traffic. Get home late. Unload groceries. Clean house. Prepare for fourteen guests.

I began dicing celery, onion, and sage at home to add to the stuffing mix like Mom used to do. My thoughts slipped back to Thanksgiving as a child and Dad's prayers. He always said he was grateful to God for what we had, and we respected—and honored— the time of prayer. Then Mom would get the last word in. "Don't forget about the roof over our heads," she'd add. I knew we were fortunate to have a home of our own.

Z-i-n-g-g-g. The kitchen buzzer jolted me back to the present. Recent Thanksgivings came to mind. Did we realize how fortunate we were? In this present day of owning much, did we truly know what it meant to be thankful? I shook my head.

Something would need to change. I'd have to come up with a plan soon.

If anyone knew how to give thanks, it was David of the Bible. This young shepherd boy gave his undivided attention—and devotion—to God. Likewise, he cared for his sheep in this same way.

His job was far from glamorous, battling cold temperatures on winter nights and sweltering heat on summer days. He likely carried a blanket or coat to gather the little lambs too young to follow the flock. There probably wasn't much time to rest at night with predators lurking to attack the sheep. Yet David remained diligent in his work.

David's humble beginnings expanded to other areas. Adept at music, he played the harp to soothe the frazzled nerves of King Saul. His diligence indicated his ability to take on grander accomplishments, such as being king of Israel.

He knew the *good things* that filled his life came from God. In 1 Chronicles 17:26, David praises God, saying, *"You, LORD, are God! You have promised these good things to your servant."*

When David became king, he took on a great responsibility. Yet, even with the authority he possessed, he remained humble as he revered, glorified, and honored God.

Awestruck with what the Lord had done for him, David wrote, *"Who am I, LORD God, and what is my family, that you brought me this far?"* (1 Chronicles 17:16). For him, there were no other gods. He worshiped only the one who calls Himself Creator, the I Am, the Alpha, and the Omega, the Eternal One. In 1 Chronicles 17:20, David declares, *"There is no one like you, LORD, and there is no God but you, as we have heard with our own ears."*

A nearly perfect host, David knew how to serve, routinely setting out a feast of praise to God. Even as king, he retained the heart of a servant, extending his thankfulness for all the Lord had done for him.

But as righteous as David was, later in life (see 2 Samuel 11), he acted on a temptation that caused significant mayhem. Instead of giving his undivided attention to God, his attention was *divided*—between the righteous life he had been living for God—and gluttony. His unruly appetite led him to indulge in the pleasures of a married woman, then arranged to have her husband killed in battle.

Sorry for what he had done, David begged for mercy and was forgiven.

In today's verse from 1 Chronicles 17:26, David accepted God's promises even though the Lord had chosen Solomon to build the temple. David could have been bitter about this, but instead, he praised God and gave Him glory. Now, that's *thanks-giving*.

My husband tended to the turkey on the morning of Thanksgiving as I cleared the counters to make room in the kitchen. Would God be on the mind of our family and guests today, or would the turkey, side dishes, and dessert take precedence, along with football, chips, and beer?

I retrieved Great Grandma's serving plate from the top shelf of the dining room cabinet. I looked down, held it in my hands, and closed my eyes. *Lord, help me make this Thanksgiving special as Mom would have.*

I set the plate on the dining room table, admiring the floral pattern I'd always loved. Serving—it was what this plate was for. But today, I wanted to do *more* than serve a meal. I wanted to have the *heart* of a servant, like Mom—and David. I wanted our prayer to be praise, our time together one of thankfulness, not self-absorption and gluttony.

I smiled as our two girls folded napkins and set out the silverware as I had done at their age. As Dad had once been, my husband was now the turkey-carving person. As Mom used to do, I arranged the turkey slices around the floral pattern in the center of the tray. It looked as beautiful as I'd always remembered.

When everything was ready, we gathered at the table. I spoke up. "Before we say the blessing, I'd like each of you to look under your plate."

Quizzical looks ensued, with a few "Whats?" and "Huhs?" Then, each pulled the piece of paper beneath their plate with a handwritten question on it: *"What are you most thankful for this Thanksgiving?"* As I gave instructions and passed out pencils, the room became quiet as everyone wrote their answer.

Then we bowed our heads. "Thank you, Lord," my husband began in his baritone voice, "for this gathering of all of us on this blessed day of Thanksgiving. I am most thankful for my family and all You have provided for us."

As a finishing element to the prayer, everyone shared what they were most grateful for—even the three-year-olds. Our grandson was thankful for his red toy fire truck, and our granddaughter was grateful for her baby doll with the pretend milk bottle. When asked what else they were thankful for, the little ones replied, "Mommy and Daddy."

My turn came last. I couldn't help but include being thankful for "a roof over our heads," as Mom used to say. I felt the corners of my mouth turn upward. If Mom and Dad were here, they would be smiling, too.

We had *reverence* last for more than a mere moment. We'd honored God for all the *good things* we had. It was much more like the Thanksgiving I'd remembered growing up. The plan had worked. We could be grateful, after all. Maybe it was there all along, but we hadn't taken the time to express it.

The seasons had changed, and so did our family. My husband and I sit in the chairs once occupied by Mom and Dad. Two new generations, including four grandsons and one granddaughter, now grace our table with their presence, seated where their great-grandparents once sat.

I look at each face, and I smile. This is our family. *This is* Thanksgiving.

And that's *one good thing*.

Worksheet for My Daily Morsel #3

Personal Insight:

For what three things are you most thankful?

1)_____ 2)_____ 3)_____

Of these three, which is most significant to you, and why?

_____

_____

_____

_____

_____

Reflection: My "One Good Thing":
What is *one good thing* you carry forward from your past or family traditions?

_____

_____

_____

_____

_____

It's normal to look back on the past; however, comparing the way things were "then" to the way they are "now" can cause disappointment or sadness. Have you ever grappled with living in your "thens" instead of your "nows?" If so, what happened, and were you able to let go of those things to focus on the present?

_____

_____

_____

_____

_____

It isn't easy to let go of the past, but here's my thought for you to keep things in perspective:

"God gives us eyes in the front of our head for a reason—to look forward, not backward!"

Today's Serving: The Goodness of Caring

Good things. Sometimes, they go unnoticed when our focus is else- where. It appeared this way for the family during their Thanksgiving cel- ebration. King David's once-good intentions were axed when his eyes roamed where they shouldn't have. Because of forgiveness, the family in today's story—and David—made a turnaround. When added to life's mix, an ounce of forgiveness cleans up some of the worst messes.

A Cupful of Reality:

What about today's story relates to your life—or the life of someone close to you? What happened, and was forgiveness a factor?

_____

_____

_____

_____

A Taste of Spiritual Nourishment:

From today's verse in 1 Chronicles 17:26 comes a key word, *servant.* How are you called to serve God? With open hands, as you help others, you are also ready to receive the *good things* God promises His servants.

The Table of Optimism:

Hope resides at the Table of Optimism. What is your hope for today?

_____

_____

_____

_____

Prayer for Today:

Dear God,

When life changes and holidays aren't like they used to be, remind me that You bring different people and circumstances into my life for a rea- son. You have my best interests in mind, even if Your plan differs from what I expected. May I learn to be a humble servant like David and give You utmost praise and thanksgiving for all You have provided. - In Jesus's name, amen.

Recipe

Prep Time

Cook Time

Oven Temp

Serves

Topic: **God Rules**

Bible Verse for Study

"Is it not from the mouth of the Most High that both calamities and **good things** come?"

Lamentations 3:38

THE PERILOUS
WALLOW FIRE

By late afternoon, we reached southwestern New Mexico. It was a long drive, but now, we were only a few hours away from our home in Arizona. The monotonous stretch of interstate prompted my husband to turn on the radio. He came across a local news station. I heard the words "fire" and "Arizona" when the reception became fuzzy.

"Did you hear that?" I asked my husband.

"No, I didn't," he remarked.

The static cleared as we descended a hill.

"They're calling it the Wallow..."

"Wait," my husband interrupted, turning up the radio.

I kept quiet so we could listen to the details. A fire in eastern Arizona prompted concern for the town of Alpine. Hearing this news, we felt worried.

"Jim and Gwen might not be home yet," my husband remarked. "They're probably still on the road. Dial his number for me, will you?"

His brother's number rang repeatedly.

"Darn," my husband said, his brow furrowing. "It's not like him not to answer—and with no way to leave a message."

Jim and Gwen had spent part of their vacation with us. We met in Texas at our daughter's house. They left at the same time as we did but planned to take extra days to explore Big Bend before returning to Alpine.

They'd finished building their dream home in the forest only two years ago. Early in their marriage, they began saving money to put a deposit on a half-acre of mountain land. It was there they'd built their cabin home. Now retired, it was their principal residence.

"What if they don't know about the fire?" I remarked.

"It's my concern, too," my husband said. "They might be somewhere off the grid."

Active outdoors enthusiasts, Jim and Gwen often embarked on adventures at the spur of the moment. They might have taken a detour to go rock-hounding or fishing. They didn't need to adhere to a schedule and could do as they pleased.

A half-hour passed—then forty-five minutes. My husband phoned again.

"Still no answer," he said, swallowing. "And voicemail won't go through." He shook his head.

A nervous feeling churned inside. I had a bad feeling about this. When we got home, we assumed our phone reception would be better than on the road. But we still couldn't reach my husband's brother.

We turned on the news—every station was covering the incident. The fire was at zero containment. The mountain burned at an alarming rate as wind fueled the flames. An emergency bulletin flashed across the screen. Alpine residents were placed on high alert for possible evacuation.

I felt sick with worry as my husband paced the family room. "Dear God, where are they?" he said, cupping his head into his hands. "Why don't they answer?"

"I'm worried, too," I said, "but there has to be a good explanation."

My husband shook his head. I looked into his piercing, dark eyes. "Let's pray," I said.

My husband nodded. We bowed our heads.

"Please, God," I said, taking my husband's hand. *"We're worried about Jim and Gwen. Be with them, Lord. Keep them safe. Keep their cabin safe. We also pray for the residents of Alpine and the firefighters as they battle this horrible fire. And we pray we will hear from Jim and Gwen soon. In Jesus' Name, Amen.*

Then, exhausted, we flopped onto the couch and closed our eyes. I had barely started to drift off to sleep when the shrill sound of my husband's phone cut into the silence.

My husband grabbed his phone. "Jim?" he said, holding the phone close to his ear. "I've tried calling so many times—we heard about the fire. Are you okay? . . . Good. So, you're at the cabin . . . What? They told you to evacuate?"

The muscles in my throat tightened.

"I'll hook up the flatbed. We'll drive out, pack your furniture and belongings, and. . . ." My husband held the phone away from his ear. "You only have how long?" my husband replied, stammering. His face turned ashen. "If there's any way we can help . . . Yes, but . . . Well, I understand you have to go . . . Dear God, we're praying for you. Call me when you can. God be with you, brother."

My husband set the phone down and slumped onto the couch. "They have to evacuate," he said, his voice breaking.

"How soon?"

"Within two hours. The sheriff came to their door to tell them."

I felt chills run through me. I couldn't imagine how they were coping. They'd just returned home from a relaxing vacation, free from worries or cares—to calamity.

I wrapped my arms around my husband's shoulders, my hand moist from wiping away tears. My husband looked like he was about to cry, too.

"Can't we do *something*?" I pleaded.

"No. There isn't enough time."

He was right. It would be unrealistic to drive five hours to their cabin when they only had two hours to evacuate.

There was nothing we could do—but *pray*.

I couldn't imagine the long, sleepless night ahead for my brother-in-law and his wife. They'd load as many possessions as possible and quickly vacate the cabin. The nearest shelter was an hour away at a school gymnasium in a neighboring town.

They didn't know how long they'd be there. They were told they'd be kept up to date on the status of the fire, but they would only be allowed to return to their home once the fire was contained and permission was granted to return—to see if anything was left.

Unfortunately, emergent firefighting efforts made communication less frequent than they had hoped.

We watched the news, but it didn't look good. Due to high winds, the fire was still at zero containment. That meant only one thing. The blaze was out of control.

We felt some relief knowing water tankers and other equipment were being utilized. Measures were taken to use water from the tankers and fire retardants to protect homes and structures and mitigate the fire's spread.

Unfortunately, the weather didn't cooperate. By morning, the wind had picked up, fueling the fire and causing it to spot up in other areas. In addition to the rugged mountain terrain, reaching some areas of the fire became nearly impossible and put the firefighters in danger. Neither Richard nor I slept well. In the morning we received a text message from Jim. It read:

"Fire less than ten min. from cabin. Pls pray."

My husband's eyes teared up. So did mine. We felt helpless to do anything—except watch, wait, and pray.

The bad news didn't end. An emergency TV bulletin reported outbuildings and cabins burned in a forest resort close to Jim and Gwen's place.

We closed our eyes and prayed non-stop for thirty or forty minutes. The phone rang. It was Jim. My husband fumbled to answer the call and pushed the speaker button.

"This might be it." Jim said in a sullen voice. "The fire crossed the barrier. Reached our neighborhood. I don't know what to think," he said, choking on words. "We might ... lose everything."

Our hope sank. Our hearts ached. How were they coping—sequestered in a gymnasium far from home—not knowing the fate of everything they owned?

Minutes turned into hours. With no further word, we suspected the worst.

—

"Wake up!" Richard shook my shoulders, then turned on the light. Bleary-eyed, I sat up in bed and tried to focus. "What's going on?"

"My brother's on the phone." He punched the speaker button and held the phone between us. I took in a deep breath. I wanted to know—and yet I didn't.

Jim's voice was shaky. "The fire . . . came within one hundred yards of our home. Can you believe it—the length of a football field? That's how close it was."

"Ohh...." Richard was speechless. I slapped a hand over my mouth in disbelief.

Jim paused, then collected himself. "The fire burned property across the road and beyond," he said, his voice wavering with emotion. "But our cabin is safe. It's standing. Praise God! Thank you for your prayers. I can't stay on the phone. Gotta' go."

Hours of worry and concern came to a halt. We couldn't believe how close the fire got to the home—yet it wasn't touched. Their cabin was safe—and so were they.

Richard and I embraced and said a prayer of thanks, but we also prayed for those who had sadly lost homes or property.

The fire had changed course, bypassing the remainder of the community. However, it was largely uncontained as it blazed through the mountains. High winds didn't decrease, causing the fire to scorch and burn over a half-million acres of forest land. It wiped out cabins, outbuildings, and businesses. Mountainous terrain proved difficult to navigate, but fire crews and air tankers did their best to save homes and structures.

We met with Jim and Gwen after the ordeal was over. Their prayers had been answered, but other questions remained: Why was their home spared when others weren't? Had it made a difference for them to keep their property free from debris and dry pine needles?

Or, as Gwen added, "Did it have to do with all the people praying for us?"

They would never know the answers to those questions. "I guess we'll have to trust God on that one," Jim said.

Gwen said she'd thought a lot about their home and belongings. "I had to separate myself from our house and all the *things*," she said. "All I could do was put it all in God's hands. I figured that even if we lost our home and everything we owned, we'd still have each other." She added, "One thing is for sure: God has been with us. I felt His peace when the fire was closing in."

Gwen's words stuck close to my heart. How would we have reacted had we been in their situation? Would we have kept that same kind of faith? I wanted to think so—but then, I'd never been through what she and Jim had just experienced.

An additional dose of angst swept through the cities and towns when the news came out about how the fire originated. Authorities announced two campers were seen where the fire had erupted. Sadly, they'd left a campfire unattended, which sparked, then rapidly spread to surrounding vegetation, igniting the forest into a raging blaze.

The carelessness of two individuals destroyed over half a million acres of forest land, cabins, homes, outbuildings, and businesses. It was a fire that could have been prevented.

The Old Testament prophet Jeremiah knew all too well about devastation and calamity. Like the hundreds of thousands of acres of forest destroyed by the fire, Jeremiah and the people of Jerusalem experienced the destruction of their city. Jeremiah's words of lament and sorrow would later become the Book of Lamentations and offers a detailed description of Jerusalem's destruction. Lamentations 1:6 relates:

"All the splendor has departed from Daughter Zion. Her princes are like deer that find no pasture; in weakness they have fled before the pursuer."

Even the most noble were powerless to do anything.

The forest land and the city of Jerusalem were places where life once flourished abundantly. There would be no homes for the people nor animals to return to without sustenance, food, or water. As Lamentations 1:6 reveals, the land that was once alive is now dead, leaving the people like deer without pasture.

The Wallow Fire could have been prevented. Campers thought they had doused their campfire well before leaving their campsite; however, the wind caused a remaining ember to ignite, setting the trees and brush around it ablaze. Sadly, the fire resulted in a loss of cabin homes, property, and businesses, and burned over a half-million acres of forest.

Likewise, Jerusalem would have been saved from destruction if the people had listened to God.

Despite the loss incurred in Jerusalem, Lamentations 3:22–26 shows hope for those who hold onto faith:

"Because of the LORD's great love we are not consumed, for his compassions never fail. They are new every morning; great is your faithfulness. I say to myself, 'The LORD is my portion; therefore, I will wait for him.' The LORD is good to those whose hope is in him, to the one who seeks him; it is good to wait quietly for the salvation of the LORD."

Today's verse from Lamentations 3:38 exemplifies God's almighty and absolute power: *"Is it not from the mouth of the Most*

High that both calamities and good things come?"

God can allow good things to occur, but in some circumstances, we may question why unpleasant things happen. It is not easy to understand, for we do not know the mind of God. However, He offers recompense: *"For no one is cast off by the LORD forever. Though he brings grief, he will show compassion, so great is his unfailing love. For he does not willingly bring affliction or grief to anyone"* (Lamentations 3:31–33).

Is there a good view of "bad"? In a sense, yes. Some of the greatest afflictions known to humanity also bring change, growth, and renewal. Likewise, the goodness in people's hearts pours out during calamities. Such was the outpouring of compassion for those affected by the Wallow Fire.

Despite the destruction of the city of Jerusalem, goodness came through redemption. Some had faith and held steadfast through the devastation. Others turned away but later repented. Jerusalem's eventual rebuilding and renewal would occur because of God's compassion and love for His people.

Lamentations 3:40 shows a change in the thinking and attitude of the people: *"Let us examine our ways and test them, and let us return to the LORD."*

God loves his children so much that, no matter what destruction they bring upon themselves, He is ready and willing to accept their return to Him.

Following the Wallow Fire, the wounded acreage was reseeded to grow new vegetation. It will take many years for the forest to return to its pre-blaze state, but little by little, the forest and the mountain communities will be renewed and thrive once again.

As God's people returned to faith, the city of Jerusalem was rebuilt and became a strong and prosperous community.

Often, we think calamities happen to others and not us; however, disaster can strike when we least expect it. It may be hugely devastating or small. Sometimes, calamities are preventable;

sometimes, they are not.

Gwen put it best when she said, "God is with us no matter what."

Land, pastures, and cities can be nurtured back to life with the good things God has in store. It is this way with God's people, too. Those who come to Him in brokenness will be renewed and replenished through His unfailing love.

Good things *can* come from calamity. Indeed, God rules over all.

And that's *one good thing*.

Worksheet for My Daily Morsel #4

Personal Insight:
Large or small disasters present us with difficult challenges. What disasters—or calamities—have taken place in your life? What happened, and how did you get through it?

_____

_____

_____

_____

_____

In what way can you personally identify with the words of Lamentations 3:22, *"Because of the Lord's great love, we are not consumed, for his compassions never fail."*

_____

_____

_____

_____

_____

Reflection: My "One Good Thing"
Name "one good thing" that you know has come out of strife or affliction.

_____

_____

_____

_____

Today's Serving: God's Rule and Recompense
Jim and Gwen witnessed the devastation in their community. Jeremiah saw the effects of the destruction of Jerusalem. Both calamities could have been prevented. If the people of Judah had listened to God, their fate would have been different. Drought conditions in Jim and Gwen's mountain community vastly increased the risk of wildfire. Sadly, forest campers did not adequately douse a campfire, causing a smoldering ember to ignite the blaze.

However, good things can come from devastation: The City of Jerusalem was rebuilt as a community of faith. And Jim and Gwen's faith helped them through a difficult time. Just when everything seemed impossible, hope remained.

A Cupful of Reality:

We may not always understand why calamities occur. But God never abandons us. Through Him, we have hope.

A Taste of Spiritual Nourishment:

From today's verse in Lamentations comes a key word, *mouth*, in reference to God's power. We take nutrition into our mouths to sustain our bodies. From our mouths come the words of our hearts. May we take in only *good things* for our physical and spiritual health!

The "Table of Optimism":

Hope resides at the Table of Optimism. What is your hope for today?

_____

_____

_____

_____

Prayer for Today:

Dear Father in heaven,

It is hard for me to understand why bad things happen sometimes. But no matter the outcome, I know You are with me and will never abandon me. Thank You for saving me in times of distress and showing me Your peace in times of turmoil. In Jesus's name, amen.

Recipe

My Daily Morsel #5

Prep Time _____   Cook Time _____

Oven Temp _____   Serves _____

Topic: **God's Goodness**

_____

_____

_____

_____

_____

Bible Verse for Study

"A good man brings **good things** out of the good stored up
in his heart, and an evil man brings evil things out of the evil
stored up in his heart. For the mouth speaks what the heart
is full of."

Luke 6:45

_____

_____

Oh, No, Not Edna!

The phone rang. It was Richard. He was at work. "No time to talk, Hon. I need to let you know Frank and Edna are coming at four o'clock instead of seven. Love you."

"Sweetheart?" I called out. Too late. I stood there in the kitchen with the phone to my ear. Unspoken words hung in the air.

Frank and Edna were coming early? *Oh, great.* Now I'd be short on time.

I blew out a heavy breath. *I bet it was Edna's idea to show up early. It would be just like her.* The muscles in my neck tensed as resentment filled my heart.

I saturated the dishrag with soap and with pursed lips attacked the saucepan with a heavy swipe. Hadn't I already done enough? Shopped, chopped, boiled, baked. Pre-cooked dinner. Okay, so the food was ready, but the house wasn't. And I certainly wasn't prepared—for the company I did not want.

I couldn't blame Richard. It wasn't his fault he'd run into Frank at an out-of-town business conference. They hadn't seen each other in years. My kind-hearted husband told Frank to look us up if he and Edna ever came back to town. Now Frank was taking him up on the offer.

Frank was fine; he was a treasure. His wife was the problem.

E-d-n-a. The thought of her setting foot in our house brought my internal thermometer to a boil.

The problem with Edna? She had no boundaries. She spoke as

she pleased, but her comments were never pleasing.

Being a Christian and knowing Edna was a dilemma for me. I was sure the good Lord loved Edna more than I could ever know. But me? How would I be able to care for her the way Jesus would? I could not find anything about her to love. I would never understand what Frank saw in her.

The day I'd met Edna—nearly fourteen years ago—was a day I wished I could have erased from my memory. It should have been a quiet summer afternoon. I'd put the baby down for a nap and poured a glass of iced tea when I heard pounding at my front door. Not just a knock, but a *Thud! Thud! Thud!* Like a sledgehammer.

I ran into the hallway. The noise stopped. I heard the baby's trembling cry and rushed to her crib, cradling her in my arms. The *Thud!* started again. I couldn't chance trouble, so I laid her back on the soft mattress.

Sweet baby, go to sleep. I glanced back before rounding the corner. My heart cried out as her tiny lip quivered.

I dashed down the hallway, sliding in slipper socks around the corner, the baby's cry muted by the constant *thud*. I approached the door. My heartbeat vibrated in my chest. Who was there? What was wrong? I froze in my steps, caught my breath, and listened. No voice outside. No sound of footsteps. Were they gone?

I slipped over to the right side of the door, peering through a crack in the drapery. Bushes in the way. The *thud* resumed.

I stepped behind the door. It was not cold in the house, but goosebumps covered my arms. "Who...is...there?" my voice shook.

A shrill, raspy voice rang out. "Your *neighbor*!"

I paused. "Who?" I didn't recognize the woman's voice.

"Your neighbor!"

"Is...something wrong?" I called out.

"Ye-s-s-s!" the voice responded adamantly.

I hesitated and took a deep breath as I placed my hand on the doorknob. I pulled the door open just a crack, enough to see a short, squat woman with grayish-brown hair and a moon-shaped face scowl at me. She had one hand on her hip, although it was difficult to define her large frame's details in the stretched pink housecoat. She held a white cloth in the other hand.

"What's wrong?" I called out. My senses reeled—scowling neighbor, baby crying. *Pull away...No...Wait.*

I pulled the door open a little more.

"About time you answered, Susie Q!" the woman huffed.

"I'm sorry, but..." I swallowed. "...I'm Nan..."

"I'm Edna. E-D-N-A. Got it?" she hissed.

She held up the cloth and waved it in front of my nose. I stepped back, almost tripping.

"Whoa...What?" I exclaimed.

"Now you see it with your own eyes," she barked. "Don't let these filthy things blow into my backyard!"

She tossed the cloth at my feet and glared at me with squinty eyes. My eyebrows lifted, my lip twisting to fathom what had just happened.

I bent down to pick up the cloth. It was a diaper. *It must have blown off the clothesline.*

Moon-face waited for my response. I searched her expression for understanding, but it wasn't there. I clamored to say anything, but the words wouldn't come out. I shook my head. The diaper was a little stiff, but it was clean.

"So disgusting!" Edna snapped. She turned abruptly and stomped down the steps. I only caught bits of her condescending mumble: "Don't have the decency...I didn't move here to...Not going to put up with..."

I felt like slamming the door but didn't want to startle the baby. I padded into my daughter's room, scooping her into a soft blanket. *I'm not going to let that mean lady bother you ever again.* My sweet firstborn quit crying and looked up at me with large, innocent eyes.

What human being would complain about a menial piece of laundry blowing into their yard?

Later, when Frank came over to visit with my husband in the garage, he apologized. "I don't know why Edna acted that way," he said, his face reddening. "I'm sorry."

Months later, Edna's mother died. Trying to be a forgiving neighbor, I left a sympathy card with a Bible verse and slipped it into her mailbox. Shortly after that, as my daughter played in the front yard, I saw Edna bolt out of her front door. Standing in her yard, she pointed an accusing finger at me.

Her hollering rang out before I could retrieve my daughter and return to the house. "So, little Missy, who believes in a 'god' of some sort," she huffed, "you need to know I *don't* believe." She paused, then yelled at the top of her voice, "Religion is just a crutch for weak people—like you!"

The heat rose in the back of my neck, but I said nothing as I scooped up my little girl.

As always, Edna had the last word. "I'm in charge of my own (expletive) life. I don't need your help!" she hollered, then slammed the door.

This was the beginning of the E-d-n-a events, and now, fourteen years later, every detail was still as clear in my mind as if it had just taken place.

Edna would again be standing at my front door in just a few hours. My only consolation was that her husband would be present.

Thinking about past Edna incidents, I was overwhelmed with disdain. I dug into the housework with a vengeance. With every swipe of the dust rag, I dished out pretend remarks to Edna, and they weren't friendly. But, as ornery as I felt, there wasn't much I could do. I didn't want to disappoint my husband or cause Frank to feel bad, but I could not think of one good thing to say about Edna.

I forced my thoughts to the present, straightened the girls' rooms, and then attended to the rest of the house. I wiped the sweat from my forehead. Exhausted, I leaned against the counter in the kitchen and then looked up at the clock.

Oh, no. *Three-thirty p.m. already.*

I rushed to leave the kitchen to change clothes but stopped short—the tie of my apron caught on the oven handle. As I untangled myself, I saw my mother's ceramic plaque above the stove. She'd given it to me when we were first married. I didn't notice it often as time passed, probably because I was constantly in a hurry. But I saw it now:

"Bless my little kitchen, God, and those who enter in.

May they find naught but joy and peace and happiness therein."

A feeling of solemness seeped into my heart. My kitchen wasn't like Mom's—especially not right now. Would my family or guests find a sense of joy or peace here? I doubted it. And happiness? Negligible. In my current state of mind, anger replaced happiness, and little good came from the thoughts in my heart.

I hadn't been attentive to Mom's plaque. I dusted it off occasionally but hadn't taken the words to heart.

Not the way she did.

I closed my eyes as tears formed. *I'm sorry, Mom. I wish I could be more like you. I wish you were here.*

Mom depended on God to get through difficult times. I needed to learn how to rely on Him, too.

When I heard the sound of the front door opening, I tossed my apron into the pantry and said a quick prayer as I walked to the entryway. *Lord, help me to find something good about Edna.*

Richard, dressed in a suit and tie, hugged me tightly despite my sweat-drenched shirt. He lifted my chin and kissed me gently. "It's going to be okay, Hon," he said.

"I hope so," I responded, trying to smile. "Are they here yet?"

"Yes. Frank is helping Edna out of the car."

"Oh, all right," I replied. "I'll be out in a minute. I'm going to change clothes."

When I returned, an older man with white hair held the arm of a gray-haired woman. Frank and Edna? Could it be? It hardly looked like them. But yes. That was Frank. Tall, thin, with hunched shoulders. He held a bony hand out to help his much leaner wife up the front steps.

I stared. "Frank? Edna?"

"It's us. Good to see you folks again." He offered a meager smile. Edna looked up but said nothing. She held on to Frank's arm tightly and gazed back at the steps.

Was this Edna? I could hardly believe how much she had aged. Her skin was lined with deep wrinkles; sagging skin replaced a moon-shaped face.

Frank was as gentle as I remembered. We hugged as he reached the top step, but I'd never seen him look so thin. His clothes looked too big.

Frank held onto Edna's arm. The rudest woman I'd ever known was now a frail old lady with a far-away look in her eyes. Only a slightly protruding stomach reminded me of her previous girth.

I could scarcely take in the change.

"Hello...Edna." I waited for a reaction. She only blinked her eyes and stared. Where was the feisty Edna I remembered? The one who pounded on my door, raised her fist at her husband, and made her voice known about not believing in God?

A lot of things can change in fourteen years.

Frank guided his wife to a chair and helped her sit. He handed me his hat and whispered, "Edna has Alzheimer's." He patted my shoulder as if to say he was sorry for all she put me through. "I'll tell you more later," he said.

On this balmy summer afternoon, an icy chill shot through me. I felt ashamed for all my anger and condemnation toward Edna. Now, it was snuffed. Extinguished. Terminated. Done.

Before the meal, my husband led us in prayer, and I noticed Frank bowed his head, too.

We made it through dessert and then relocated to the living room. The girls came in and sat down next to Edna. My oldest daughter lovingly took Edna's wrinkled hand in hers. Edna did not resist. She sat very still, closing her eyes. It was hard to tell if this was comforting or if she was tired.

Frank joined my husband and me across the room. "I should have told you this before," he said in a low voice, "but Edna had dementia a long time before we knew about Alzheimer's."

Frank paused and wiped a wisp of white hair to one side. "I didn't tell you then, but when Edna would come to your house, I felt so embarrassed. I didn't know why she acted the way she did." He lowered his gaze. "I didn't want to admit anything was wrong, but it was the beginning of dementia."

"We're so sorry, Frank," my husband replied. I nodded in agreement, but words would not come—a knot formed in my throat. I felt as low as a speck of dirt. I would never have guessed Edna had dementia. Was this the reason for the pounding on the door, the unruly behavior, and the uncouth language? It would explain a lot.

Right now, I felt like the unruly one, but at the same time, who could blame me for having been judgmental toward Edna?

Frank confided he and Edna needed a place to stay for a few days because they'd lost their home in foreclosure. He and Edna still owned a two-bedroom rental in town, but it would be a few weeks before he could move.

He swiped at the wetness beneath his eyelids. "Edna can't live with me anymore," he said, his lip quivering. He explained that she'd wandered out the front door and into the street. "Fortunately, she wasn't hit by a car," he exclaimed.

Frank's eyes looked misty. "I have to put her in a care home," he whispered, turning away. He pulled a handkerchief from his pocket.

We helped settle Frank and Edna for the night, but I could hardly sleep. Guilt leeched through every pore of my skin. I'd focused on everything wrong with Edna and grumbled about the impending visit. I'd pre-set my mood to the tune of highly undesirable. I'd neglected what was needed—a forgiving heart.

Instead of forgiveness, I'd stored resentment, anger, and unhappiness. I hadn't focused on the good things—like the words on Mom's plaque.

The verse for today, from Luke 6:45, are the words of Jesus and what he had to say about what comes from the human heart, either good or evil: *"A good man brings good things out of the good stored up in his heart, and an evil man brings evil things out of the evil stored up in his heart. For the mouth speaks what the heart is full of."*

The verses before this relate that a good tree doesn't produce bad fruit, and a bad tree doesn't produce good fruit (see Luke 6:43-44).

Jesus is comparing the heart of a good man to a tree that bears good fruit and the heart of an evil man to a bad tree that does not bear good fruit.

The key phrase Jesus used in the verse from Luke 6:45 is: "stored up." One good (or bad) action does not dub a person either good or bad. But note that Scripture uses the words *"stored up"* when referring to the heart of the good man and the evil man. The effect of good—or evil—comes when it is stored up in the heart.

Our words originate from the heart. A good man speaks kind and encouraging words, while an evil man speaks harshly and critically. The words from our lips reveal the truth of our hearts. The mouth acts as a spigot for what is inside the heart.

I thought of the poor attitude I had before Frank and Edna arrived. The truth would come out about all the wrong things I'd stored inside. My heart, spiritually speaking, had become my emotional storage shed. It was not a pretty place. It was falling apart, and it needed repair.

Our brain stores emotional memories; however, the Bible indicates the heart is home to the very root of our being. And within our hearts is the capacity to store good or bad things.

I have taken notice of Mom's plaque above the stove a lot more often. If I could see her now, I imagine her smiling and telling me to depend on God for the answers I need.

I pray more often now, saying, *I'm sorry, God. I wish I could be more like You. But one good thing I know—You are always with me.*

Maybe it was good I had that horrible, lousy day many years ago—God needed my attention. Maybe my apron getting caught on the oven door made me notice Mom's plaque above the stove.

One day, I'll give the plaque to one of my daughters. I can see it now. I smile as I hand it to her, and she places it on her kitchen wall. I give it to her with the same hope Mom had for my brother and me—to store good things in our hearts and accept others as Jesus does—even the Ednas of the world.

And that's *one good thing.*

Worksheet for My Daily Morsel #5

Personal Insight:
Did you ever dread preparing for an event or guests you did not care for? If so, what happened? Explain the outcome.

_____
_____
_____
_____

Reflection: My "One Good Thing"
What one good thing came out of the situation you were in? If nothing good resulted, would there be anything that could have been done to turn it around?

_____
_____
_____
_____

Name one of the good things you store in your heart:

_____
_____
_____
_____

If there is one thing you'd like to clear from your heart, what would it be?

_____
_____
_____
_____

Serving for Today: God's Goodness and the Freedom of Choice
Understanding how God could love anyone like Edna was hard for me. I'd pointed a finger and proclaimed she wasn't a good person. Indeed, Jesus could have pointed the finger at me for claiming such a thing. God gives us freedom of choice, but it can get us into trouble. Not knowing the whole picture, I was wrong to judge Edna. If I had known about her

cognitive decline, her behavior would have made sense, and I wouldn't have judged her as I did.

A Cupful of Reality: We're imperfect beings. Sometimes, we say or do wrong things. Have you caught yourself saying or doing the wrong thing? What happened? Were you able to turn a not-so-good situation into something better—or even good?

_____

_____

_____

_____

A Taste of Spiritual Nourishment:
From today's verse in Luke comes a key word, *overflow*. May the gracious words from your heart build your spiritual resilience to anything negative.

The Table of Optimism:
Hope resides at the Table of Optimism. What is your hope for today?

_____

_____

_____

_____

Prayer for Today:
Dear Father in heaven,

You know my innermost thoughts and misgivings. Encourage me to store only good things in my heart and purge all that is not good. May I think before I speak, use words wisely, and accept—and love—those different from me. In Jesus's name, amen.

Recipe

Prep Time

Cook Time

Oven Temp

Serves

Topic: **God's Sacrifice for Us**

_____
_____
_____
_____
_____

Bible Verse for Study

"The law is only a shadow of the **good things** that are coming—not the realities themselves. For this reason it can never, by the same sacrifices repeated endlessly year after year, make perfect those who draw near to worship."

Hebrews 10:1

YOUR SHADOW: A GLIMPSE OF YOU

Remember the first time you saw your shadow? Was it a moment of great delight, mystery, or fear? For me, it was all three. My friend came to my backyard to play on a sticky Virginia afternoon. We sat on the short brick wall dividing the driveway from the yard. Boredom set in, and I flitted my fingers back and forth in the sunlight.

It was then I first noticed my shadow—my twin. My friend laughed, copying my actions. We purposely moved our bodies in odd contortions, watching with glee as our shadows danced. The fun lasted until looming gray clouds blocked the sun.

Later, the sky cleared, and I went to the garden with my father. He handed me a wicker basket. "Hold it steady," he said, placing the fresh beans in the basket. I was drawn to the long, lean shadow of my father. He was not tall, but his shadow extended across the garden. My short stature grew big, too, and I wished I could be that height! Unfortunately, I was so distracted I spilled the basket's contents. Then, my father came over, and we picked up the beans—filling the basket to the brim. I loved the fresh, sweet smell of the vegetables we'd picked.

The bright orange and pink hues of the sunset dimmed, and with it, I watched the dusk gently erase our shadows from the ground. The blanket of the night stretched out over the sky. All the shadows were gone.

Later, I lay awake, thinking about my fun time watching my shadow. Then sudden blackness dampened my excitement, as the light from the hallway went dark. I could not see my hands in front of my face or anything else. I panicked. I couldn't see! My small, shaky voice pierced the quiet with a wail: "Mommy!" My fears were relieved as a flood of brightness entered my doorway. My mother came to the rescue with a flashlight, which I happily tucked under my bed-tent covers.

I wasn't afraid anymore. I felt safe and secure in the light.

The discovery of my shadow continued to intrigue me. My shadow *looked* just like me. It had my exact shape and form. It was a *glimpse* of who I was, but I knew it could never be the "real me." One night, as my mother and I knelt beside my bed to pray, I asked her if God made the shadows.

She said, "Yes, he did." Then I asked her *why*. "He must have had a reason," she said, kissing my cheek. She turned off my lamp and left my door open just enough to let in some light, and soon I was fast asleep.

Later, the importance I'd placed on my shadow gave way to other interests as my discoveries became a mere childhood memory. Reminiscing one day, I thought about the question I'd asked my mother so long ago: "Why did God make shadows?" She never knew the answer, but it made me think of the possibilities. What was the value of a shadow? I shrugged it off as a silly thought until I imagined living in a time without modern conveniences, cell phones, clocks, or watches. How would you know the time?

The light streams through the window at the break of dawn. There is no question about what time to get up in the morning. And when darkness comes, so does slumber.

Telling the time of day without clocks would turn you into a keen observer of sunlight and shadow, and this would quickly become second nature. Your "timepiece" might be a familiar object, a wall or post outside your home, or a stationary marking on the ground. As the day passes, you notice the shadows' position and length. It might signal the time to meet at the river to wash clothes, watch the children play together, and gather with other women in the community.

Later in the day, you must allow enough time to prepare the evening meal and tend to the garden and the animals before sunset. Otherwise, it would be too dark to continue working outside unless the moon provided enough light.

Today's verse from Hebrews 10:1 speaks of shadows from the view of Old Testament law.

As a child, I realized my shadow was nothing more than the form or shape of me. It was merely a *representation* of me and would never be more than that. Just as we distinguish between the reality of who we are and our opaque, temporary shadow, so, too, the Bible distinguishes between the Old Testament law and shadows. Hebrews 10:1(a) tells us: *"The law is only a shadow of the good things that are coming—not the realities themselves."*

The law existed as a "foreshadowing," a *glimpse* of something better to come. God brought the law to His people with the first covenant, which served a purpose for a certain period; however, as we know, the guidelines coming from the law were temporary. Something would have to change.

Many of God's people would not listen to His law and did not obey Him. The value of the law was only of a temporary duration, however. Its foreshadowing points to Christ with the words from Hebrews 10:1. The God of creation would bring something of much greater value to His people than the law—He would bring them Jesus.

Old Testament law established rules for the rites of worship. God desired that His people would behave in a manner pleasing to Him, so rules were set in place as standards for His expectations. If God's people held to their faith and followed the law, they could expect to receive His favor and blessing. On the contrary, those who did not submit to the law paid the consequences for their disobedience.

In the Old Testament, the atonement of sin was achieved using the blood of sacrificed animals. The practice was done only by the High Priests each morning and night. Animal sacrifices were repeated to cover the sins of the people. The establishment of biblical law provided an opportunity for people to receive God's favor—if they obeyed Him.

Unfortunately, numerous accounts of Old Testament history bear witness to sinful and wicked behavior. The request made by God was simple. He wanted His people to *listen* and *obey*; however, the stain of human sin blotted out any intended efforts of goodness or kindness.

But what about forgiveness of sin? In the Old Testament, animal sacrifices were carried out by the high priest to grant forgiveness. The nature of this practice is revealed in Hebrews 10:1(b): *"For this reason it can never, by the same sacrifices repeated endlessly year after year, make perfect those who draw near to worship."*

God's forgiveness of His people under Old Testament law was a temporary measure, and the sacrificial rituals performed by the High Priest of the Tabernacle represented a shadow of something better to come—Jesus Christ.

Jesus was the true High Priest (Hebrews 8:1-2): *"...who sat down at the right hand of the throne of the Majesty in heaven, and who serves in the sanctuary, the true tabernacle set up by the Lord, not by a mere human being."*

The words in today's verse from Hebrews 10:1(b) ring true: *"For this reason it can never...make perfect those who draw near to worship."* The sacrifices were ongoing, repeated year after year. It was as if the sinner could not feel he was ever completely forgiven.

The first covenant God made with His people did not take effect without the shedding of blood, evident in Hebrews 9:22: *"In fact, the law requires that nearly everything be cleansed with blood, and without the shedding of blood, there is no forgiveness."* Another reference from Hebrews 9:18 reveals the use of blood for sacrifice: *"This is why even the first covenant was not put into effect without blood"* (Hebrews 9:18).

Our answer to why the animal sacrifice was not enough to clear the sins of the people lies in this verse from Hebrews 9:9: *"...the gifts and sacrifices being offered were not able to clear the conscience of the worshiper."*

The Bible explains that animal sacrifices were related only to food, drink, and ceremonial washings. The ceremonial rituals were carried out to absolve sin. However, because they were not part of the believer's *conscience*, the act of forgiveness, according to Old Testament law, was not enough to effectively touch a person's soul.

Just as our earlier discussion of a shadow's limitations in revealing anything more than a shape or an outline of an object or person, the Old Testament law, too, was only a glimpse of the "real thing," but not the reality itself. The Old Testament law and its provision of cleansing foreshadowed something better to come: the cleansing of sin by Jesus Christ.

The repeated offerings of animal sacrifices were not enough to ease the sinner's conscience. The laws of the first covenant were continually broken, and God was unhappy with the rebellion. But He didn't give up on His people. Instead, he created a new covenant, as described in Hebrews 9:11–12:

"But when Christ came as high priest of the good things that are now already here, he went through the greater and more perfect tabernacle that is not made with human hands, that is to say, is not a part of this creation. He did not enter by means of the blood of goats and calves; but he entered the Most Holy Place once for all by his own blood, thus obtaining eternal redemption."

The earthly tabernacle referred to in the book of Hebrews is used to explain the first covenant regulations. As we read the story by the author of Hebrews, learning of the great wickedness permeating the land, we realize something had to change. A new covenant—a new agreement—*would* take place between God and His people.

Hebrews 8:5 refers to the earthly tabernacle as a *"copy and shadow."* In other words, the earthly Tabernacle replicates what is in heaven.

Hebrews 10:1 uses the term "shadow" in describing the Tabernacle. It was merely a foretaste of better things to come through Jesus Christ. His death and resurrection on the cross would provide the means and connection to eternal life for those who believed and followed Him.

Thinking back on the childhood memory of our shadows, we weren't far off in recognizing them as an indication of something better: the "real me" or the "real you," the "real thing." For God's people, the shadow of the good things to come came from Jesus's death and resurrection. The shadow was only a representation of what could be. Jesus' life was the final sacrifice for all humankind.

How dim the light may have been at Calvary, beneath the cross a shadow, the painful reminder of the death of our Lord. Also, beneath the cross was Mary's shadow—and the shadow of others with her, in despair at the loss of Jesus. They had been courageous to stand by the cross. They were bold in their faith and believed Christ was the good that God sent to His people from heaven.

Jesus—He's *the One Good Thing* God gave us. In His light, we do not need to fear the dark or the shadows.

And that's *one good thing*.

Worksheet for My Daily Morsel #6

Personal Insight:
Do you recall what thoughts came to mind when you first discovered your shadow?

_____
_____
_____
_____
_____

Reflection: My "One Good Thing"
List one good quality or characteristic about you that is not revealed by your shadow:

_____
_____
_____
_____
_____

Today's Serving: God's Sacrifice for Us
Young children may be frightened by their shadow, while older children may find it intriguing. But the darkness of a shadow is no comparison to the pitch darkness of night if there is no available light. With this in mind, imagine the darkness felt by those who loved Jesus as he died on the cross. Fortunately, the inner darkness these people experienced at Calvary lasted only a little while—until Jesus's resurrection into heaven. The darkness, then, in the hearts of those who mourned, was turned to light as they realized their Lord and Savior was not dead but alive and sitting at the right hand of God the Father. The light had come to overtake the darkness.

A Cupful of Reality:
Our lives are filled with both dark and light moments. Describe a dark time in your life. Did anything change to cause that period to turn into something positive?

_____
_____
_____

A Taste of Spiritual Nourishment:
From today's verse in Hebrews comes a key word, *perfect*. We are not perfect due to sin; however, God forgives us and sees us as pure and without blame when seeking His forgiveness. Knowing He sees us in a perfect light is a wonderful feeling. May this thought warm your spirit better than a steaming bowl of oatmeal on a winter day!

The Table of Optimism:
Hope resides at the Table of Optimism. What is your hope for today?

_____

_____

_____

_____

Prayer for Today:

Dear Father in heaven,

You see beyond every shadow and know every detail of my comings and goings. Sometimes, the way is not clear when my faith is shadowed. Still, I know You have a plan for me. Because of You, I do not need to fear the shadows, the darkness, or the unknown. In the light of Your love, I am safe and secure. In Jesus's name, amen.

Recipe

Prep Time _____   Cook Time _____

Oven Temp _____   Serves _____

Topic: **God's Favor** _____

_____

_____

_____

_____

_____

Bible Verse for Study

"For the LORD God is a sun and shield; the LORD bestows favor and honor; no **good thing** does he withhold from those whose walk is blameless."

Psalm 84:11

_____

_____

_____

DISASTER IN AISLE FIVE

"It's all your fault!"

Mom's words grated at my tender ears. I wasn't always the cause of wrongdoing; my brother was often guilty, too. But I was first to be blamed; I was three years older.

I vividly remember the day my brother and I "helped" Mom shop for groceries. The grocery cart was filled to the brim. Mom turned away just as my brother climbed onto the end of the cart. My brother jumped off, but it was too late.

C-r-a-a-s-s-s-h! Bang! The cart toppled, smacking onto the tile. Glass bottles of orange juice and milk busted open. My brother and I jumped backward to avoid the unleashed, swirling, milky orange fluid and glass shards shooting toward us. Canned goods rolled in every direction, some denting upon impact. The eggs had no chance, adding additional goo to the concoction. What a disaster!

Eyes wide, Mom whipped around. *"Oh!"* A scream came out as her mouth formed in the shape of the eggs that had dropped. Onlookers gasped.

My mother shot a cold glare in my direction as she struggled to turn the cart upright, her high heels splattered with the sticky mess. A storekeeper came running over and signaled to an associate for assistance. A deep voice came through on the intercom: *"Cleanup on Aisle Five."*

I stepped close to help, but Mom shooed me away.

"Never...mind!" she huffed.

She was so mad she hardly got the words out.

Split seconds unfolded like a time-warp in slow motion as the lake of goo spread to the next aisle. Mom's cold hand landed on my shoulder as the associate finished mopping the sticky residue. "If you'd been paying attention to your brother, this wouldn't have happened," she snapped.

Why was I responsible? Because I was older?

Mom looked at me through squinted eyes. *"It's all your fault!"*

My brother was three years younger, so I became the scapegoat for any trouble he caused. It wasn't fair.

One afternoon, while Mom and Dad were at work, my cousin and brother got into a cabinet above the refrigerator. I was naïve, believing them when they said they were drinking a concoction of "soda" (which turned out to involve liquor). I was supposed to know what they were doing. I was blamed—again.

Being a scapegoat followed me into adulthood. Once, while working an office job, a hysterical and difficult boss blamed me for losing a document. "It's all your fault!" he raved.

The document was later found in the boss's office. One instance in which I was *blameless*—but I couldn't prove it.

When I came upon the verse from Psalm 84:11, the word "blameless" stuck out like a neon sign. I fretted. If God bestows favor and honor and does not withhold any "good thing" from me, how would I ever measure up to be *blameless*? It seemed impossible.

I didn't realize it then, but I wasn't alone. We're all in the same boat because we're subject to sin.

Still, the thought of having been blamed for so much wrongdoing made me feel insecure. How could I receive the good things God had in store for me if I was the cause of trouble?

Worksheet for My Daily Morsel #7

Personal Insight:
With your understanding of Psalm 84:11, how has God shown you favor
and honor as you follow Him?

_____

_____

_____

_____

Reflection: My "One Good Thing:"
What "one good thing" has come from your walk with God?

_____

_____

_____

_____

Today's Serving: Caretaking Through Forgiveness
If we are blamed for something we've done wrong, we may react negatively. But, according to Psalm 84:11, God will not withhold "any good
thing" from us when we walk with Him. Thus, our "negatives" become
"positives" when our sins are forgiven, and we then can be called _blame-
less_.

A Cupful of Reality:
"You're to blame!" The words sound harsh; they're not what we want to
hear. Describe an experience when you were blamed for something you
didn't do. Was forgiveness part of the solution?

_____

_____

_____

_____

A Taste of Spiritual Nourishment:
From today's verse in Psalms comes a key word, _shield_. Picture God
shielding you wherever you are and whatever you do.

The "Table of Optimism":
Hope resides at the Table of Optimism. What is your hope for today?

_____

_____

_____

_____

Prayer for Today:
Dear Father in heaven,

Help me understand the meaning of Your Word, which I know to be true and just. Increase my understanding as I meditate on the scriptures. Thank you for forgiving me when I make mistakes and help me to forgive others. In Jesus' name, amen.

Part One: God as Master Caretaker

Recap of Morsels #1-#7

Congratulations! You have just completed the first seven Daily Morsels—Part One of this book—showing God's care for you. Now that you have read the stories, completed the worksheets, and your *One Good Thing* journal entries, the following questions will help you assess your progress:

1. What insight have you gained from the stories?

_____
_____
_____

2. In what way(s) have you been encouraged to be optimistic?

_____
_____
_____
_____

3. How have the Bible verses about "good things" applied to you? Give an example.

_____
_____
_____
_____

4. Which stories did you favor, and why?

_____
_____
_____
_____

5. How are you doing with your daily *"One Good Thing"* journal entries? If you've kept up, good job! If you've missed a few, don't worry. You're putting "good things" to work and making progress! Fill in missed

entries if you can. Otherwise, go on to the next day. Do your best to be consistent and save time by keeping your entries short.

6. Using the following scale, how would you rate your optimism now? (zero = none; ten = 100%)

0   1   2   3   4   5   6   7   8   9   1 0

7. How has your outlook changed from when you began this book?

_____

_____

_____

_____

8. Have you noticed any difference in your ability to avert negative thoughts? If so, how? (If not, are you recording your daily journal entries? They will help you develop the habit of thinking positively).

_____

_____

_____

_____

9. Looking back at your previous Table of Optimism responses, which desire for hope is most important to you now?

_____

_____

_____

_____

10. If you need encouragement to finish the stories, worksheets, or journal pages, what goal can you set to complete them?

_____

_____

_____

_____

11. What goal do you have in mind when you finish this book?

_____

_____

_____

_____

Prayerfully consider how God can help you reach your goals.

PART TWO
GOD AS MASTER PROVIDER

GOD AS MASTER PROVIDER

Providers are givers, granters, suppliers, and preparers. In short, they supply the needs of others.

Can you imagine our lives if we couldn't depend on others for what we need? *Depend* is the keyword. We want to think we are self-sufficient, but it would be hard to exist if we had to go one day without using something someone else provided or made.

Some things come from family or friends, but most of what we own comes from someone—or someplace—outside of our network.

We need connections with others to thrive.

Intangible needs often come from others, such as being cared for or loved.

We may not have everything we want, but there is One who supplies what we *need*. God is our Master Provider. He loves us, cares about our needs, and endows us with gifts and talents to enrich our lives and the lives of others. Furthermore, he bestows His favor upon us so we might also use our hearts and hands to share what we have with others.

In Part Two, the stories in "God as Master Provider" account for God's provision for His people.

As you read these stories, note how God has provided *good things* for His people—including you!

Recipe

My Daily Morsel #8

Prep Time _____   Cook Time _____

Oven Temp _____   Serves _____

Topic: **Spiritual Food/Hunger & Thirst**

_____

_____

_____

_____

_____

Bible Verse for Study

"...for he satisfies the thirsty and fills the hungry with
good things."

Psalm 107:9

_____

_____

_____

_____

Still bothered by the incident at work, I flipped open my Bible to Psalm 84:11. There was one question I couldn't get out of my head. *How could I walk the road to salvation blamelessly as a sinner?*

Before delving deep into the verse, I investigated its origin. As far as we know, David (shepherd, musician, and king) was the primary author of the Psalms.

David was skilled on the harp and sought after for his musical ability. He soothed King Saul's troubles by plucking tunes on its strings, and Saul found solace through the music. David praised God with his heart and soul, expressing his love through poetic psalms and harp music. But later on he also committed grievous sins. He certainly couldn't be *blameless*, could he?

So, what does this have to do with walking the road of salvation "blamelessly?" We can begin by looking at one of many descriptions of the nature of God in today's verse from Psalm 84:11:

"For the LORD God is a sun and a shield..." Yes. The Lord is like the light of the sun. His light represents all that is good. Love emanates from Him. The world revolves around the need for sunlight, just as we have a quest to believe in a power higher than ourselves. No life on earth can survive without sunlight. So, as people of faith, how would we prosper without God as the light of our souls?

God is also our *shield*, our protector against the forces of evil in the throes of everyday life. He provides *favor and honor* to us for our reverence and faithfulness to Him. To be favored is to be "chosen and special," another way God shows His love for us.

To be *honored* is a way God shows we are His own. Is it not ironic the God we serve, love, and honor, also honors *us*? This is because He desires to have a relationship with us, a giving and receiving reciprocal relationship. When we honor God, He also honors us.

Getting back to being "blameless," as we read Psalm 84:11, it might be easy to assume that David spoke of an ideal situation in which a believer walks blamelessly. Still, I was conflicted by the term and prayerfully thought about its meaning. I wasn't perfect. I made mistakes. The problem? Being human. Subject to sin.

But I realized my mistaken thinking. Focused on my faults and sins, I was missing the point. It's no wonder I was stuck in the "blameless" trap. It is likely others have fallen into this trap, too. An answer came to my heart. I realized I needed to stop looking within myself and instead look to Jesus for the salvation He provides for my sins.

I tend to make things complicated. I know others do, too. It's easy to overthink, analyze, and blame ourselves for making mistakes. God provides us with a simple answer: His salvation. This enables us to go from being "blamed" for sin or wrongdoing to being "blameless."

God is our helpmate. He can untangle the complicated messes we create. You may recall the macramé wall hangings that became popular years ago and resurfaced recently. Intricate patterns required artisans to cut cords of many lengths, which easily tangle. Knotting instructions were not always easy to follow. One mistake might result in having to untie many rows of knots—a frustrating effort (I've been there). Those jumbled knotting episodes remind me of the messes that result from life's complications and the tangled webs we sometimes create for ourselves.

But God, the mastermind of all, can untangle us from the most jumbled messes. He provides simple answers, such as salvation, if we follow His way and not our own!

Finally, I took the knotted, worried mess I'd created—worrying about blame and my mistakes—and gave it up to God and asked for forgiveness. The result of being "untangled" was a freeing feeling.

A beautiful verse about forgiveness comes from Isaiah 1:18: " 'Come now, let us settle the matter,' says the LORD. 'Though your sins *are like scarlet, they shall be white as snow; though they are red as crimson, they shall be like wool.'"*

We are forgiven when we confess our sins—beautifully so!

As long as we are walking this earth, we will never be free from the temptation of sin; however, through Christ's redemption, we can walk confidently and remain "blameless," all because of Him.

If we look back on the stringent laws of the Old Testament, the laws weren't well met. People failed to live up to them. But, because of God's great love and compassion, He offered redemption for those who were sorry for their sin—and later pardoned all of mankind's sins through the death and resurrection of His Son, Jesus Christ.

The forgiveness of sin is the crux of the Christian faith. Jesus atoned each of our sins to save us from the demise of a world filled with wrongdoing. There is freedom through the cross!

To walk uprightly is what God asks us to do. He knows our imperfections, but when we seek His forgiveness, in His eyes, we become blameless (and "white as snow," as mentioned in Isaiah 1:18). We become righteous in God's eyes, and He bestows favor and honor as we walk with Him.

Through Christ's forgiveness, our sins are erased and blotted out. We are purified through Jesus—cleansed indeed!

At last, I was happy to understand the full meaning of being blameless. I'd struggled with the term. I was sure others had, too.

The Lord will not withhold *good things* from us when we live in a manner pleasing to Him. His goodness shines through.

When I was twelve, I did not understand the far-reaching extent of God's care and compassion. It took a long time to realize I could go from being blamed—to being *blameless*.

David lived in a time before Jesus walked the earth, but He called out to God in desperation when he had done things he shouldn't have, and the Lord pardoned him. Centuries later, I called upon God and received God's forgiveness. May we have the faith David had as we walk the road of salvation—free from blame!

When I got in trouble for the "disaster in aisle five" episode, I felt that "trouble" had become my middle name. Was I stuck in it forever? Later that day, my mother and I talked. I told her I was sorry but didn't think I should have been blamed for something I didn't do. I saw my brother step on the edge of the cart, causing it to tip. To my surprise, Mom apologized. She said she was having a bad day, leaned over, and kissed my cheek. She felt bad she'd blamed me. As perfect as I thought she was, she made mistakes, too!

It's been many years since the grocery store incident. Mom is no longer with us. I credit her for raising my brother and me in a Christ-centered home. She had a tough-as-nails nature but loved us and only wanted us to do what was right.

The toppled grocery cart was just one minor incident among many that provided a life lesson. I learned about my mother's love—and God's love.

Indeed, God is like the sun—His love is brighter than anything we can imagine, and He is our shield, the protector of our souls.

Because of *Him*, we can walk blamelessly in His sight.

And that's *one good thing*!

A DIET UNINTENDED

When I was growing up, our family gathered for meals at the dinner table every night. For most families in the 1960s, sitting at the dinner table was more than a tradition—it was expected.

Fast food was a rarity, so Mom cooked almost everything from scratch. She made nutritious meals, usually meat, potato, vegetables, and bread and butter. Mom made applesauce, too. My mouth still waters as I think of the aroma of apples and cinnamon simmering on the stove.

While my mother provided well for our nutritional needs, she wanted to ensure that my brother and I grew up to be spiritually fed, too. She provided a healthy menu for instruction by taking us to Sunday School and church every week.

We lived just a few blocks from church and walked there when the weather was nice. Before we went home, Mom made sure we had our Sunday School papers in hand. At bedtime, she would read the Bible verses from the lesson with us before we said our nightly prayers.

We participated in church activities with other families in the congregation, joining in Sunday picnics at a nearby park, or indulging in special dinners or celebrations related to the liturgical church calendar.

During the summers, Mom enrolled my brother and me in fun-filled weeks of Vacation Bible School. I have fond memories of exciting visits by a family who brought ponies for us to ride, the performance of a "Jolly Green Giant" clown who squeezed his tall form into a Volkswagen Beetle, and lively music and sing-alongs, concluding with an assortment of cookies, cake, and fruit punch.

When I reached seventh grade, Mom enrolled me in Confirmation (catechism) class, which met on Wednesday evenings of the fall and spring semesters.

As a young teen, I wasn't exactly jumping for joy about having to attend Confirmation class through seventh, eighth, and ninth grades.

I already had plenty of homework, in addition to Pastor's requirements of weekly reading assignments from a textbook and quizzes. Despite grumbling, I met the requirements, nervously answered questions in front of the congregation, passed the final exam and became a confirmed church member.

Following Confirmation, I continued to attend the monthly youth group gatherings, which consisted mainly of kids I'd grown up with.

We had great youth directors, a young college grad and his wife. I liked them a lot, and we did many fun things, so I couldn't say anything was lacking. But something had changed. It wasn't the leadership. And it wasn't the other kids. It was me.

Maybe it had something to do with being seventeen. The times were changing. I questioned the values I'd been taught. Along came the Vietnam War, political turmoil, and radicalism. The Hippie movement was in full swing. They promoted freedom, peace, and love. *Who wouldn't want those good things?*

I wanted to fit in, so I looked up to my peers. I adopted some of their ideas, one of which was to quit the church youth group. I wanted freedom just like they did—to be released from the hold of the "establishment" and authoritarianism (including controlling parents).

I followed a few of my friends' paths and questioned why I attended church. Then, when Mom would come to wake me up early on Sunday morning, I'd make excuses for not going. The truth was, I didn't want to go to church anymore.

One Sunday morning, my mother rapped on my door. "Time to get up!" I didn't want to go to church, but didn't tell her. "Five minutes," she said. I covered my head with the blanket and closed my eyes.

Five minutes flew by. Mom returned. "Your time's up. Get out of bed!" she exclaimed.

I needed to tell her the truth. "Mom," I said, hesitating as I pulled the covers off my head, "I don't want to go."

"What's wrong?" she asked.

"Nothing," I replied. "I just don't want to go to church today— or any other day." *There. I said it.*

Mom's mouth dropped open as if she would say something, but no sound came out. Her ordinarily soft, round face now looked as tight as barbed wire. She was on to me now, with all the excuses I'd made for not going. She glared at me as the edge of her lip turned downward.

"All right. Have it your way," she snapped and shut my door with a thud.

That didn't go well. What did I expect? Now, she'd tell Dad. Oh, what did it matter? He didn't attend church but expected my brother and me to go with Mom. He'd be mad.

While Mom and my brother went to church, I stayed in my room and wrapped up in my blanket in bed. I was sure Dad would give me a hard time if I left my room.

I felt bad about making Mom upset, but it was no one's fault but mine. After she and my brother got home from the worship service, she'd cooled off enough to come in and talk to me. More than anything, she felt hurt—and disappointed.

"I don't condone your decision," she said, "but I'm not going to force you to go to church." She was wise, knowing it wouldn't do any good to coerce me.

My deflated attitude about church followed me to college. My appetite for worldly passions intensified. My campus was approximately five hours away from home, so I enjoyed doing what I wanted without my parents badgering me.

However, I soon learned that freedom of choice led me to do things that got me into trouble. I partied with friends until the wee hours of the morning, drank, smoked, and missed my classes the following day. I spent time with the kind of people my parents had warned me about.

I filled up on all the wrong things and dismissed church and God. I was no longer seeking His Word—or His guidance. I loved my freedom, but something was lacking, and I didn't know what it was. I tried to dismiss it but couldn't.

Maybe it's because I'm feeling guilty.

But it was more than guilt. I had an empty space inside, an unsettling void that yearned to be filled. I didn't know it then, but I was on a diet I'd never signed up for. My spiritual plate was empty, the cupboard of my soul bare. I was deficient in God's Word and no longer interested in the good things He had in store for me.

This diet—*a spiritual diet*—is not one anyone would want to choose.

I was at fault. I'd ingested all the wrong things and served up a heaping quantity of excuses to justify my bad behavior.

One evening, as I returned to the campus apartment I shared with my roommate, Breanna, I opened the door. "Breanna?" I called out. No answer. It wasn't like Breanna not to tell me where she was going. The phone rang. It was Breanna. She could hardly speak. Her brother had just died in a horrific accident. A semi-truck had collided with his car, killing him and critically injuring a passenger.

I was taken aback by the sudden loss of my roommate's brother. I looked hard at my life and how I'd pushed aside my parent's values. My friends and I had been with Mason in his car the previous week. He'd sped around the mountain curves so fast I faked nausea to get him to slow down. That was then. Now, he was *dead*. I shuddered to think we'd been in the car just a week before with him. It could have been all of us.

When my roommate returned to school a few weeks later, she asked if I would go to the worship service with her on Sunday morning. She attended a small congregation a few blocks from campus. I didn't want to go but thought maybe she needed some company during a difficult time.

I decided I wouldn't let it change my life—just because I was attending a church service with her.

In the weeks following, I attended Sunday worship with Breanna but told her I was only going because of her. A spark of joy returned to her face. *Maybe this is doing her some good.* I didn't realize God had a plan—to help her—and to help me.

It took time, but my taste for God's Word germinated like a planted seed and began to take root. During one sermon, I swallowed hard to keep tears at bay as the Pastor talked about parental love for children. I didn't want the reminder because I felt ashamed for being so distant from my parents, but I knew he was right.

After the service, the pianist who usually played was absent during the young adult Sunday School class, so my roommate volunteered me. I was embarrassed because I hadn't played the piano in a long time, but I agreed to play.

The requested hymn was the one about our Father's world.

Of all the hymns, why this one? It had been one of my favorites while growing up, but I hadn't heard or thought about it for a long time. As voices blended in harmony, warm tears escaped, swirling inside the lower frame of my glasses and down my cheeks. A chord struck within my heart as I played the melody, touching the empty, tender spot inside me.

I managed to get through the song without sobbing, but my

heart cried. *I'm sorry, God. I need You!* When the class was through, Breanna noticed my puffy, red eyes.

"What's wrong?" she asked.

I pursed my lips as we walked down the church steps to keep a whimper at bay.

By the time we reached the sidewalk, I couldn't hold it in anymore. "I've been wrong...all this time..." I held my head with my hands and wept. Breanna wrapped her arms around my shaking shoulders.

"It's going to be okay," she whispered.

I felt sure she was right as I wiped the moisture from my eyes. "When I started playing the hymn," I sniffed, "I felt God's presence." I felt my lips curve into a slight smile.

As we returned to our apartment, I spilled out my story: how I'd stopped attending church, distanced myself from my parents, and slid away from God. Somehow, I think Breanna had known it all the time. It wasn't until that Sunday morning I realized what I'd been missing.

My lack of sustenance, my "spiritual diet," wore me down to the bone. It took a tragedy in my friend's life for me to realize I was ingesting all the wrong things. Mom and Breanna had been praying for me. And one thing was certain: God intervened at the right time.

I'd slipped away, but God had never moved away from me. Empty spiritual plate? Bare cupboard of the soul? No more. I'd been renewed, spiritually fed, and loved beyond measure. I had peace and a different kind of freedom I never thought possible. Who could want more? I had God's recipe—His provision of good things for me.

I'd been on an unintended spiritual diet, but God rescued me before it was too late.

◆

The world never offers enough—but God does. He feeds us

and quenches our spiritual thirst. Numerous verses in the Bible address the topic of hunger and thirst: physical—and spiritual.

God provides. When Moses and the Israelites wandered through the Wilderness of Sinai, God revealed to Moses He would send down "bread from heaven" (Exodus 16:4) when the people complained of hunger. Manna appeared on the ground every morning, offering enough to sustain the people daily. The book of Exodus describes the taste as a wafer-like substance made with honey.

Other instances of God's provision include Jesus's turning five loaves of bread and two fish into enough food for five thousand or turning water into wine at the wedding of Cana. These are just a few instances of God's provision in time of need.

Other Bible verses refer to hunger in a spiritual sense in Matthew 4:4 when Jesus said, "It is written: 'Man shall not live on bread alone, but on every word that comes from the mouth of God,'" and in John 6:35, when Jesus declared, "I am the bread of life. Whoever comes to me will never go hungry, and whoever believes in me will never be thirsty."

Examples of Bible verses about spiritual thirst are in John 4:14, "but whoever drinks the water I give them will never thirst," and Psalm 42:2, "My soul thirsts for God, for the living God." These are just a few verses showing how God supplies spiritual refreshment.

God loves you, and He loves me. He doesn't give us "leftovers." Instead, he gives us the full measure of His love, the whole spread, the entire feast, the tastiest morsels for our souls' nutrition. What better way to be fed?

On that Sunday morning long ago, I rekindled my relationship with God. I learned to trust Him again. He filled my spiritual plate to brimming, and the cupboard of my soul soon overflowed.

I celebrated victory over spiritual depletion. Once empty, now

I was filled—because of Him. I was shocked by the successful results and the life-changing effects.

I hope I will never experience spiritual emptiness again, but I wouldn't mind just a twinge of spiritual hunger and thirst for God now and then, a yearning to continually seek Him and stay close to Him.

The world can never offer enough, but God can. He is our portion. He is all we need.

And that's *one good thing.*

Worksheet for My Daily Morsel #8

Personal Insight:
If you have ever felt hunger or thirst for God's Word, in what way did you seek Him?

_____
_____
_____

Have you, or someone you know, ever succumbed to anything resembling a "spiritual diet?" If so, describe:

_____
_____
_____
_____

If you answered "yes" to the above question, what was the result?

_____
_____
_____
_____

Reflection: My "One Good Thing"
What is *one good thing* God has supplied for your own spiritual needs?

_____
_____

Today's Serving: Provision Through Sustenance

God provides. He cared for Moses and the people as they wandered through the desert with manna and quail. Likewise, Jesus provided for the people, performing a miracle as he turned a few fish and loaves of bread into enough to feed thousands. God still provides for us today. He supplies us with spiritual nourishment and can fill our plates with good things when we are depleted. And this is one good thing to be optimistic about.

A Cupful of Reality:

The shelves of our spiritual kitchen may not always be as well-supplied as we would like. How can you personally "restock" your supply with spiritual nourishment?

A Taste of Spiritual Nourishment:

From today's psalm comes a key word, *satisfies*. When we have enough food to eat, we feel satisfied. So, likewise, when we feed our souls with God's Word, we can be spiritually fulfilled. So, the next time you have a meal or snack, open your Bible and find a verse to feed your spirit. *Bon appetite*!

The Table of Optimism:

Hope resides at the Table of Optimism. What is your hope for today?

Prayer for Today:

Dear Father in heaven,

I want to trust in You for the good things you supply in my life. Keep me spiritually hungry and thirsty enough to continue seeking You. Guide my path and direct my steps to keep my focus in Your direction. Thank You for providing spiritual food to nourish my soul, giving me hope through Your Word, and loving me just as I am. In Jesus' name, amen.

Recipe

Prep Time _____

Cook Time _____

Oven Temp _____

Serves _____

Topic: **God Rescues Us**

_____
_____
_____
_____
_____
_____

Bible Verse for Study

"Jethro was delighted to hear about all the **good things** the LORD had done for Israel in rescuing them from the hand of the Egyptians."

Exodus 18:9

_____
_____
_____

D. J.'s Rescue

*R*escue. The word incites action, emotion, and reaction. If you were held captive against your will, seeking release, liberation, or deliverance from impending peril would be human nature. It was this way for my father-in-law, who was held as a POW for thirty-nine months in a Japanese prison camp during World War II.

My father-in-law, "DJ," was a spry young man. Raised on a farm in the Midwest with eleven siblings, he knew what sharing space with a large family meant. His father was a strict disciplinarian, so DJ learned the value of hard work early. Hundreds of acres of farmland and caring for and feeding cattle, sheep, and other farm animals required daily attention. As a result, there was little time off, except for family outings, which consisted of a monthly excursion to town for supplies or the occasional visit to a neighbor a few miles down the road.

By age eighteen, DJ did what so many others did during the war—he answered the call to serve in the U.S. military. Inducted into the Marines before his mother had a chance to see her son fully grown, DJ looked forward to this civic duty. He wanted to make his family proud. Little did he know the events that followed would later challenge every ounce of courage and strength he had within him.

Fourteen months after the Pearl Harbor attack, the Japanese attacked the Philippine Islands of Corregidor, a U.S. military outpost. A specially built underground passageway called the

Malinta Tunnel provided a safe space for offices, including barracks and a hospital to house U.S. and Philippine troops and allies.

As weeks passed, the bombings increased in intensity. The coastline provided little protection, despite barricades set up as gunnery stations. As the frequency of the attacks escalated, fewer ships made it to deliver artillery and rations to the island.

Heavy shelling often caused blackouts, enabling the Japanese to encroach upon the island easily. With decreased supplies, U.S. troops were unable to keep up. Once tanks invaded and the Malinta Tunnel was bombed, the Americans were forced to surrender the island to the Japanese.

On May 6, 1942, the Japanese captured hundreds of troops and took them as POWs. This included DJ and his men. They were transported to regional prisons—filthy encampments—where they were treated brutally.

A high barbed-wire fence prevented escape. The punishment for trying to escape was immediate execution, so few dared to try.

The soldiers were stripped of their clothing and degraded to wearing rags as loincloths. An infestation of flies and insects brought about by leaking sewage and an overall lack of sanitation contributed to disease.

The men became emaciated on a diet of meager portions of uncooked rice infested with insects. DJ was no exception. He suffered from dysentery, a manifestation of the squalid conditions, and scurvy and malaria were not uncommon.

POWs were forced to perform physical labor for long hours each day. Already weak from malnutrition, many collapsed from exhaustion, and some died. In addition, those who suffered injuries from the war were often not treated. As a result, infection was rampant, and when it progressed to sepsis, death was usually imminent.

Vision loss was also common due to malnutrition. DJ could no longer distinguish depth as he had previously. As his health issues increased, his expectation of survival diminished.

If only they could be rescued from this suffering, he thought. The guards' interrogation and belittlement were ongoing, as were beatings and atrocities DJ didn't want to think about.

His lowest point came when a guard overheard him complaining about the dilapidated conditions. The guards mocked him and laughed, telling him he would soon have his own place. He was pried from his cell and shoved into solitary confinement. The space in the tiny cell was no longer than the length of his compact legs.

The dirt floor flooded when it rained, and there was no way to keep the thin straw mat on which he slept, dry. Tropical humidity and flood water seeping in after the rain turned the mat moldy. He had no recourse but to use what he had.

A sliver of light filtered through a vent in the cell block, the only light available, as there were no windows. Winters were freezing, and summers were sweltering. He had no contact with anyone other than guards mocking him for seven months. However, he could hear occasional footsteps approaching his cell to deliver the meager ball of rice shoved through the bars of a small, locked compartment. Sometimes, he heard screams. He could hardly bear the sound and covered his ears.

He could do nothing in the darkness, so DJ reminisced to keep his mind off the suffering. He thought about his family's farm when he and his brothers helped his father seed the fields, harvest the crops in the fall, round up cattle and sheep, and milk the cows.

He missed the sweet aroma of his mother's corn cakes baking on the griddle in the morning and the homemade apple pie she'd make for him on his birthday.

Work on the farm was grueling at times, especially when the family didn't have enough money, and DJ and his brothers had to skip school to work on the farm. But that was nothing compared to the grueling existence plaguing him now. Whether he'd ever make it out of here, he didn't know.

At night, DJ had a recurring dream of having a complete set of teeth. When he awoke, he'd run his tongue across the bottom and top of his mouth. Months of chewing uncooked rice caused his teeth to erode down to the gums, exposing the nerves and causing him pain. Additionally, he had sores in his mouth that wouldn't heal.

He thought of how he had complained to his father about how hard the work was on the farm. It was nothing compared to now.

DJ longed to know about his family. How were his mother and father, his six brothers and four sisters? He grieved he might never see them again, and if worse came to worse and he died, would they know how much he loved them?

When he was released from solitary confinement, he could barely walk, weak from the prolonged confinement. He shielded his eyes from the light as two guards rifled him into a holding cell. This was a larger room. The conditions were no better, but at least he had contact with others.

DJ struck up a friendship with a fellow soldier named George, who shared his cell. They had something in common, as George had grown up close to DJ's hometown. They spoke but kept their voices low. Sitting as far away as they could from the iron bars, they became silent if guards approached.

George had studied to be a pastor before the war broke out. DJ admitted he wasn't a believer but agreed to hear what George had to say.

The pastor and DJ tended to a soldier in their cell whom the guards had whipped for not standing at attention. The soldier was severely injured. Efforts to give him sips of water resulted in it running out of his mouth.

DJ had seen his share of death, but it hit too close to home this time. He'd befriended the soldier; they'd been through a lot together.

The pastor sat by the ailing soldier, praying over him. DJ sat nearby. *What good will it do to pray? The man is dying.*

The pastor glanced at DJ. Did he know what DJ was thinking?

"I'm praying for his comfort," George whispered, "to ease his transition."

"His transition?" DJ questioned.

The pastor nodded. "Yes. Passing from this life to the next. He'll be in God's hands and no longer have pain or suffering."

DJ hung his head. It wouldn't be long before his comrade was dead. A knot formed in his throat. His eyes began to sting as emotion welled inside him, but there wasn't enough moisture in his body to form tears. He shuddered. Who would be next? George, others, or perhaps he himself?

The pastor's words grated at DJ. Was it possible there was a place that offered life after death? Maybe death wasn't so bad. It's not that DJ desired it, but to be in a place without suffering or pain would be a relief from his current state of misery.

DJ watched George's lean frame reach out to help their ailing cellmate.

A glimmer of hope? Were those the words he heard? George was as emaciated as the rest, receiving the same meager rations. Something about him was different, but he didn't know why.

DJ had questions for the pastor in the weeks following the cellmate's death. He didn't want to admit it, as he'd never been a believer, but some of the things George told him were beginning to make sense.

The seed of faith was planted—and grew. In time, DJ concluded his pastor friend was right. He felt the effect of prayers and a peace he had never known. He became hopeful that he would survive if he didn't give up. He'd seen too many men attempt—or complete—suicide. At one point, DJ didn't care if he lived or died, but now he'd changed his mind. He wanted to live.

Hope came true after three years and three months of imprisonment in the POW camp. On September 1, 1945, President

Truman announced the Japanese surrender to the United States.

Liberated. Delivered. The POWs were rescued. As pleased as DJ and his comrades were in regaining their freedom, it was with heavy hearts that they departed camp. Far fewer men left than had entered those gates. DJ knew he, the pastor, and others were lucky, numbering only a few hundred. Over two thousand soldiers who entered the prison camp never made it out.

After discharge, DJ was hospitalized and then returned to the family farm when he was well enough to go home. He would never be the same. It took months for his body to recuperate from physical deterioration, and the emotional scars ran deep. DJ eventually adapted to civilian life, married, and raised two stepsons.

DJ would never forget the pastor—the reason he didn't lose hope. He'd not only befriended George, but befriended the God who rescues—and delivers.

—

Peril: DJ and his men knew it well, having lived through the horror of war and the dehumanization and suffering as POW's. for thirty-nine months.

The Israelites lived in peril for over four hundred years, the enslavement passing down through generations of their sons and daughters.

The timeline of our Bible verse for today, from Exodus 18:9 (when Moses's father-in-law, Jethro met with Moses at his encampment in Midian), takes place after the Israelites were released from captivity in Egypt by Pharaoh. To glean the significance of today's Bible verse, if we backtrack a bit, we will see how the difficulties faced by Moses and the Israelites would later contribute to their spiritual lives in a positive way.

Under Pharaoh's harsh rule, the enslaved Israelites were treated badly. Exodus 1:13 describes their treatment by the Egyptians as "ruthless." Men were forced to grueling hours of hard labor, and women were taken as slave servants.

Going back further in the timeline, peril was evident even at the birth of Moses. Pharaoh, threatened by the growing presence of Israelites in the country, mandated that male infants born to Hebrew women were to be killed. However, Moses's life was spared, for midwives helping with the births feared God and did not want to kill the infants. They hid Moses for a period of time, then for his safety, he was placed in a basket in the Nile to be discovered and cared for.

Moses was safe, but his life did not get easier. When he became a grown man, he witnessed an Egyptian beating up one of his own people. Enraged, he murdered the Egyptian. When Pharaoh found out what Moses had done, he was furious and planned to kill Moses. However, Moses fled to Midian, where he stayed for many years and escaped harm.

While in Midian, Moses was tending to a flock belonging to his father-in-law. He took the flock across the wilderness to Horeb, known as the "mountain of God" (Exodus 3:1). There, Moses was awestruck by the unusual sight of a burning bush that was not consumed by the flames. The Angel of the LORD appeared in the bush, and God spoke to Moses through the burning bush. God told him to remove his sandals, for he was standing on holy ground. Moses did so, but fearing God, he hid his face.

God told Moses He knew the people were suffering and said He had come to rescue them from the hands of the Egyptians. He told Moses to go before Pharaoh and tell him to let the people go. Moses was afraid that Pharaoh wouldn't believe him, but God assured Moses of His presence, saying, "I will be with you" (Exodus 3:12).

The Lord was with Moses as He promised. He instructed Moses and Aaron how to perform the signs he had told them about in the presence of Pharaoh. However, God hardened Pharaoh's heart so that God's power would be revealed. This became apparent when He brought the plagues upon Pharaoh and the Egyptians. When Pharaoh had enough of the pestilence, death, and destruction of his people and country, he ordered the Israelites to leave.

Finally, the Israelites were free from bondage, for God had come to their rescue.

Now that we've backtracked, let's move forward and revisit the scene from our verse for today from Exodus 18:9. Moses' father-in-law, Jethro, arrives to see Moses at his encampment in Midian. Now, instead of worry, fear, or sorrow, they delight in joyful celebration, as *"Jethro was delighted to hear about all the good things the Lord had done for Israel in rescuing them from the hand of the Egyptians."*

Truly, God provided many good things for the Israelites. He protected them and showed His concern for them. He assured Moses He was with him, He spoke to him and made His presence known in a very unexpected way—through a burning bush that was not consumed by fire. He used His miraculous powers to demonstrate that He was—and always would be—the Great I Am. The perilous effects of the plagues He set in place finally convinced hard-hearted Pharaoh to set the Hebrew people free.

Truly, the Lord Almightly rescues His people in their time of need.

We may never understand why DJ and his men faced extrenuating circumstances, or why the Israelites remained in bondage for generations. But, God's timing is different than ours (2 Peter 3:8).

If there is one thing we can be sure of, it is that God cared for His people then, just as He cares for us today. The tasks or difficulties we experience may be different from Moses's situation, but just as Moses did, we, too, can rely on God's Words of comfort from Exodus 3:12, when He told Moses, "I will be with you."

What comfort God's Word provides!

The POWs and many others rejoiced the day they were set free at the culmination of World War II.

Jethro rejoiced and praised God for rescuing His people from the hands of the Egyptians.

Rescue. Release. Liberation. Deliverance.

Moses and DJ are prime examples that when God acts, it is in no small way.

And that's *one good thing.*

Worksheet for My Daily Morsel #9

Personal Insight:
Was there a time when you needed to be rescued or delivered from a perilous situation (physical, emotional, or spiritual)? If so, did anyone help you? If so, what kind of assistance did you receive, and how were you rescued or delivered from harm?

Reflection: My "One Good Thing"

If you have ever needed God's rescue, how did He help you, and what one good thing came from this?

Today's Serving: Provision Through Deliverance
Enslavement is a thread of dehumanization that has woven itself throughout history. Today, we looked at two different circumstances: one during World War II and the other during the life of Moses. Despite the travesty, God provided for Moses and His people. He loosened the hardened heart of Pharaoh to deliver the Israelites from enslavement. And His hand was at work when DJ and a few hundred POWs were freed from the hands of the enemy.

A Cupful of Reality:
We usually associate "enslavement" or "imprisonment" with historical events. However, enslavement or imprisonment can take place in a mental or spiritual sense. We can be trapped if we let negative thoughts or circumstances rule, and the resulting "war" is real. When we call out to God, He comes to our rescue. I have personally experienced this. Perhaps you have, too.

Space is provided on the next page if you wish to write your thoughts or describe your experiences:

A Taste of Spiritual Nourishment:
From today's verse in Exodus comes a key word, *delighted*. Jethro was delighted for all the good things the Lord had done for the people of Israel. What is one thing that brings delight to your heart?

The Table of Optimism:
Hope resides at the Table of Optimism. What is your hope for today?

Prayer for Today:
Dear Father in heaven,

I am so thankful that You come to the rescue of your people when they are in need. Thank You for rescuing me from danger and delivering me from sin through Your precious Son, Jesus Christ, Our Lord and Redeemer, amen.

Recipe

My Daily Morsel #10

Prep Time _____   Cook Time _____

Oven Temp _____   Serves _____

Topic: **Fulfillment/Renewal**
_____
_____
_____
_____
_____
_____

Bible Verse for Study

"Praise the LORD, my soul; all my inmost being, praise his holy name. Praise the LORD, my soul, and forget not all his benefits—who forgives all your sins and heals all your diseases, who redeems your life from the pit and crowns you with love and compassion, who satisfies your desires with **good things** so that your youth is renewed like the eagle's."

—Psalm 103:1-5

THE WORST BEST
CHRISTMAS EVER

It was always my husband's dream to own a restaurant. After extensive market research, we made the purchase. It was a small but well-established venue with a thirty-five-person crew already on board.

Our lifestyle went from mediocre to extraordinary. Suddenly, we made more money than we ever imagined possible. We bought things we'd always wanted and padded our savings account.

Initially, we didn't do anything different than usual. We attended church as we always had. My husband worked long hours at the business, and I kept busy with our two elementary-school-aged daughters.

Then, things changed. We no longer needed to stay on a grocery budget, and we splurged on gourmet food. Clothes shopping was no longer limited to buying items on sale; we bought whatever we pleased. We purchased a new truck, furniture, appliances, and home decor. We even paid off the mortgage on our home. If there was a need, we filled it. We lacked for nothing.

Unbeknownst to us, a small seed called "greed" took root. It started out tiny, then grew exponentially.

I wouldn't have believed if anyone had ever predicted we'd become self-reliant instead of God-reliant. But it happened. We relied on ourselves—and not on God. We attended church, so we thought we were being faithful. But deceit entered in as money became our gain.

At an earlier time, we had barely scraped by financially, so we didn't feel we had the ability to tithe. However, once money was not an object, we were overtaken by our newfound financial freedom and the many choices we had to spend money as we pleased. We increased our giving at church, but felt guilty, knowing we could have done better. Then, less than a year later, our fortune was gone.

As I read the psalm for today's lesson from Psalm 103:1–5, the part about *"...and forget not all his benefits..."* evoked a memory. Revisiting the details, I searched the closet for my box of old journals. Sifting through the contents, I spotted the hardback volume with the black fabric cover. I opened the journal to the entry I'd written about the day our life turned inside out.

Thursday, June 24th:

My husband pulled the thick chain taut, clamping down on the shackle of the heavy padlock. It made two clicks. Click one. Our business was closed. Click two. I closed the door on my faith.

The impending loss was final—goodbye income, investment, and hope—hello, sadness, despair, and depression. I open the door to you unwillingly as you force your way in. I have a feeling you'll be staying for a while.

The downfall was so subtle that we hardly knew we were in trouble. Then everything went downhill. Fast. Cash reserves dwindled, and we took money from our home equity to stay afloat. But it only worked for a while. We made one last payroll. Our funds were depleted.

For a while, we had it all. Then our fortune was gone.

I wanted to forget about today as much as I wanted to forget about faith. Where had it gotten us over these past months? Nowhere. If God had been watching out for us, our restaurant would have been spared. Right? And where was He this morning when my husband padlocked the doors to our business?

Friday, June 25th:

Daylight peeked through my bedroom window this morning. It filled the room with light, but I felt only darkness inside. I'd been through bleak times, but right now was the bleakest.

What had happened? I used to believe in good things. I used to have faith. I used to feel happy. Now, those things feel far away. Everything changed. Our dream became a nightmare.

Memories flooded my heart. I closed the journal, unable to read further. Why rehash the past? Shouldn't I leave it alone? Maybe the memories surfaced for a reason, but one thing I didn't want to do was store them in my heart.

On a scorching summer day in June, my husband and I were suddenly without a source of income. Before closing the business, we had to take out another mortgage on our home. But now, with the business shuttered, we needed money to make mortgage payments and care for young mouths to feed.

While job searching, I landed an interview for an office job. "I am a person of little patience," my prospective boss said. It wasn't what I wanted to hear, but desperate for work, I accepted the position.

I was saddened by the changes our losses had caused. Long ago, we'd decided for me to stay home with the children, even though it meant we'd forfeit income. But now, I didn't have a choice. I had to work—with a boss who yelled and screamed. No one was happy—especially not me.

By December, my husband was still looking for work. What would we do about Christmas? I grieved our loss of income. Sadness loomed over me. Our girls were six and nine. I couldn't bear the thought of disappointment on their faces. But I had to be realistic. We'd be lucky to pay bills, much less have anything left over.

Moving from a state of affluence to a state of impoverishment changed everything. I humbly fell to my knees in prayer each night. Prayer was a place I hadn't visited for some time. Would God forgive me?

The pageantry of Christmas decor made me want to roll up

into a little ball and disappear from the world. I avoided shopping centers, but even the food mart was decorated, a painful reminder of things we couldn't afford. Lights and garlands adorned our neighbor's homes. I put up decorations only because of our girls.

Daily prayer was becoming a habit. I prayed every morning on the drive to work. I didn't know if it would help, but I didn't know what else to do. Christmas was only three weeks away.

On the drive home one afternoon, a thought popped into my head.

Sew coats for Christmas.

Caught off-guard, I couldn't imagine it. Me? Sew coats? I'd never sewn anything other than "straight lines," making simple curtains from rectangular material. Turn under the edge. Stitch. *Press with the iron.* Done. But making a coat? I argued with my conscience. It was unrealistic, considering my lack of sewing skills.

I thought about it. The girls needed coats. But how would I manage interfacing, sewing a lining, pockets, cuffs, and collar? Then, placing buttonholes and zippers? I'd never done any of those tasks. How could I do them now?

I couldn't get the idea out of my head as I lay in bed that night. The thought of the coats nagged at me. But so did inspiration. Was there a reason for this? I knew I had to try. If I could make these coats, the girls would have a Christmas gift and stay warm through the winter.

Inspiration called—and I answered. I found a pattern at a garage sale, just the sizes I needed. I found denim tucked away in a storage closet and soft material for the lining. I would make quilt squares from the girls' old dresses and use denim for the remainder.

I threaded the dusty sewing machine and pressed the foot pedal. The machine kept stalling. *Oh, no. Please help me, Lord.* I didn't give up. The wheel of the motor finally turned, and I could stitch without interruption. As I sewed, I chuckled. All the pieces so far were "straight lines." I felt hopeful.

I stayed up late to work on the coats every night after the girls went to bed. I got frustrated, though. I made a mistake and had to rip out all the seams of the lining and start over. The seam ripper became my worst enemy—and best friend. By the time I started to work on the zipper, I was ready to scream. The hours went by while the machine needles kept breaking. The material was so thick the machine couldn't handle it. And neither could I.

I wanted to give up, but I couldn't let our little girls down for Christmas. I committed to sewing the coats. Nothing would stop me now.

It was a proud moment as I put the finishing touch on the jackets. They looked homemade, but I felt they were special because the quilted fronts were made from the girls' old dresses. I'd sewn them with love—and a fair amount of sweat over many nights.

I received a revelation when my husband found employment a few months later. I hadn't used the sewing machine since making the coats. Now that we were both employed, I took the machine in for routine maintenance. I told the repairman I'd initially had trouble with the machine, but it finally began working.

The repairman set the machine on the counter and looked it over. He slid off the faceplate and removed a piece from the bobbin chamber. He held it up to get a closer look at it. He looked bewildered.

"Ma'am, when did you say you last used this machine?"

"About five months ago," I replied.

"Did you notice anything unusual about the bobbin case?

"No," I shook my head.

"Did any small part fall out, or was the machine dropped?"

Again, I shook my head. "No...neither of those happened."

He held up a metal part.

"See this?" The repairman pointed to a jagged edge.

I nodded.

He shook his head. "Ma'am, there is no way this machine should have sewed anything."

Words would not come, but the corners of my mouth turned into a slight smile. Some things are only possible with God.

As the years passed, our daughters outgrew the coats, and I donated them to charity. I hoped whoever received them would be as blessed as we'd been.

If we hadn't lost our business, I might not have known the real meaning of the benefits God could provide.

It wasn't easy then, but now I smile when I think back to that December. I thought it would be the worst Christmas ever, but it was the most memorable. We didn't have money, so we weren't focused on things. Instead, we focused on our faith in God and the time we spent together as a family.

Losing our business was one of the most challenging things we ever went through. I sometimes wonder if we had not experienced loss if my faith would be what it is today. At the time, we thought we had it all, but we didn't. We gained wealth but let go of faith. As it slid away, so did the benefits that would have come from God.

Like David, we learned through experience. God provides good things for His people. *His* benefits far outweigh any treasure on earth.

David had good reasons for writing Psalm 103. First, he wanted to praise God wholeheartedly. Secondly, he desired to remind others not to forget God's benefits. Likely, it was because he had been through adversity himself.

We often receive reminders. There is a good reason to receive them—and give them.

I thought of all the times I've been a "reminder." As a mom: "Don't forget your homework!" As a spouse: "Remember to pick up your suit from the cleaners." Or as a supervisor: "The deadline on paperwork is by five o'clock today."

We have many things to remember; getting a reminder is good. I'm always happy to get them and equally glad to help others remember things.

Maybe David felt the same way. He had a lot on his plate. We don't know if he had anyone reminding him of what he needed to do. But if he did, he might not have been listening when he got himself into trouble. He'd forgotten about God's benefits. He'd strayed from faith, stepped out on his own, and fell into the pit of sin. He may not have noticed when the door to his faith quietly closed behind him.

Later, David grieved over his sin. He pleaded for forgiveness, which God granted. It is no wonder David wanted to remind us not to forget about the good things God provides. He learned the hard way about forgetting—and remembering. However, once he renewed his faith, he allowed the door of his heart to be open again for God to dwell within.

David provides an essential lesson for us in Psalm 103:1–5. He writes about six benefits God delivers: 1) forgiveness of sin, 2) healing, 3) redemption, 4) being crowned with love and compassion, 5) having one's desires satisfied with good things, and 6) renewal.

A description of each benefit follows:

God Forgives
David wrote in Psalm 103:3 that God *"forgives all your sins."* There is nothing small about the way God works. David's sins were great, but so was God's forgiveness. David was exceedingly sorry for what he had done. He pleaded for forgiveness, and God accepted his plea. We have such a forgiving God!

God Heals
David stated God is the one who *"heals all your diseases"* (Psalm 103:3). Some might argue this point, but think about this: Is it our job to decide whether disease might cause death or whether, in God's grand scheme, it might be His will for our earthly life to

be complete? None of us is immune to death, and we don't know when our time will be.

Also, we don't know God's definition of disease; we only know our perception of it. We want simple answers to complex questions. We can make assumptions, but they might not be correct. We cannot know the mind of God.

Disease is often considered physical but can manifest as a mental—or spiritual condition.

We don't know what type of disease David refers to in his writing or how healing occurred. Did he witness healing in others? Did he experience healing of his own? We don't know, but David believed in God's healing power, whatever that healing might entail.

God Redeems

David wrote that God *"redeems your life from the pit"* (Psalm 103:4). Redemption, the act of being saved, kept David from further destruction. Although he lived before the time of Christ, God provided redemption for those who sought Him—as David did.

In David's time, many people strayed from God's Word or did not follow Him. Compared to today, times haven't changed. And neither has God. He remains the same today as always. He is our source of love and redemption.

God Crowns with Love and Compassion

In Psalm 103:4, David says God *"crowns you with love and compassion."*

If anyone deserves honor, it is God. Yet He turns things around and honors us with love and compassion.

Imagine how David must have felt. He'd committed terrible, lowly acts. He must have felt like a speck of dirt before God for his actions. But because David sought forgiveness, the Lord spared him, forgave him, and crowned him with love and compassion. What an amazing God!

God Satisfies Desires with Good Things

We do not know what "good things" David might have wished for, but understanding the sensitive nature of his writing, it's easy to imagine his desire was good, and perhaps he was referring to the benefits God provides. Clearly, David believed God provides good things for those who seek Him.

God Renews

David wrote that God is the one *"who satisfies your desires with good things, so that your youth is renewed like the eagle's"* (Psalm 103:5).

One of the strongest winged creatures, the eagle is swift, flies at great heights, and builds its nest in high places to protect its young. A caring parent, this majestic bird teaches its little ones to fly by catching them on its wings.

Because of its strength, it serves as a symbol of youth. David equated renewal to gaining strength—like the strength of an eagle.

Because he wrote about renewal, we can be certain David knew what it felt like. Sin led him to a low place, but God allowed him the opportunity to start over. What a great feeling—to be renewed with such strength, and what great strength it would be!

—

Renewal came for me when I was at my lowest point after we lost our business. God heard my plea when I fell to my knees in prayer. He rescued me, answered my prayers, and encouraged me as I searched for employment. And miraculously, he enabled an old dusty sewing machine to operate as I sewed coats for our daughters.

God provided renewal for David, too, comforting his aching heart and giving him strength for the path ahead.

I never imagined learning to sew coats for Christmas would bring renewal, but it did. Likewise, David probably never imagined he'd be saved from the nature of his sin, but he was.

In my weakness, God showed me I had a strength I didn't know

I had. Battling sadness, I sewed coats I never thought I could make.

If God could rescue David—or me—He can save anyone who calls on Him in need.

Such is God's love. He unlocks the shackles of sin, renews, and fulfills us.

And that's *one good thing.*

Worksheet for My Daily Morsel #10

Personal Insight:
David's devotion and willingness to follow God's commands made him a faithful servant, ruler, and worker. He made mistakes but learned from them. He focused on what God wanted him to do instead of what others wanted. He "worked for God" instead of "working for people." In what way do you see yourself working for God instead of working for people?

_____

_____

_____

_____

_____

What changes, if any, might you make in your day or how you perceive your work?

_____

_____

_____

_____

_____

Reflection - My "One Good Thing"
Of the six benefits mentioned by David (Forgiveness of Sins, Healing, Redemption, Crowning with Love and Compassion, Satisfying Desires with Good Things, and Renewal), which most closely speaks to your heart and why?

_____

_____

Today's Serving: Provision Through Renewal

David asked for forgiveness, which God granted, and then David's life was renewed as he rebuilt His faith in God. My renewal came through prayer with the loss of our business. God provides for His people and gives them hope for the future. He did this for David. And He did it for me. And he can do this for you, too.

A Cupful of Reality:

David thought he had it all but got caught up in sin. I thought we had it all but lost our business. Sometimes, we live through adversity. It may be our fault—or not. How has God provided you with a sense of renewal in a time of loss, big or small?

A Taste of Spiritual Nourishment:

From today's verse in Psalms comes a key word, *redeem*. Rejoice, for through Christ, you are redeemed, justified, saved, rescued, absolved, and made new. Now, that's something to smile about—a dose of joy for your soul!

The Table of Optimism:

Hope resides at the Table of Optimism. What is your hope for today?

Prayer for Today:

Dear Father in heaven:

Thank You for making David's faith an example for me: his heart of love to praise You, the gift of his songs and psalms, and his reminder of Your great benefits. David suffered through difficult times, and so have I. It was during those times that I drew close to You. Thank You for coming to my aid. You renewed my spirit when I needed it the most. In Jesus's name, amen.

Recipe

My Daily Morsel #11

Prep Time

Cook Time

Oven Temp

Serves

Topic: **Goodness and Reward**

_____
_____
_____
_____
_____
_____

Bible Verse for Study

"From the fruit of their lips people are filled with **good things**, and the work of his hands brings them reward."

Proverbs 12:14

_____
_____
_____

AN UNFORGETTABLE VACATION

When I was nine, one small incident on a family vacation changed my life.

My parents loved to travel, so Mom agreed when my father suggested Carlsbad Caverns. When I saw the brightly colored brochure, I was hooked.

Mom added, "They have a gift shop, too."

I grinned.

As we drove to our destination in southern New Mexico, my father, a scientist, taught us the difference between stalagmites and stalactites and explained how the caves were formed.

I fidgeted during the day-long trip, which seemed to take forever, as I was ecstatic about seeing the caverns.

The sun began to set as we pulled into the campground, the sky a brilliant pink and orange. After Dad backed our travel trailer onto the concrete slab, we went to the visitors center to purchase tickets for the cavern tour for the following day.

The next morning, I awoke to sunlight peeking through the window curtain in my bunk. I wanted to get up, but everyone was asleep. I thought about poking my finger into my brother's cot above me to get him to wake up but decided it might not be a good idea. He'd be cranky if he didn't get enough sleep.

I pulled out the brochure for the caverns from the magazine rack next to my bunk. I occupied myself by re-reading every pamphlet caption and descriptive paragraph and studying the photos. I'd practically memorized it when my parents' alarm clock sounded an hour later.

After breakfast, we drove to the visitor's center to meet with the tour group. The park ranger led us down a steep, winding path to the cave entrance and finally into the cave. We walked single file on the narrow semi-lit trail. Dad smiled when I recognized two major rock formations he'd told me about. I looked up in awe at the smooth, towering stalagmites rising from the cave floor. The air smelled damp and musty.

The minute my mom turned away, my brother climbed over the railing and onto a rock at the trail's edge. Fortunately, she grabbed him in time before the ranger noticed.

I stood beside my father, watching him set the F-stops on his 35-millimeter camera, adjusting for the low light level. Dad's interests were mine, too. He bought me a Brownie camera for Christmas, and I loved taking pictures as much as he did.

As the guide led us into the biggest cavern, the "Big Room," we came to a standstill. I looked up, my mouth dropping open at the sight of what appeared to be a cascade of frozen waterfalls. It was so massive I couldn't get the entire formation to fit in the viewfinder of my camera, but my father had a special lens on his camera to capture the whole spectacle.

As the tour guide wrapped up his talk, I wished the tour didn't have to end; however, my feet were already sore from walking. It was chilly in the cave, too, so the warm spring air felt welcoming as we stepped outside.

Our next stop was the gift shop. I couldn't wait to look for rock samples to add to my collection. My favorite piece was Iron Pyrite—it looked like gold. I liked books, too, and thought about buying one about the Caverns.

I rushed to the gift shop and looked in the windows as I waited for my parents and brother, noticing my reflection in the glass. Short, blonde wisps of hair out of place didn't bother me, but my blue-framed eyeglasses showed up as bright as a neon road sign.

The rims turned up into a point on each side. I didn't like being the only student in my fourth-grade class to wear glasses. Kids stared as if something was wrong with me.

I inched up to the window, pressing my nose against the pane.

Mom's voice bellowed from behind. "Don't make a mark on the window!"

I stepped back. "I was only trying to look at the rocks," I replied.

"Well, hurry up, then," she called. "Don't be so slow."

Mom was always telling me to hurry up. I puffed up my cheeks with air, then blew it out. I did that when she bugged me. Mom and my brother entered the gift shop first, but Dad waited, holding the door.

I marveled at the many aisles of merchandise and found rock samples. I thought one was from the cave. Dad said it wasn't, but it looked similar in composition.

Mom didn't enjoy the shopping because she had to discipline my brother, who was misbehaving. "Keep your hands to yourself, Danny," she hollered. He wasn't listening, so she took him outside while Dad and I shopped.

Dad found a sticker from the Caverns to put on the back window of our travel trailer. He didn't need to buy anything but gave me time to look for a souvenir.

The rock display was one aisle away from the cash register. Then, in a loud voice, I heard the lady at the cash register say, "We don't have anything for retarded children."

My father quickly grasped my hand. "We need to go," he said, whisking me out of the store. I barely kept up. His face looked red.

"Why are we leaving, Daddy?"

My father hesitated. "I'll tell you later, Honey."

Once we were in the car, it sank in. The cashier was talking about me. I was the only child in the store. My heart sank, and deep inside, I felt like my soul had just been wrung out in an icy river. I sucked in a ragged breath. *The lady thought I was "retarded."*

I trembled. Was something wrong with me—and no one had ever told me the truth?

Now it made sense—the many times my mother and teachers told me to hurry up. Evidently, I was slow in more than one way.

The joy usually bubbling inside me burst, fizzling like the dying embers of a campfire. A blanket of sadness covered the surface of my heart. Every good thought I had about myself had just been extinguished.

We drove in silence to the campground. My mother usually fixed lunch, but Dad said he'd fix the sandwiches. I think he needed something to do. He looked sad. He didn't think I noticed—but I did.

In the afternoon, as Mom rested and my brother played quietly, Dad came outside to the picnic table while I was coloring pictures in a nature book.

"Hi, Sweetie," Dad said, sitting across from me.

"Hi, Daddy." I looked up for a quick second. I didn't want him to catch on that I knew what had happened. I steadied my hand as I traced the outline of a tree trunk with a brown crayon.

Pretending I didn't know, I looked up. "Daddy," I asked, "Why did we have to leave the gift shop?"

My father cleared his throat.

"Hon," he began, his voice soft, "some people aren't nice and shouldn't be in business."

"Oh," I replied, looking down and continuing to color.

"I'm sorry you didn't have time to get your souvenir."

"It's okay, Daddy," I replied. Pressing down with the green crayon, I colored the last pine trees in my picture.

My father was quiet for a moment. "That's a beautiful picture," he said and put his hand on my shoulder.

I took a breath as my eyes caught the intensity of his gaze.

"Honey, do you know how much Mom and I love you?"

"Yep," I nodded, keeping my head down. I pressed my lips together. I didn't want to cry. I stuffed the crayons into the box. "I love you, too, Daddy," I said.

"I know, Sweetie," he said, patting my head. He returned to the trailer.

I'd played the actress. I guessed I was good at it because my father didn't suspect I knew the entire story of what happened in the gift shop.

At bedtime, Mom reminded me I was special. We exchanged our nightly "I love you" statements with hugs. I closed my eyes but couldn't sleep.

"Special." There was that word again. I'd heard it as an endearing term for my parents' love for me. But I'd also listened to my teacher talk about "special" kids who needed a lot of help. The lady at the gift shop thought I was one of them. Maybe she was right. I was terrible at math and had to stay after school every day for math tutoring. I wasn't catching on. Evidently, I was one of the kids my teacher was talking about.

The day at the cavern started out being fun, but after the incident at the gift shop, I wished we'd never come here. It changed everything. Instead of leaving with a souvenir, I left with a damaged sense of self—all because of one person's careless words.

I didn't know until years later that my memories of the caverns would produce something good until I came across the Bible verse from Proverbs 12:14:

"From the fruit of their lips people are filled with good things, and the work of their hands brings them reward."

My experience at the gift shop was the opposite of the words in the verse, but I couldn't get the scripture out of my mind once I discovered it. Then it struck me. When we see what is not good whether it refers to things or people—we can better appreciate the good things.

As I thought about it, I remembered things others had said

about me that were good. My best friend's grandmother told me the artwork I'd created at school was some of the best she'd seen, and a neighbor said I was "sweeter than candy."

My mother assured me I could do anything I set my mind to, even if difficult. My father encouraged me to write a poem, which my teacher shared in class. And Mom and Dad always told me they loved me. These were all good things.

God is the creator of good things. Take the apple, for instance. It invokes a flavor bursting with sweetness and is loaded with vitamins and minerals. God created it as something that would be good for us. The verse from Proverbs 12:14 uses fruit as an example, but it refers to the goodness that comes from one's lips, which is as sweet and succulent as fruit.

My mother used to say, "One rotten apple spoils the bunch." It is a true statement. It only took one woman's thoughtless words to cause hurt that extended far beyond what came from her mouth. Perhaps the words slipped out by accident, but even if so, the damage was already done.

Did the woman at the cash register ever regret what she said? Did she know I was within earshot of my father? Did she understand the implications behind her comment? I would never know the answers to these questions, but one thing was sure. Her words left a deep scar.

In sixth grade at the end of the school year, I was honored as "Student of the Week." I was surprised, but happy, for in our small class others had been nominated, except for me—until I finally received the honor. A story I had written had been posted on the bulletin board for other students to see. I loved to write, so I felt good about that. I lagged behind in other subjects, such as math and history, but managed to pass my exams. It took a long time for me to realize I was as worthy as anyone else.

Looking back on the Carlsbad Cavern trip, I realized there were some good memories. Dad was enthused when I demonstrated what he'd taught me about rock formations, and I will never forget his love and encouragement as we sat at the picnic table together. Then, there were Mom's frequent reminders. "You're special," she'd say. I knew I was loved.

My parents' words were like what I imagined from the verse in Proverbs—sweet as fruit, coming from the goodness within them. In the end, that was all that mattered.

I didn't mention the surprise. After we got home from our trip, my father handed me a small box wrapped in gift paper and a bow. I excitedly opened it. As I unwrapped the brown paper, I squealed with glee and thanked him. It was one of the sparkly rocks from the gift shop that he'd seen me looking at. He'd remembered. I was thrilled. Now I had a souvenir. A few years later, the rock was lost when we moved. But the best souvenir of all was the memory of our time together as a family, which would last forever in my heart.

As Christians, we hope what we say will be beneficial, worthy, honest, truthful, and pleasing, but we are imperfect. Words of frustration or anger may slip out of the mouths of the best of us. Unkind words may erupt in the heat of a disagreement, and these outbursts may cause us to feel sorry or ashamed afterward.

It is believed that King Solomon wrote much of the Book of Proverbs. According to Proverbs 1:2, he writes "for gaining wisdom and instruction; for understanding words of insight."

The words from today's verse in Proverbs 12:14 say the "fruit" that comes from one's lips is filled with good things, relating this to the work of one's hands as a reward. Essentially, this is interpreted as goodness from within extending to one's actions.

Fruit that is not good can come from hurtful words, whether they are intentional or uttered by mistake. I would never know if the cashier's remark was a slip of the tongue or whether she thought she was being helpful to my father. I hoped she hadn't intended to be spiteful, but whatever the reason for her comment, it was hurtful.

—

Many Scripture verses have to do with the words that come from our mouth, tongue, or lips. In Matthew 15:11, Jesus says, "What goes into someone's mouth does not defile them, but what comes out of their mouth, that is what defiles them."

Other Scripture of instruction about the words we use come from Colossians 4:6, "*Let your conversation be always full of grace, seasoned with salt, so that you may know how to answer everyone,*" from Ephesians 4:29, "*Do not let any unwholesome talk come out of your mouths, but only what is helpful for building others up according to their needs, that it may benefit those who listen,*" and from Proverbs 31:26, "*She speaks with wisdom, and faithful instruction is on her tongue.*"

—

My mother's comment, that there will always be "a few rotten apples in the world," was true. But I didn't have to live with the effect of hurtful words. And neither do you. Instead, we can be encouraged by the *good things* that come from others' lips, from those who speak from the goodness of their hearts.

And that's *one good thing.*

Worksheet for My Daily Morsel #11

Personal Insight:
It has happened to most of us—someone said something, either by a slip of the tongue or by wrongful words, that caused us to feel hurt. If this has happened to you, did you recover from the hurt? If so, did forgiveness play a role in your recovery?

_____

_____

_____

_____

_____

Reflection: My "One Good Thing"
What one good thing has come from words aptly spoken by you or someone who spoke kindly to you?

_____

_____

_____

_____

_____

Today's Serving: Provision Through Goodness
Proverbs says that the goodness within us extends to our actions and work. Essentially, then, it affects all that we do. As this Scripture states, being "filled" with good things is rewarding. In today's story, my parents demonstrated that good could come out of the face of despair and hurtful words.

A Cupful of Reality:
Who has come to your aid in a time of need, demonstrating the kind of goodness depicted in today's Scripture?

_____

_____

_____

_____

_____

A Taste of Spiritual Nourishment:
From today's verse in Proverbs comes a key word, *fruit*. Think of your favorite fruit as you visualize biting into its juicy sweetness. Now, think of that same sweetness that comes from your lips when good words come from your heart. Savor that goodness as you go about your day!

The "Table of Optimism":
Hope resides at the Table of Optimism. What is your hope for today?

_____

_____

_____

_____

Prayer for Today:
Dear Father in heaven,

Please help me forgive those who say hurtful things and guard my lips against saying unkind things. Your saving grace is my rescue. May I routinely commune with You, for You cleanse me from all unrighteousness. I choose to rejoice in You and fill my heart with the good things that come from trusting in You. In Jesus's name, amen.

Recipe

My Daily Morsel #12

Prep Time

Cook Time

Oven Temp

Serves

Topic: **Joy/Gladness**

_____
_____
_____
_____
_____
_____

Bible Verse for Study

"On the twenty-third day of the seventh month he sent the people to their homes, joyful and glad in heart for the **good things** the LORD had done for David and his people Israel."

2 Chronicles 7:10

_____
_____
_____
_____

Joy Ride

My father was an avid outdoorsman. As I grew up, I wanted to be just like him. We shared the same interests: fishing, camping, and off-road Jeeping in the mountains. A man of firm conviction, my father believed in hard work and doing everything right. He was a perfectionist, and his nature was tough as nails. He upheld the Finnish cultural ideal of *"Sisu,"* just like his father did. This meant he would do his best to persevere through adversity.

Dad didn't talk about it often but once told me about his difficulties growing up. His parents were poor, but despite affliction, they were resilient. They had *sisu*—but they also had a strong faith in God.

My father's cultural heritage had rubbed off on me by the time I was fourteen. I wanted to be solid and grounded, just like him. He was proud of me for this and encouraged me to have that same strength of character.

We lived in a small town at the base of a mountain, so it only took an hour or two to reach the higher elevations. Dad liked taking us to obscure places for Jeep rides, and we were always excited to go with him. It was a fun way to explore the outdoors and was a welcome reprieve from weekend chores.

Dad invited a family friend, Johnny, to ride along with us. Little did I know, on that warm June morning, that my desire to be grounded like a rock would be tested more than I could imagine.

Removing the top from the Jeep, my father replaced it with the simple canvas summer top. With no sides, doors, or windows, it left the Jeep in the open air. My brother grinned as he jumped into the back seat. I don't think he had a concern in the world, but I did—I feared we might fall out. But Dad checked our seatbelts to ensure they were snug and made us promise to keep them on.

As we turned onto the highway, I was pleasantly surprised at how freeing it was to ride in the open air. My short blonde hair blew every which way in the wind. What a joyride!

The Jeep was a workhorse for its age. It didn't travel very fast, but we reached an elevation of approximately 8,300 feet after an hour and a half. Then, we turned off on a dirt road that took us from tall pines to a meadow of Aspens, where the tracks from the road became almost invisible in the grass.

The smooth ride was short-lived as we headed toward a steep, rocky incline. The engine whined as we ascended the hill. Small rocks gave way to larger ones and then to boulders. I leaned over to look down. We no longer had tire tracks to follow.

"Dad?" my voice raised an octave. "What happened to the road?"

My father turned toward me, his lips parting into a full grin, and Johnny let out a belly laugh.

"We're making our own road, Sweetie!" Dad replied.

I rolled my eyes. I laughed on the outside, but I wasn't sure how I felt about not having a road to follow. We'd been on Jeep rides before, but those had been tamer.

Dad maneuvered the Jeep over one boulder, then the next, gripping the steering wheel with both hands. I could see his expression in the rear-view mirror. He squinted and pursed his lips as he struggled to maintain his grip as we climbed over the massive rocky mount.

I held my breath as the jeep tilted to the right and was relieved when it came back to center. However, the hill was getting progressively steeper. My brother and I held on tightly to the roll bar.

Danny was quieter than usual, and I could tell he was scared.

As we got close to the crest of the hill, the Jeep wouldn't advance. I heard the whirr as my father gunned the engine.

Johnny looked down. "Front tire is spinning, Carl."

My father turned the wheel as far as he could. *Whew.* The tire grabbed hold. I sighed a breath of relief as we reached the summit.

As we descended the other side, Dad put the Jeep in low gear to slow the engine. There was a lot of loose soil beneath the rocks, and he was concerned it could cause us to slide. Fortunately, we made it safely to the bottom of the hill as the rocky landscape eased us back onto smaller stones, then pebbles. Finally, the Jeep tires made tracks over wild grass and green moss.

Dad put his foot on the brake as we rolled to a stop. He flipped off the ignition.

"Time for lunch," he said. We unhooked our seat belts and piled out of the Jeep.

While Dad retrieved sandwiches and sodas from the cooler, I stretched my legs and marveled at the tiny purple and yellow wildflowers at my feet. They looked delicate against the background of the massive rock hill we'd climbed.

I was relieved to be on flat ground again. We sat on a fallen log beneath the shade of a pine tree. The bologna and cheese sandwich Mom made tasted pretty good now, even though I was not fond of bologna.

I finished my lunch. Dad and Johnny talked, and Danny played with a toy truck in the dirt. I decided to walk back toward the rocky mount from where we'd come. I stopped and looked up. The hill was steeper than I realized, and I was amazed we'd made it over.

The sun played hide and seek behind the clouds as I rubbed at the goosebumps on my bare arms. I was glad we'd brought our sweatshirts.

Dad summoned us back into the Jeep. He decided it would be

best to try another route down the mountain. I was glad to hear that because I didn't want to go over that crazy hill of boulders again.

"Will we be on a *road* this time?" I asked.

My father half-smiled and raised his eyebrows. I knew what that meant. We'd be making our own road again. I sighed. *Here we go again.* "*Sisu,*" I reminded myself. *Be as solid as a rock in cement.*

We drove through the clearing of Aspens and slowed to a stop. Dad and Johnny stepped out of the Jeep to look at the terrain.

"Wait there," Dad told us. We watched as they walked ahead to survey the landscape. Dad nodded, and then they returned to the Jeep.

"Are we going to the *right*, Dad?" I asked.

"No, Hon. It drops off too steeply."

"What about the meadow ahead?"

"Fenced off," Dad responded.

"So, I guess we're going *left.*"

Dad nodded. It was our only option.

Soon, we passed through the Aspen meadow and descended downhill through the forest. We reached a flat area that looked like a creek had run through.

"Is this a creek, Dad?"

He nodded. "This will serve as our *road*. We'll be driving through the stream bed, Hon."

Now, I wished we could have gone back the way we came. "What if it *rains*?"

My father gave me that "look," a downward turn of his lips and widening his eyes. That meant I shouldn't worry—and trust him.

"*Sisu,*" I reminded myself.

It wasn't exactly flat as we drove slowly over the streambed. The Jeep tilted slightly to the right, then to the left. Sometimes it dipped in the middle. Riding in a streambed seemed like an odd thing to do, but I trusted my father.

I diverted my attention to the small plants, moss, and wildflowers that grew along the bank. As we rolled along, the tires made a crunching sound like broken glass. I noticed reddish agate and wished we could stop to collect some of it.

I overheard Johnny ask where the streambed would lead. Dad responded, saying it would lead us to the reservoir, and from there, we could access the highway that would take us home.

I knew the reservoir Dad was referring to. He had taken us fishing there before, although we'd never taken *this* route to get there.

I looked over at Danny, who was busily defraying the end of a rope tie Dad kept in the back of the Jeep. At least he wasn't bugging me like he did on long car trips.

Dad seemed to have a good handle on getting us through the streambed, and now the Jeep was moving along a bit faster. Occasionally, he'd have to slow down for a large rock or two, but these were nothing like the large rocks we'd encountered earlier.

Afternoon clouds, some turning gray, now replaced the warmth of the morning sun. I looked up through the pines, watching clouds move together, closing out areas of blue. As the wind picked up, I zipped my sweatshirt and pulled the collar over the back of my neck.

Dad looked relaxed and confident as he maneuvered us through the stream bed. He and Johnny talked and laughed, as they usually did, telling each other fish stories.

The hum of the Jeep motor lulled me into a state of sleepiness. I closed my eyes and leaned against the backrest, the sway of the Jeep moving my upper body like a rag doll. It felt as if we were heading downhill at a steeper grade than before, but I was too tired to open my eyes to look.

I dozed off, unaware of how much time had passed. I was startled as the Jeep came to a sudden halt, the sound of gravel flying from underneath the wheels.

"What are we doing?" I mumbled, squinting at the brightness

as I opened my eyes.

"Stay there. Don't move!" My father's voice was stern. I watched as he carefully stepped out of the Jeep and looked down.

I gasped. This wasn't a stream bed. It was a crevice, and it was deep.

"Dad!" I yelled.

My father didn't answer. Instead, he walked to the front side of the Jeep. "Keep your seatbelts on, stay still, and listen to Johnny!"

My brother and I complied. If we made the Jeep move, I didn't want to think about what would happen.

"What's my father doing, Mr. Rickman?" I asked as I inhaled a deep breath.

"Deciding how we're going to make it over this hole," Johnny said calmly.

How could he be so calm? A couple of large boulders were the only thing keeping the Jeep in place against the sides of the ravine.

All I could think about was my dad's accident with friends in Canyonlands when a tire on their Jeep got stuck in quicksand.

I craned my neck to see out the front window. What was my father doing? He'd walked ahead, then back toward the Jeep's driver's side. His hands were on his hips. That wasn't a good sign.

Dad and Johnny came to the back of the Jeep where my brother and I sat.

"What are we going to do?" my voice squeaked shakily.

"I'm going to stand back here," Dad said, his arms reaching toward my brother. "Now, Hon, stay where you're at and carefully unbuckle your brother's seat belt." I did as Dad asked. He told Danny to be still, and then he and Johnny grabbed his shoulders and pulled him from the Jeep.

Next, it was my turn. A nervous energy shot through me as Dad and Johnny reached over to pull me out of the vehicle. He didn't want to take a chance to create any more movement than possible.

"Sit on that rock under the pine tree over there," Dad said.

Johnny directed us to the spot to which Dad had pointed.

"And stay there," he warned, easing himself into the driver's seat. "We're going to get this Jeep back on track."

"But Dad," I cried, "it looks like it's going to *fall!*"

My father raised his hand in the air. I knew what that meant. *"Do as I say. Don't ask why."*

I covered my mouth as a sob erupted. I watched as Dad gripped the steering wheel from where we were sitting. He turned his head in my direction. "Have a little faith, okay?" he called out.

I nodded, sniffling. I wasn't so sure about that. How was I going to persevere with sisu—and faith?

I shook my head. *Faith.* Mine had just sunk to the bottom of that crevice. What if something happened to Dad? *No!* I couldn't think about that. Not here. Not now.

Johnny stood nearby. His task would be to signal my father how to turn the wheel to get out of the aperture. Just a few hundred feet ahead, the depth of the ravine lessened. The challenge would be to get it to that safety point.

My brother and I sat on the rock. We did what we were told. To stay put. What else could we do? I felt helpless.

At this moment, I wasn't sure I even had as much as a *little* faith. All I could think of were the "what ifs." What if Johnny told my father to turn the wheel the wrong way? I didn't want to think about the consequences. The wheels wanted to slide, not grip, the raw edges of the boulders.

The crevice was deepest toward the front of the Jeep. To go backward was not an option.

Johnny signaled my father to turn the wheels to the right. I clasped one hand over my mouth. Then Danny screamed, "He's going to fall in!"

I sucked in a raspy breath and pursed my lips. "He's *not* going to fall in," I replied, grasping my brother's hand.

Dad slowly gunned the engine to get the Jeep to inch forward. "Stop!" Johnny shouted, shooting up his hand. My father put on the brakes. "Can't hit it on the left," Johnny called out, "or else..."

I knew what that meant. The Jeep would go down—with my father in it.

My brother's eyes widened. I tightened my grip on his hand.

"Dad said not to worry, Dan." I tried to console my brother. "Remember...*Sisu*." But I wasn't sure I believed my own words.

Johnny signaled for my father to turn the wheels in the other direction. The Jeep gears began to grind like a saw on metal. I could tell Dad was struggling to make the steering wheel turn left. Then,

Clunk! Scrape!

I screamed as the Jeep fender smacked against the boulder. The Jeep tilted left...Oh, dear God...

"Daddy, don't fall!" Danny sobbed.

Johnny shot both hands into the air. "Pull to the right, Carl!" he yelled.

I drew in a deep breath, and then the prayer tumbled out. "*Please, God, don't let the Jeep fall with Dad in it...*"

Tears flooded against the inside of my glasses. I pulled them off, shook out the salty fluid, and swiped at the stream running down my cheeks.

"Daddy!" we cried. The Jeep tilted, then slumped.

No more clunk or scrape. The Jeep rested where it was. I could see Dad's hands gripping the steering wheel like a vise, his face pale, his expression pained.

I couldn't take any more of this. I stepped down off the rock. "Dad!"

But Johnny yelled to go back. Then I realized my brother was trying to follow me.

Danny and I returned to the rock, my vision blurring with tears. Before a sob could erupt, a small voice inside me spoke. *Get a hold of yourself—have faith!*

I breathed in and closed my eyes. I couldn't watch anymore, so afraid of what would happen next. Then, strangely, my fear began to subside as peace washed over me like a soft ocean wave, and words of comfort came to my heart. *Do not look back. Instead, look forward with faith, which brings joy.*

Is that you, God?

I opened my eyes and noticed my father reach down and pick something up from the Jeep floor. He summoned Johnny and handed these things to him.

And what were they? Rubber floor mats from the Jeep. My father told Johnny to slide a mat under the front of each tire. Then Johnny signaled for my father to inch the Jeep forward. Yes! The rubber mats were holding; they were keeping the tires from sliding.

Johnny motioned for my father to inch forward just a little. Then again. A little more. And again. My brother and I watched in anticipation as the front tires gripped the mats, allowing the Jeep to ride over the boulders.

Within a few hundred yards, the stream bed would be accessible. We cheered and clapped as Dad reached the other side of the ravine. He was safe now, back into the streambed—free from the deep crevice. Danny and I hugged and cried out for joy. Because of his Finnish heritage, my father didn't shed a tear, but his eyes looked a little watery.

Floor mats...*Ingenious!*

As Dad said, all you need is a little faith. My lips curled into a smile. Yes, my father was right. That's all I had, but even a little faith was enough. I thought of Jesus's parable of the mustard seed and that even faith as small as a mustard seed makes a difference.

We resumed our journey. It was dusk when we reached the access road to the reservoir. We were tired and hungry, but we made it home feeling relieved and *joyful* for the good things that came to pass that day. We were safe and arrived home just in time for Mom's pot roast dinner.

A thought came to me as I laid my head on the pillow to sleep that night. *Sisu* was a quality inherent to my father's culture, but his real strength came from his faith.

I always wanted to be like Dad. He is no longer with us, but I think of him often. He taught me that even a little faith could make a difference, and true joy comes from the Father above.

•—

King David and his son, King Solomon, were men of great faith. David desired to build the temple and gathered supplies for over a decade. However, it wasn't part of God's plan for David to accomplish this. Instead, Solomon was chosen to construct the temple, Israel's first house of the Lord.

The temple was constructed of cedar, large stones, and gold, and it took seven years to complete. Much of the material had to be secured from distances far away and required the employment of hundreds of thousands of workers, craftsmen, and artisans.

If there ever was a reason to be overwhelmed, frustrated, or have doubts about undertaking such a massive project, this was it. However, Solomon had prayed fervently for wisdom—which God gave him, along with the earthly treasures needed to construct the magnificent temple.

Suppose David and Solomon lived in today's times. In that case, I am sure my father would have nodded in agreement that they had "*Sisu*." They were stoic, determined, and they persevered, just like my father and his Finnish heritage. My father would also be the first to tell you that David and Solomon were great men of faith.

•—

I know how faith can be. Even just a little bit of it helped me during a frightening time. Fortunately, in the end, the Jeep adventure was a good one.

Talk about a *joyride*!

And that's *one good thing.*

Worksheet for My Daily Morsel #12

Personal Insight:
Joy cannot be stored in your pocket or bank account for later use. The only actual "bank of joy" is through our Redeemer. Describe what this type of joy feels like for you:

_____

_____

_____

_____

My "One Good Thing" – Name one thing that brings you joy that is not material in origin:

_____

_____

_____

_____

_____

Today's Serving: Provision—Joy and Gladness
Our eyes are in the front of our head, not in the back, so we are meant to "look forward," not backward. This is something to remember if we dwell on past events or things we can't control, such as peril or danger. By looking forward with faith and trusting God, we can also look to joy— and hope.

A Cupful of Reality:
Has your faith ever faltered and interfered with your ability to experience joy? If so, describe what happened.

_____

_____

_____

_____

_____

If your faith faltered, how did you find faith again?

_____

_____

_____

What is one thing you can do to remind yourself to "look forward" with hope instead of looking back to the past?

A Taste of Spiritual Nourishment:
In today's verse from 2 Chronicles comes a key word, *heart*. Joy is a state of being, as opposed to happiness, which can be fleeting. What brings joy to your heart?

Think of *Joy*—as spiritual nourishment.

The "Table of Optimism":
Hope resides at the Table of Optimism. What is your hope for today?

Prayer for Today:
Dear Father in heaven,

Please remind me to take one step at a time. I cannot take tomorrow's steps today, just as I cannot retrace yesterday's steps. Help me focus on the *good things* You provide for me so that my eyes may be fixed on You. Enable my feet to walk the path that leads to faith and joy, for this is the true *joyride*. In Jesus's name, amen.

Recipe

My Daily Morsel #13

Prep Time

Cook Time

Oven Temp

Serves

Topic: **Peace, Prosperity, and Provisions**

Bible Verse for Study

"Then this city will bring me renown, joy, praise, and honor before all nations on earth that hear of all the **good things** I do for it; and they will be in awe and will tremble at the abundant prosperity and peace I provide for it."

Jeremiah 33:9

"Way To Go, Jerry!"

After school, Jerry hurried to the locker room to change into his red gym shorts. He retrieved a basketball and dashed out the back door. Rounding the corner of the red brick building, he headed straight for Skyview High's old basketball court. There was no need to rush. No one played on the old court anymore—except him.

The new basketball court in the gym looked enticing, with its shiny floors and state-of-the-art equipment. But Jerry didn't mind playing on the old court, even though weeds poked through the cracks in the cement and the basketball hoop was rusted. He liked having the place to himself.

Jerry took the first shot. Swoosh. Then, eleven more baskets without one miss. As he turned to dribble the ball, he saw two guys watching from the chain-link fence at the far side of the court. One of the guys yelled something, but he was too far away for Jerry to read his lips—probably some snide remark. In Jerry's world, that was nothing new.

He turned his back, ignoring the onlookers. He was relieved when they left.

On the next shot, the ball bounced against the rim of the hoop. Jerry caught it before it hit the concrete. Dang. Oh, well. Even a less-than-perfect practice was better than being at home when his father was there.

—

Mark and David walked down Martin Drive as they did every

167

day after school. David had a lot on his mind and didn't feel like talking.

"What's with you?" Mark asked. "You've got that look on your face. Are you mad?"

David paused. "Yeah, I am," he exclaimed. "I can't believe what you said about that guy."

"The new guy," Mark interrupted, "that—Jerry, what's his name?"

"Yeah. You were going to call him a 'retard,' weren't you?"

"Pshh." Mark rolled his eyes.

"You're forgetting," David said, lowering his gaze, "what I went through."

"But you weren't retarded just because you had braces on your legs."

"Yeah? Well, guess what? That didn't keep kids from calling me the 'R-word,'" David huffed. "It was humiliating."

"Hmph." Mark shrugged his shoulders.

As they reached the intersection where they'd go their separate ways, Mark hopped off the curb and rushed across the street without saying goodbye.

David wasn't going to let his cousin get the best of him.

"Did you forget everything you ever learned, Mark?" he yelled. "Like 'Do unto others?' Can't you have a little compassion?" David's breath caught. He inwardly fumed when Mark ignored him and kept walking.

The next afternoon, David realized Mark had left school without him. Just as well. He'd stop by the basketball court. Maybe Jerry would be there.

But the court was empty, and there was no sign of Jerry. All was quiet—until David heard a door slam and a man yelling. He rushed through a stand of pines, then hid behind a tree. A few hundred feet away in the parking lot, he watched a man in a suit shaking his fist at a boy. "No son of mine disobeys!" he yelled. The boy in red shorts cowered, his head bent low.

David gasped. *It's Jerry.* He watched helplessly as the father yanked his son by the collar and pushed him as he got into the back seat of a Cadillac.

As the car sped out of the parking lot, David prayed. *Dear God, please help Jerry and keep him safe.*

—

Jerry locked his bedroom door. His face burned where his father had slapped him, but the sting of his father's words, "You'll never amount to anything," hurt the most.

He peeked through the curtains of his bedroom window, relieved his father's car was gone. *Probably off to some meeting.* It would be another two hours before his mother got home from work. He worried about how she'd take the news of what had happened.

Jerry pulled a textbook out of his backpack. He sat down to read, but the anger inside kept him from focusing on his homework. His neck hurt, too, when he tilted his head to one side.

Thank you, Father, for that! Jerry slammed the book closed and wiped tears with his sleeve.

He threw himself onto the bed and sunk his face into the pillow. Things used to be different when his father would say, "I love you, kid." But that was before Jerry got sick with Meningitis when he was six. His mother said he'd almost died. He knew he was fortunate to survive; however, the disease caused him to lose his hearing. And not just for a while. He became deaf.

After that, his father always seemed disappointed in him.

Jerry punched his fist into the mattress. *"Take that, Father!"* he cried.

In their small community, assistance for Jerry was limited. There was no school for deaf students, as in the bigger cities. Instead, a teacher from a neighboring town taught Jerry and his mother to use sign language. Unfortunately, few people in town knew how to sign, and their communication ability was limited if they did. Later, Jerry learned to read lips.

Whether there was help or not, it didn't matter. Jerry knew he would never be the son his father wanted.

—

Mark finished his morning classes and rushed to the cafeteria. He was glad David had accepted his apology for his unkind remarks. He promised to do better. But, right now, he had something important to say.

David had just sat down with his lunch tray when Mark tapped him on the shoulder.

"You're not going to believe this," Mark said, pulling up a chair. "Your basketball hero can't hear," he said quietly. "When I walked by the front office, I saw him speaking in sign language with some lady."

"Really?" David's mouth dropped open. "Jerry's *deaf*?" he whispered.

Mark nodded.

"No wonder he didn't respond the day we were at the court, and I yelled, "Way to go, Jerry!""

Now, it all made sense.

—

Jerry hesitated as he stepped onto the court, sucking in a deep breath. It had only been two days since the confrontation with his father. He glanced around nervously. He'd be dead meat if his father showed up. But he'd thought long and hard about it and had a plan. But, if he stayed on the west side of the court, flanked by thick pine trees, he wouldn't be visible from the parking lot.

As Jerry warmed up, he couldn't get his father's words out of his mind. The hateful comments still ate at him. Sitting on the splintery wood bench at the sideline, he rested his head in his hands. Would he ever amount to *anything*?

His father was right about one thing. Jerry struggled in school, and lip-reading was not easy. But he wasn't going to let his father's wrath destroy him. There had to be a way to prove he was worthy—if only his father would give him a chance.

Fortunately, Jerry had a compassionate mother who encouraged him to pursue other interests. She was his rock, his inspiration, and a woman of faith. She'd taken Jerry to church and Sunday School for as long as he could remember. She always told him she loved him, and before he got on the bus to go to school, she'd say, "I said a prayer for you today."

Jerry's thoughts reverted to the present as he dribbled the ball to avoid the broken places in the cement. *Broken.* Just like the relationship with his father. Ire rose inside, his spine stiffening. He grabbed the basketball and heaved it, watching it slam with a thunderous *Bang* against the backboard.

Take that, Father!

Loose screws rattled, and splintered backboard pieces scattered into the air as the ball dropped through the hoop.

He inhaled ragged breaths to control his anger. Being mad wasn't going to help anything. Jerry sighed, then tilted his head back. He looked up at the sky as glistening rays of sunlight burst forth from a bright opening in the clouds.

Were his mother's prayers riding along those beams of light that reached toward heaven? He brushed the dark hair from his eyes as he stared into the sky. A sense of peace washed over him. The beauty of the light traveled right into the deepest places of his heart.

As he stood in the center of the basketball court, feeling the sun's warmth on his shoulders, he bowed his head and closed his eyes.

❦

David and Mark cut across the shiny new basketball court, their tennis shoes squeaking. Mark signaled directions as they stepped into the hallway. "Coach's office is the first door on the right."

David knocked. There was no answer. The coach had probably left for the day. He hesitated, then slipped the envelope under the door. He looked up at Mark, then smiled. "I can't wait for Coach's reaction."

Mark nodded. "Yeah, same here."

The next afternoon, 87-degree temperatures and a sprinkling of afternoon rain were not deterring Jerry's practice. He felt he had been filled with extra energy, courage, and confidence today. And if his father showed up, he wouldn't sit on the curb and sulk. Instead, he'd stand his ground. He'd defend himself if he had to. No one would keep Jerry Steiner from playing basketball—including his father.

Jerry shot a series of baskets, stopped for water, and wiped the sweat from his forehead and neck. Suddenly, he noticed the movement of a shadow on his left. He froze. Someone was standing behind him.

Jerry clenched his fists. Expecting confrontation and filled with a mixture of determination and fear, he spun around, prepared to defend himself.

But it wasn't his father. His mouth dropped open in surprise. *Coach Michelson. What is he doing here?*

Jerry felt a lump rise in his throat. Was he in trouble? Had his father called to complain? The coach didn't look mad, but he wasn't saying anything.

The coach motioned with a curled finger to follow him. Jerry had to walk fast to keep up. He followed Coach past the old court, around the building's corner, and to the gym entrance. They walked around the perimeter of the gymnasium. Guys on the court waved. *They must really like Coach,* Jerry thought.

They stepped into the office. Coach offered Jerry a seat, then sat in a tattered swivel chair behind his desk. A burly man with plump cheeks and a thick jaw, Jerry couldn't decipher the expression on his face.

Coach pulled an envelope from the drawer and slid it across the desk to Jerry.

"Take a look at this," he said.

Jerry swallowed. He looked at the cursive inscription. *"For Coach Michelson."*

He didn't recognize the handwriting. It wasn't his father's, but maybe his father's secretary had written it.

His hands shook as he unfolded the letter on yellow notebook paper. He read silently.

Dear Jerry,

You don't know my cousin or me, but we've seen you play basketball after school. You're awesome! We told the guys on the team, and then everyone watched you shoot baskets from the classroom overlooking the old court. We wanted Coach to know, too, so we wrote this letter.

Keep up the great job! You're going to be a star!

Sincerely,

David Halloran, Mark Embry, and the Skyview Basketball Team

As Jerry finished reading the letter, his vision blurred from tears stinging his eyes.

Coach tapped him on the shoulder so Jerry could read his lips. "Congratulations, Son."

"Thank you," Jerry struggled to get the words out, swiping at the moisture beneath his eyes. He hoped Coach understood. He managed to get out a few more words. "Can read...lips," he gestured, pointing to his mouth.

Coach's shoulders relaxed. "Good, Jerry." "Now," he said, looking Jerry straight in the eyes, "How about trying out for the team?"

This was a dream come true! Jerry felt his mouth burst into a broad grin. "Yes!" he nodded excitedly.

"If it hadn't been for David and Mark, I wouldn't have known about you," Coach said.

Jerry didn't think he had any friends, but maybe now that was changing.

Exchanging a handshake with Coach, Jerry couldn't stop grinning. He'd never felt happier. Maybe God was listening, after all?

There was a knock on the door. Coach answered, glanced at Jerry. "Meet your new friends, Son," he said, motioning for the guys to step forward. "Jerry, I want to introduce you to David Halloran and Mark Embry."

These were the guys who wrote the letter. Jerry vigorously shook hands with both boys.

"No time to spare. To the court, guys." David and Mark gave Jerry a thumbs-up and shooed him behind Coach as they walked into the gymnasium.

Jerry stood in place before running onto the court, saying a silent prayer. He felt peace fill his heart. He was sure everything was going to be okay now.

❦

God had plans for Jerry, just as he had plans for Jeremiah. Both men shared something in common. They were unable to look at themselves in a positive light and lacked confidence because of it.

The Lord wanted Jeremiah to share an important message with the people. However, it would not be a message of hope, salvation, peace, or joy. Instead, the message God wanted Jeremiah to share was one of impending doom. Judah's people were wicked, and God was unhappy with them because they would not listen.

We can only imagine what Jeremiah's thoughts might have been about delivering such a message. Was he shocked, surprised, afraid? In his heart, did he question how God could trust him to carry out such a monumental task? Doubting his abilities to bring such terrible news to the people, might he have thought, *"Why me, Lord?"*

Jeremiah feared he wouldn't accomplish what God wanted him to do. But he prayed. And God answered by sending Jeremiah to a potter's house. There, he watched as the potter shaped and formed a vessel. He noticed how the potter could instantly build up the clay—or tear it down. In this way, Jeremiah understood how God—the Master Potter—could build up a kingdom—or tear it down at will.

Now, Jeremiah understood the importance and urgency of the message God wanted him to relay. And with confidence, he did as God had asked him to do. He warned the people of Judah to repent, or their city would face destruction.

But the people mocked Jeremiah when he delivered the message to them. The authorities found out what he was doing and threw him into a cistern filled with mud.

When King Zedekiah learned of Jeremiah's imprisonment, he secretly sent a servant to release him. He brought Jeremiah before him and told him to explain the message he had been given.

As Scripture tells us, Jeremiah warned King Zedekiah as the Lord had instructed him. The army of Nebuchadnezzar would indeed come to destroy them, for they continued to be disobedient. Then, the land of Judah was destroyed just as God said. The hands of the Master Potter tore down that which was not good.

Jeremiah and Jerry prayed to God for help, and the Lord empowered each of them with strength and courage. As a result, they both accomplished what they didn't think they could do. Jeremiah's answer to prayer came through his visit to the potter's house and the courage to deliver a message to the people. Help for Jerry came through David and Mark—people he didn't even know—who became his friends.

God provided for both Jeremiah and Jerry. As a result, they gained the courage and confidence to do what they thought was impossible. Jeremiah might have been shaking in his boots, but he approached Judah's people to impart God's message of impending doom. Likewise, Jerry overcame his fear of his father and proved his worth.

Jeremiah discovered that good things—like courage, confidence, and prosperity—await those who believe, listen, and obey the Master Potter, who molded him as God intended.

Good things came Jerry's way. Life was peaceful for him after his mother and father divorced. Later, his mother met a lovely man who became like a father to Jerry, encouraging him to excel at basketball. Jerry was good enough to have played professionally; however, he wanted to make a difference in another way—to coach teens with special needs.

And that's *one good thing*.

Worksheet for My Daily Morsel #13

Personal Insight:

1). Everyone has a talent or gift that can be shared. What is one talent or gift that you share?

_____

_____

_____

2). How have you refined your skills or knowledge when using your gifts or talents?

_____

_____

3). Have you faced obstacles in using your skills or abilities as Jeremiah or Jerry did? If so, what were they, and what did you do?

_____

_____

_____

4). In what way is God molding you to become the best you can be?

_____

_____

Reflection: My "One Good Thing":

When have you needed extraordinary confidence to accomplish an important task? What *"One Good Thing"* enabled you to complete what you set out to do?

_____

_____

Is there a time when you turned to God for confidence or courage? If so, what was the result?

_____

_____

Today's Serving: Provision Through Peace

Jerry was thankful he overcame a wounded spirit caused by his father's negative behavior. His prayers did not go unanswered. Likewise, Jeremiah's needs were met, enabling him to look at the tasks ahead with hope and optimism. Armed with peace and courage, each prospered from God's goodness.

A Cupful of Reality:

Negative influences impact us, whether they are situations or people, just as they did for Jerry and Jeremiah. Describe an experience when you overcame adversity. What happened, and what changed to turn it into a positive outcome?

_____

_____

A Taste of Spiritual Nourishment:

From today's verse in Jeremiah comes a key word, _awe_. Commonly appearing in the Bible, it is a mix of amazement and reverence. Imagine a miniature box in your heart where you could store moments of awe on a tiny piece of paper. What would your "moment of awe" say?

The "Table of Optimism":

Hope resides at the Table of Optimism. What is your hope for today?

_____

_____

Prayer for Today:

Dear Father in heaven,

As You helped Jerry and Jeremiah through difficult circumstances, please also help me when I face obstacles. Whether the challenges are the size of boulders or minor inconveniences that occur daily, please grant me the patience and perseverance to handle them. I am not alone; You are with me and will help me. I appreciate Your confidence in me so I may grow in faith and become the person I was meant to be. In Jesus's name, amen.

Recipe

My Daily Morsel #14

Prep Time

Cook Time

Oven Temp

Serves

Topic: **Do You Have a Great Need?**

Bible Verse for Study

"When you give it to them, they gather it up; when you open your hand, they are satisfied with **good things**."

Psalm 104:28

TAKING THE RIGHT PATH

I stood on the forest road, the tips of my new hiking boots brushing against the meadow grass. I couldn't help but smile. My parents had recently purchased ten acres of forest in the Rocky Mountains. It all seemed like the best dream I could ever hope for.

Today, I'd hike the perimeter of the acreage. I lined my right foot up with the property marker. It was easy to spot, a wooden stake with a plastic orange tie around it.

The sun warmed my shoulders as I stepped through the tall grass in the meadow. I passed through the aspen grove as it gave way to the pine forest. I spotted another orange marker. I was on the right track. The stakes were not close together but were easy to spot.

Such peace! It was quiet, a stark contrast from our home life in town. The only sounds here were those of nature: the chirp of a sparrow, the chattering of blue jays, the soft buzz of bees in the wildflowers, and the hushed whisper of a gentle breeze swishing through the pines.

Things that had been grating on my nerves—starting tenth grade at a new school and expectations of teachers and my parents—dissipated with each step.

My father was a knowledgeable outdoorsman. He'd taught me a lot over the years. My promise to him came to mind:

I'll be careful, Dad. As you told me, I'll follow the boundaries by watching for the orange stakes.

Dad had the same concerned look on his face as he always did. Being the father of a teenage daughter certainly wasn't easy. He must have been having a parent moment: *Do I let her hike alone? . . . She should be okay if she stays on our land."*

Finally! I felt I'd won this time, maybe because I was sixteen, and Dad decided it was okay. I wasn't a little girl anymore.

I felt an increasing sense of exhilaration as I walked farther into the forest. I was free from my parent's concerns, free to be alone. I'd done my share of helping Dad set up camp. I deserved a break. I was delighted my parents had purchased the land. They'd taken my brother and me camping when we were small. Now, it seemed like a dream—to camp on our land.

I was curious to see where the national forest backed up to our ten acres. My parents had "walked the stakes" with the realtor. But unfortunately, I didn't get to go since it was a school day. But now, it was my turn to explore the boundaries of our property.

Inhaling the crisp mountain air, I felt revived and invigorated with each step. My mind drifted away in thought. Not watching where I was going, I tripped over a jagged rock, but caught myself before falling.

It had been a while since I'd seen an orange property marker. I'd been captivated by the beauty of the forest and hadn't thought about looking for them. *There must be one close by.*

I came to a cluster of granite boulders and climbed to the top. I needed to rest, anyway. My feet hurt, and my right toe pinched— dang new boots. I should have broken them in before I came to the mountains. I could have opted for a softer pair, but these— the stiff, heavy-duty ones—were the latest rage at school.

Turning, I shielded my face from the sun. How far had I hiked? I didn't know. I couldn't see the forest turnoff; the trees were too dense.

I wasn't wearing a watch, either. I guessed that I'd been away for over an hour. I looked up at the horizon. Bright coral clouds swirled between patches of vivid blue sky. The sun would be setting soon.

I'd better get back to camp.

Climbing down from the boulder, I scouted for an orange stake as I proceeded, keeping my eye on where I'd just walked. No stake. I crossed to the opposite side of the boulder, then ventured in each direction, using it as a center point. I shook my head. Not one orange stake was in sight. I began to worry.

Something should look familiar. I scanned the terrain, but it looked the same as I turned in each direction. The only difference was the cluster of rocks. *I can retrace my footprints.* However, it wasn't possible. Pine needles had cushioned my steps, and my boots had not left an impression on the ground.

A gripping thought entered my mind.

Am I lost?

I argued with my conscience. How could I get lost on my parent's property? I hadn't passed the stakes bordering the national forest. *Or had I?*

A knot tightened in my stomach. *I need to find the stakes.*

Keeping the cluster of boulders within view, I walked a large circumference around the rocks in search of a marker. I was careful not to walk too far, propelling myself deeper into unknown territory.

The sun's warm rays gave way to a chill in the air as the sun inched its way over the horizon. I'd been comfortable in hiking shorts and a tee shirt, but I'd shiver in these clothes once the sun went down.

Most of the time, I wanted to get away from my parents, but now I was thinking about them. I'd promised Dad I would follow the stakes. I'd messed up. Would he and Mom be wondering where I was by now?

Emotion building up inside me broke loose as tears came. I didn't feel like the strong person I thought I was. How stupid I felt for losing my way! If Dad knew I was lost, he'd be so upset.

A sting of guilt embedded its tiny dagger into my heart. I hadn't been very agreeable lately. Especially to Mom; I told her I didn't want to attend church anymore, and she got upset. I heard her crying in her room at night. She was disappointed in me. All I knew was that I was laying my feelings on the line and being truthful. Church was boring, and the youth group, well, not so cool.

I can still believe in God and not go to church.

But guilty feelings and tears weren't going to help me now. I needed to do something to find my way back to camp quickly.

I cupped my hands around my mouth and yelled as loud as possible. "Mom! Dad!" But there was only silence.

I yelled again, this time screaming out the words. But, again, all was silent except for the chirping of a distant bird and my breathing.

Sitting down on a rock, I choked back tears. The sun would be setting. It would be dark soon. And I had a great need—I needed help.

I thought about when I was little and afraid of the dark. I'd lay in bed and cry. Mom would come to my room, and we'd fold our hands and pray. I hadn't done that in a long time. I folded my hands and looked up.

God, are you there? I need help!

I wiped away tears with my shirt sleeve. Crying would be of no use. Time was ticking away.

Stay where you're put. The words of my brother's scoutmaster came to mind. "If you get lost," he'd said, "stay put."

Stay put. It didn't feel right! I felt the urge to walk away from the rocks. I questioned my thinking. Was this the right thing to do, or was I reacting to my panic?

I couldn't sit any longer. I couldn't just wait out in the dark and cold all night. So, I got up, took a deep breath, and began walking toward a dense stand of pines. It felt eerie, but maybe I'd see something beyond the trees. The foliage was so thick only bits of light reached the forest floor. It seemed foreboding—and dark. I wasn't sure why I kept walking through the brush, but it felt like the right thing to do.

A Bluejay swooped down onto the tree branch next to me, cackling at me. *Ack, ack, ack.* Annoying bird. It was so loud, that my ears hurt, so I walked quickly through the pines, avoiding getting caught between tangled branches. Finally, the dense pines gave way to a clearing within a few hundred feet.

A ridge of rocks lay ahead. I felt winded. My heart pounded beneath my ribs, and I heard the labored breathing echo in my ears. Adrenaline must have been at work because I felt a sudden burst of energy to get my tired feet over the rocky ridge. The clunking sound of my boots provided a rhythm to which I stepped: *Clunk, clunk, scrape.* The sound helped me keep my mind off the nervous feeling in my stomach.

I came to an embankment, which sloped gently upward. I felt a sense of hope. Maybe there would be something I'd recognize as I reached the top.

Nothing but flat brush and pine.

I let out a sigh. Why had I trusted my instincts? I was wrong. I felt angry with myself. Why hadn't I watched where I was going? Then, I wouldn't be in this predicament.

I continued walking across the flat landscape of scrub brush and pine and came upon a ravine that dropped off sharply. The ground was soft beneath my feet. The loose soil gave way, and I lost my footing. My heart raced as I stumbled down the ravine, landing on my knees in the gravel. I felt the sudden sting of scraping rock. I brushed myself off. Both knees were scraped, and the right one was bleeding. I had nothing to wash the blood off and hadn't brought water—dumb decision. I never thought I'd be gone this long.

The ravine was deep; I'd have to climb out the other side.

Some of the rock ledges would serve as a foothold. It was a laborious process; I tested each before putting my total weight on it. The ascent was more challenging than I anticipated, and thorny burrs stuck to my socks as my feet slid into patches of weeds.

A hint of orange glow from the sky scattered its rays of light randomly across the ridge. There was still a little bit of daylight left, but not much.

Nearing the top of the ravine, I was breathing so hard, and I felt slightly dizzy and sick to my stomach. I stopped to rest but didn't want to waste time.

Please, God, no more ravines.

I continued across a flat area of ground, which gradually inclined. A hill...

As I reached the top of the ridge and looked below, the burden of my worries released with every breath I took. As I looked down between the trees, I noticed an open area. *Could it be? Yes—a dirt road!*

A burst of renewed energy propelled me down the hill. I slid on the soft soil and gravel but didn't fall this time.

There were no cars or people on the road. It was quiet here, just like the forest. I was elated to reach this road—a sure sign of civilization.

I didn't know where I was but began walking down the road. I saw a wooden structure behind the trees—a cabin. I was overjoyed. I didn't see or hear anyone, so I thought it was vacant. I walked past a front screened porch but could not see inside the window.

I'll try the other side.

Then I heard a door opening. I prayed it might be someone who could help me.

"Excuse me..." I called out.

A middle-aged woman with blonde hair and glasses stopped abruptly on the steps. I must have startled her. I was a sight, covered in dirt, with bleeding knees.

The woman pushed up her wire-frame glasses. "Oh, my...do you need help?"

"Oh, yes, please!" I held back tears. "I'm lost!"

I was never so glad to see another human being in my life. The woman was patient and kind. She retrieved some moist paper towels to clean the blood from my knees and gave me band-aids. As I put on the band-aids, I explained what had happened and gave her the location of my parent's property.

"I know where that is," she said. "Come with me," she signaled as I followed her to a small car. "I'll give you a ride."

The woman introduced herself; her name was Sue. She said she'd lived on the mountain a long time. We passed neighboring cabins dotting the forest edge as we drove along the bumpy dirt road, but there were no signs of other people.

"How far is it to my turnoff?" I asked.

"About four miles," she said. "That's all road and not forest, so you walked a long way from your property, young lady."

"Yeah. Guess I kinda' got turned around," I replied. Pride kept me from admitting how I got lost and how scared I was.

I asked Sue to drop me off at the corner as we approached Pine Glen Road.

"I don't want my parents to know I got lost," I said.

"Where is your parent's property?" she asked.

"Around the corner past that knotted pine," I replied.

Sue let me out on the corner and wished me well. I thanked her profusely.

Through the aspen grove, I walked past the knotted pine and up the path leading to our campsite. I hoped Mom and Dad wouldn't notice how late I was.

Dad stepped out from behind the woodpile.

"Where in the world have you been?" he exclaimed. His eye-brows furrowed in the firelight. "I kept calling, but you didn't answer. Your mom and I were worried." His hands were braced against his hips—not a good sign. "I was getting ready to look for you—do you see how dark it's getting?"

"Yes, Dad. I'm sorry," I responded.

"You should have been back sooner," he said, turning away, gathering a handful of kindling from the woodpile.

"Hon, she's home," he said, calling out to Mom. She rushed out from the door of the trailer as I walked up.

"Where were you? Dad said you'd be home by dinner!"

I was glad the kerosene light on the porch was dim. It helped mask the lie that came from my lips.

"Sorry, Mom...I was over *there*." I pointed to an area beyond the meadow. "Guess I didn't hear you. I went to the lean-to." I rationalized this as part truth because I had built a small lean-to from tree branches the day before, far from the view of our campsite.

"Dad and Charlie were going to go looking for you." Her voice broke. I could tell she'd been crying.

Mom looked at me and shook her head. "Go get washed up."

It was getting dark, and I was glad she didn't notice my banged-up knees.

As Mom set the table outside, I washed up in the bathroom and changed into jeans to hide my bandaged knees.

I sat at the picnic table on the deck as Dad lit a second lantern. Mom served the ribs and dropped a dollop of mashed potatoes onto my plate.

We said grace. Dad looked calm now. "So, how was the hike?" he asked matter-of-factly.

"Oh, the hike..." I hesitated, pushing the spoon into my potatoes.

"Um...It was fine."

"You followed the stakes?"

I nodded, shoveling potatoes into my mouth, avoiding eye contact. Besides, the way I figured it, the hike did turn out fine. I was home, safe and sound. I purposely changed the subject, asking Dad about his recipe for the smoked ribs. Fortunately, he didn't ask me any more questions about the hike. Thank heavens I got home before he went searching for me.

I had difficulty sleeping that night because of a few things Sue told me. The conversation played over in my mind.

"Do you know about the bear sightings?" she'd asked.

"Bear sightings?" I'd replied, gulping.

"The drought is forcing bears to forage for food in our community. Last night, a black bear, larger than my Husky, got into my garbage can and ripped it apart."

I shuddered to think of what might have become of me had I not found my way out of the forest.

Sue said she'd been house-sitting for a friend. "If I hadn't forgotten the mailbox key," she said, "I wouldn't have been at my cabin this afternoon."

And I might not have found a way home.

Finally, out of exhaustion, I went to sleep.

In the following days, I thought about the prayer I'd said. Maybe it had made a difference.

It took me a long time to fully understand the power of prayer. As I reminisced about the events of that day, I was certain divine intervention was the reason I remained safe.

I don't think it was a coincidence when the screeching, cackling Blue Jay got my attention. It made me move quickly through a dark part of the forest. It wasn't a coincidence when I spotted the dirt road, the cabin, and Sue. It wasn't a coincidence that I returned safely to my parent's land and was spared spending the night lost in a national forest where bears and other wild animals roamed.

I used to believe in coincidence. Now, I believe in prayer.

God provided good things for our family. We were blessed

to have our plot of land, food, clothing, shelter, education, employment, and a house in town. Out of all the things we had ever owned, the land in the mountains brought us the greatest joy. It was a place of peace, a refuge from the stress of daily city life, and a place of great beauty. It was a place where we spent time together as a family, and it was a place for making memories—even my getting lost in the woods.

As believers, we gladly gather what God has in store for us. The words from Psalm 104:28 ring true: *"When you give it to them, they gather it up; when you open your hand, they are satisfied with good things."*

When God opens His hand, we prepare to receive the good things He provides us. He knows our needs—and the best way to supply them.

The Bible shows how God provides good things for His people in many ways. One example is when the Israelites wandered through the wilderness and complained of hunger. God provided manna, a wafer-like substance covering the ground for the people to gather daily; however, it was to be consumed the same day and not stored, or it would go bad and attract maggots (Exodus 16:4; 13–16; 19–20).

When people complained about not having enough water, God enabled Moses to retrieve water from a rock (Exodus 17:6). When the five thousand gathered on a hillside to see Jesus, He performed a miracle, turning five loaves of bread and two fish into enough to feed the multitudes (Matthew 14:18).

As God did with the manna, we gladly gather what the Lord has in store for us and happily await His good gifts for us, according to our needs.

I'd found myself lost and alone on the mountain late in the day. I had a great need but also a great God who filled that need.

He answered my prayers. It wasn't just a coincidence that I found the dirt road, the cabin, and Sue. I call it a "God-incidence." The Lord knew my circumstances and enabled me to find a way home to safety with Mom and Dad.

I'm grateful I was "on receive" when God opened His hand to provide direction for me. Indeed, He is the giver of goodness.

And that's *one good thing*.

Worksheet for My Daily Morsel #14

Personal Insight:
1. Did you ever get lost or fear losing your way? If so, what happened?

_____

_____

_____

_____

_____

2. When in your life have you had a great need? What took place?

_____

_____

_____

_____

_____

3. In response to the above question, did you receive help? If so, what influence did it have on you?

_____

_____

_____

_____

_____

Reflection: My "One Good Thing"
What good thing—or things—have come your way during a difficult time in your life?

_____

_____

_____

_____

_____

Today's Serving: Provision Through Need
When we are open to receiving from God, He supplies our needs. This was the case for His people throughout the Bible. It started with Adam and Eve, extended through the Old and New Testament, through the resurrection of our Lord, and into the life of God's people thereafter. Add to that a young lady lost in the mountains. God is always with us.

A Cupful of Reality:
Have you experienced a "God incidence"—a time when you were certain God led you in the right direction?

A Taste of Spiritual Nourishment:
In today's verse from Psalms comes a key word, *gather*. When someone gives us a gift, we open our hands to receive it. Imagine you are opening a gift that God is giving you. You open your hands gladly to gather what He hands you. Picture the gift in your mind. What might it be?

The "Table of Optimism":
Hope resides at the Table of Optimism. What is your hope for today?

Prayer for Today:
Dear Father in heaven,

Often, I have been lost, either not knowing what to do or straying away from You. Thank You for watching over me and caring for me in times of need—and all other times. Guide my footing as I maneuver the straight and narrow path to salvation. In Jesus's name, amen.

Part Two: God as Master Provider

Recap of Morsels #7-#14

Congratulations! You have just completed the first fourteen Daily Morsels—Part One and Part Two of this book—showing how God provides for you. Now that you have read the stories, completed the worksheets, and your *One Good Thing* journal entries, the following questions will help you assess your progress:

1. What insights have you gained from the stories?

_____

_____

_____

_____

2. In what way(s) have you been encouraged to be optimistic?

_____

_____

_____

_____

3. How have the Bible verses about "good things" applied to you? Give an example.

_____

_____

_____

_____

4. Which stories did you favor, and why?

_____

_____

_____

_____

5. How are you doing with your daily *"One Good Thing"* journal entries? If you've kept up, good job! If you've missed a few, don't worry. You're putting "good things" to work and making progress! Fill in missed en-

tries if you can. Otherwise, go on to the next day. Do your best to be consistent and save time by keeping your entries short.

6. Using the following scale, how would you rate your optimism now? (Zero = none; ten = 100%)

    0   1   2   3   4   5   6   7   8   9   1 0

7. How has your outlook changed from when you began this book?

_____

_____

_____

_____

8. Have you noticed a difference in your ability to avert negative thoughts? If so, how? (If not, are you recording your daily journal entries? They will help you develop the habit of thinking positively).

_____

_____

_____

_____

9. Looking back at your previous Table of Optimism responses on the worksheets, which desire for hope is most important to you now?

_____

_____

_____

_____

10. If you need encouragement to finish the stories, worksheets, or journal pages, what goal can you set to complete them?

_____

_____

_____

_____

Prayerfully consider how God can help you reach your goals now—and after you finish this book.

PART THREE
GOD AS MASTER TEACHER

GOD AS MASTER TEACHER

Educators, tutors, guides, mentors—and teachers—are held to high standards. They not only teach, but they communicate, nurture, enlighten, and advise their students.

Many people guide and instruct us throughout our lives, whether in the classroom, on the home front, at church, in places of employment, or in other capacities within our communities.

James 3:1–2 reveals this higher standard to which teachers are held:

"Not many of you should become teachers, my fellow believers, because you know that we who teach will be judged more strictly."

Proverbs 22:21 indicates they must "speak the truth" and provide "truthful reports."

The distribution of the types of gifts given by the Holy Spirit (1 Cor. 12:28) includes teachers: *"And God has placed in the church first of all apostles, second, prophets, third teachers, then miracles, then gifts of healing, of helping, of guidance, and of different kinds of tongues."*

Jesus's ministry was one of instruction. He was addressed as "Rabbi," which means "teacher." Jesus taught His Father's will to His disciples, the people in the temple, and throughout cities, villages, and the countryside.

As Master Teacher of all, God also provides instruction through the Holy Spirit, as indicated in John 14:26: *"But the Advocate, the Holy Spirit, whom the Father will send in my name, will teach you all things and will remind you of everything I have said to you."*

When Jesus's life on earth was finished, the power of the Holy Spirit provided the disciples with the help they needed when Jesus was no longer physically present.

As you read each of these stories, note how God's instruction leads His people to understand the *good things* He has in store for them—and this applies to you, too!

197

Recipe

My Daily Morsel #15

Prep Time

Cook Time

Oven Temp

Serves

Topic: **Do Not Forget the Lord**

Bible Verse for Study

"When the Lord your God brings you into the land he swore to your fathers, to Abraham, Isaac, and Jacob, to give you—a land with large, flourishing cities you did not build, houses filled with all kinds of **good things** you did not provide, wells you did not dig, and vineyards and olive groves you did not plant—then when you eat and are satisfied, be careful that you do not forget the Lord, who brought you out of Egypt, out of the land of slavery." Deuteronomy 6:10-12

For Rent Only

Morning light shot through my window. I woke up, blocking the brightness by covering my eyes with my hand. There was one spot in the curtain where the sun peeked right through. Nature's wake-up call. No need for an alarm clock.

I didn't want to get up, but I had no choice. I was the adult. The children needed prodding out of bed. There was breakfast to make and sack lunches to prepare. I felt so tired of the routine. Why did I feel so weary? The day had barely begun.

I caught a glimpse of a glum face in the hallway mirror. Was that me? Something wasn't right. I pretended not to know what it was, but I knew the truth deep down. I felt as if God was far away. Maybe I should clarify this. It wasn't because of Him. It was me.

What happened? I'd always attended church, read the Bible, and practiced prayer. As I looked back, I realized the change had been gradual. Now, I was living in a spiritual void and doubting my faith. Guilt took up residence. I didn't feel like going to church. What would my children say if I didn't take them to Sunday School?

I felt estranged for a wife and mother who seemingly had it all—a loving husband, two beautiful little girls, a home, two cars, and friends and family nearby.

I had a big question for God. "If you're real," I begged, "please show me a sign."

I waited. There was no answer.

But then, unexpectedly, one morning, as I opened my dresser

drawer, I felt as if an "instant message" slipped into the inbox of my heart.

Wood from trees I created.

I dismissed the thought and shook my head—silly me. Was I dreaming? But the words came again, flashing quickly yet clearly into my mind.

Your clothing, woven from thread; thread spun finely and delicately from sheep, which I made.

Mystified, I knew this was real. This wasn't a dream. I was wide awake, out of bed, fully conscious. The words were not mine.

I went to my closet and pulled out my brown penny loafers. *For your feet, shoes from the hide of a cow.* I looked down at the loafers I'd put on. They had long been a comfort for my feet, providing warmth and protection. I paused in disbelief but knew the words that came to my heart were real. A surge of joy exploded inside me. My prayer was being answered.

I went to the kitchen. Fixed coffee. Water from the tap...God's. Coffee beans, not just from the supermarket, are grown in the soil of God's earth. I poured milk into my coffee. The milk—the cow—back to God again.

Dropping bread into the toaster, I analyzed its ingredients: grain turned to flour, yeast, salt, and water. God provided it. And don't forget butter—back to the cow.

I went into my backyard and pulled two fresh navel oranges from the tree. I'd nurtured it and watered and fertilized it as needed. But somehow, it wasn't mine. God owned it. He'd created it. And it was His water and nutrients in the soil that fed it.

I marveled at the flagstone rock patio beneath my feet and the sturdy brick that formed the walls of our home. The house wasn't mine, either, despite mortgage payments. Someday, I would leave the earth. I was merely renting space for a while—from God.

Rain clouds gathered and watered my yard—God's rain. I drove to work, adding gas to my car—fuel—another creation of His.

At work, I grumbled about mounting paperwork piled onto my desk. I wasn't happy with my job and lived for weekends. God showed me otherwise. My job provided money to make the house payments, maintain the car, and put food on the table.

Friday arrived, and I awaited a boat trip with relatives to Lake Mead. We sailed to a quiet cove; a brilliant fire-orange sunset surrounded us.

No flashlights needed. A full moon provided light. I lay in the sand in my sleeping bag and looked up, amazed at God's artistry in star constellations. Then, the sounds of waves touching the shore lulled me to sleep.

At daybreak, God woke me up. His sun was in my eyes. I got up—gladly. I, too, was His creation. He'd wrapped me in His righteousness and presented me with a gift: a new start—a new day—in Him.

On the sandy beach that morning, I recommitted my relationship with God. He'd answered my prayers in more ways than one. He'd brought renewal to my heart and refreshment to my soul. He'd given me many good things I could never have supplied myself.

The verse from Deuteronomy 6:12 became an important reminder: "...*be careful not to forget the* LORD..."

It is never too late to reconnect with God. He is ready and waiting with open arms to provide for all we need.

God provided for His people long ago, just as He provides for us today. He promised to give Canaan, the Promised Land, to Abraham, Isaac, and Jacob, and their descendents. Deuteronomy 6:10–12 spells out some of the things God provided: large flourishing cities, houses filled with "good things," wells, vineyards, olive groves, and nourishment for the people, so they could eat and be satisfied.

At an earlier time, as Moses, Aaron, and the Israelites traveled through the harsh land, the people became angry when there wasn't enough water. The Lord instructed Moses to take Aaron's staff in his hand and to speak to the rock so it would bring forth water. Instead of speaking to the rock as God had instructed, Moses struck the rock twice with Aaron's staff and talked to the people as though he had provided the miracle instead of God. God was displeased because Moses had disobeyed.

Moses did this out of anger kindled by the people's incessant complaining and lack of faith. Still, he disobeyed God's command, and he paid dearly for his disobedience. In addition, Moses's actions dishonored God in the presence of the Israelites (Numbers 20:1–12).

The resulting punishment for Moses and the Israelites originated from a culmination of separate incidents: Moses's disobedience and ignoring God's instruction when retrieving water from the rock, the Israelites's continued grumbling and disbelief, and their rebellion and contempt for God when they heard the report of the leaders' journey of espionage into enemy territory (the Promised Land of Canaan).

As a result of their mistrust and disobedience, God would not allow Moses and the people of his generation to enter the Promised Land.

Instead, Joshua, who had lived with the Israelites through years of wandering, succeeded Moses as the leader of the people. Then, Joshua (along with his companion, Caleb) led the younger generation into the land of plenty, known at the time as the land of Canaan.

The land of Canaan had long been pledged to God's people— if they obeyed Him. Due to the sins of Moses and his people, Joshua, Caleb, and the new generation of Israelites benefitted from God's promise to settle in the "land of milk and honey."

Canaan was a rich and fertile land, starkly contrasting the harsh environment the people had been accustomed to. Imagine their joy and excitement as they entered this land of plenty.

Indeed, it must have felt like a dream for these new residents of Canaan. Unlike the desert, this land provided the needed water and fertile soil to grow crops. No longer nomads, now they had stability. They settled down with their families and lived in prosperity. God was good.

However, even though they settled comfortably into their new homes, they were given a reminder in Deuteronomy 6:12: *"...be careful that you do not forget the LORD, who brought you out of Egypt, out of the land of slavery."*

Life was now good, but God had a concern. When the people had all they needed, they might get "too comfortable," leading to complacency. It was precisely what the Lord wanted His people to avoid. He wanted His people to remain faithful and obedient and remember He was the reason for their prosperity, bringing them from a life of bondage into freedom. The Lord desired that His people would not only worship Him in difficult times but also in good times.

Imagine what it must have been like for the people to go from living in scarcity to living in plenty. Perhaps it was overwhelming; would their attitudes have become grandiose? The challenge now would be for God's people to remain humble and not forget about Him, for He brought them out of bondage and provided them with good things.

I was most fortunate when I realized all God had provided me. He revealed His presence when I searched for Him. I had taken many things for granted: the clothing I wore, the food I ate, and the roof over my head. The truth was that all I needed came about because of Him.

God provided for His people long ago, and He provides for us today.

Dawn is the first appearance of the Lord's creation in our

waking hours. His presence is always with us. Every second. Every minute. Every hour of the day—even when we think He has forgotten us. His path leads to righteousness, love, peace, and comfort. And His joy—as bright as the dawn—will fill our hearts.

That morning, many years ago, as I lay on the sandy beach of Lake Mead, I awoke to the brightness of God's sun in my eyes. And I smiled, for His Son was once again the focus of my heart.

And that's *one good thing*.

Worksheet for My Daily Morsel #15

Personal Insight:
Have you ever forgotten about God? If so, what were your thoughts? How did these feelings compare to the times you have acknowledged Him?

_____

_____

Reflection: My "One Good Thing"
What good thing (or things) has God provided for you today?

_____

_____

What items in your home or environment remind you of God's presence in your life?

_____

_____

Is there a time when you were blessed with more than you'd ever had in monetary value, possessions, or a time when you prospered greatly in some other way? If so, describe:

_____

_____

_____

If you have ever received anything in abundance, were you able to remain humble, focusing on God as the giver of good things?

_____

_____

Today's Serving: God's Instruction Through Attentiveness
The Lord God provided instructions for Moses to give to the people regarding His decrees and commands so they might live abundantly. This meant that they would have to listen, be attentive, and not forget about Him.

The same holds true in today's story, revealing what God supplied in one person's life and realizing these provisions existed because of Him. God provided for His people in Moses' time and continues to supply for His people's needs today.

A Cupful of Reality:
Just as a teacher tells students to pay attention, God also expects us to pay attention to Him. What life experience has taught you the importance of paying attention?

_____

_____

How would you best describe your ability to be attentive to God's Word?

_____

_____

A Taste of Spiritual Nourishment:

From our verse in Deuteronomy comes a key word, *vineyards*. If you've ever had the opportunity to visit a vineyard or grow grapes, you understand the time and attention it requires.

The Bible reminds us that Jesus is the vine, and we are the branches. When well tended, the vineyard produces good fruit. And when we remain in Him, we "produce good fruit."

No nutrition is better than God's crops—or His spiritual food!

The "Table of Optimism":
Hope resides at the Table of Optimism. What is your hope for today?

_____

_____

Prayer for Today:
Dear Father in heaven,

I pray my faith will shine for You, Lord, as bright as the morning sun. Thank You for loving me and never forgetting me, even though sometimes I don't think about You. I am grateful for all I have been given and praise Your Holy Name. In Jesus's name, amen.

Recipe

My Daily Morsel #16

Prep Time _____   Cook Time _____

Oven Temp _____   Serves _____

Topic: **Staying Close to God**

_____

_____

_____

_____

_____

Bible Verse for Study

"No sooner had Gideon died than the Israelites prostituted themselves to the Baals. They set up Baal-Berith as their god and did not remember the LORD their God, who had rescued them from the hands of all their enemies on every side. They also failed to show loyalty to the family of Jerub-Baal (that is, Gideon) despite all the **good things** he had done for them."

Judges 8:33–35

An Honest Mistake

The phone rang. I didn't want to pick it up, figuring it was probably another sales call. But I took it anyway.

"Hi. It's your mum." My mother-in-law's voice sounded unusually deliberate. Something didn't sound right, but I dismissed the thought.

"Oh, hi, Mom, how are-"

"I'm *sure* it was just an honest mistake," she interrupted. "Am I right?" Like barbed wire, her words stuck sharply to make a point.

"A mistake?" I repeated, scratching my head. "What mistake?"

"Why didn't you come over yesterday?" Mom accented the word 'yesterday' as if it had a downward turn, ready to fall from the sentence.

I was perplexed. "I thought Rich talked to you."

At that moment, the glimmer of a memory emerged. Mom had phoned last week, and I'd forgotten to tell my husband she'd called.

My mother-in-law was a woman of many words. She was rarely quiet, but now there was silence on the other end of the line. The communication gap was uncomfortable. I fidgeted, twirling the phone cord around my wrist as if this would fill the void. I wanted to say something but fumbled for the right words.

Finally, Mom broke the silence.

"Yesterday was Dad's birthday."

The missile of words had been launched.

Another pause. This time it was my own.

My heart dived. "Oh, no, Mom, I'm so sorry...how could we forget?" I clasped a hand over my forehead—Dad was always excited about his birthday. "It makes me feel special," he always told us.

The mistake! Somewhere between my husband working ten-hour days, attending college full-time at night, and I, as the primary caretaker of our two little girls, my father-in-law's birthday had slipped by us. If I hadn't forgotten to tell my husband about Mom's phone call the previous week, he would have been reminded of Dad's birthday. He depended on me to keep us on track, and I'd erred.

My mind raced in review mode. What had we done the previous day? I scanned my memory. We came home after church and had lunch, as usual. I put our little one down for a nap, helped our older daughter chase down the parakeet that escaped from its cage, and gathered piles of laundry to load into the washer.

I vaguely remember my husband's voice trailing in through the back room. It was one solitary place where he could focus on schoolwork.

"No, not today, Mom," he said. I heard a click as he put the phone down and explained to me, "Mom wanted to know when we were coming over. I told her not today."

"Okay," I responded. It didn't occur to me anything was out of the ordinary. Mom often expected us to come over, even if it was not in our plans.

The disappointment in Mom's voice brought me back to reality, to the crux of the moment. If she was this upset, I couldn't imagine how Dad must be feeling. We'd not only forgotten his birthday; we'd forgotten *him*.

We made the hour-long drive over the one-lane patched asphalt road the following weekend, past the many rows of flower gardens beautifying the landscape. We pulled into the worn neighborhood, parking in the gravel drive of Mom and Dad's meager home.

Mom was in the kitchen, preparing Dad's favorite meal, a pot roast. The girls were excited, unwrapping small toys Mom bought at the grocery store.

We greeted my father-in-law, who occupied the dingy blue recliner, his pride and joy of the old-fashioned living room furniture. A thin man with wispy sand-gray hair, his bouncing, bird-like voice matched his stature. His wisecracks extended beyond teasing. It was as if his vocabulary was laced with miniature daggers right at my husband and me. Despite our numerous attempts to apologize for missing his birthday, it seemed nothing we could say or do would suffice. The damage was done.

Little did we know the fragile nature of human life would change our lives only months later. We got the phone call in the middle of the night. Dad had suffered a massive stroke. Unfortunately, he was unable to respond and lapsed into a coma. We took turns sitting at his bedside for hours. We left the room. We were only away for twenty minutes, but when we returned, he was gone.

The last birthday Dad knew was the forgotten one we made up to him a week later. How I regretted our mistake. I wished we could have told him again, "We love you, Dad, and we're sorry we missed your birthday."

My mother-in-law was right. We'd made an "honest mistake." We felt badly, because we cared about Richard's father. It was an innocent forgetfulness, but it carried a crushing blow.

Looking back, I wonder how we could have forgotten such an important event. How had we fallen short and been so inattentive? There was no way we could make up for it now.

The lesson from the Book of Deuteronomy in the previous Morsel reminded us not to forget the Lord. In today's verse, Judges 8:33–35, the Israelites turned "forgetting" into "completely forgotten." It was as if they had erased God from their hearts and minds. Their actions were not a mistake, as they'd made a conscious decision to worship idols.

Even with Gideon's persuasion to obey God's laws, they turned to idolatry and forgot about the Lord.

In any society, whether in Bible times or the present day, some people break the law. Depending on the degree or severity of the injustice, some are fined or charged for their wrongdoing. Others cross a more serious line, committing the most detestable of sins, and are imprisoned.

The Israelites crossed a serious line over time. Their forgetting turned into disobedience, resulting in them turning away from God. They chose a path that led to darkness and destruction.

The dark-hearted nature displayed by some people is the reason laws exist. It is also why judges and rulers were chosen in those times. God picked Gideon to be one of the rulers over the Israelites, but the Lord was unhappy the Israelites had forgotten about Him.

As Judges 8:34 tells us they *"did not remember the LORD their God, who had rescued them from the hands of their enemies on every side."*

The Bible warns against forgetting about God. Did the wrongdoing of the Israelites begin as a simple, innocent mistake, such as forgetting? To forget now and then is one thing, but if left unchecked, it could become a big problem.

We don't know the onset of the Israelites' forgetting about the Lord, but it probably started small and progressed into something much bigger. They took forgetting to a whole new level when they looked for—and worshipped—false gods.

There were profound implications for evil behavior. In the sixth chapter of Judges, scripture reveals the Lord handed the Israelites over to the oppression of the Midianites for seven years.

The Bible warns us not to forget the Lord. Proverbs 2:17 reminds us of God's covenant with Abraham and his descendants. Psalm 103:2 reminds us of the benefits of the Lord. Deuteronomy 8:11 says, *"Be careful that you do not forget the Lord your God, failing to observe his commands, his laws and his decrees that I am giving you this day."* Deuteronomy 6:10–12 reminds us of the Lord's provision, referenced in our previous daily morsel.

If only the Israelites had heeded God's warnings! Instead, they were swayed by false teachings and refused to hear the truth. They turned their backs on the One who could have rescued them from peril.

God rescues those who slip away or forget about Him if they are willing to return to Him. From Jeremiah 3:21:

"A cry is heard on the barren heights, the weeping and pleading of the people of Israel, because they have perverted their ways and have forgotten the Lord their God."

A simple act of forgetting, like a forgotten birthday, causes hurt feelings. On a grand scale, forgetting due to willingly distancing yourself from God causes calamity, as it did when the Israelites rebelled against God.

Gideon's own father was not immune, for he was a worshiper of idols. The Lord instructed Gideon to destroy the altar his father had erected for Baal and build an altar to God. The people were enraged when they suspected Gideon had torn down their altar. They pursued him, but the Lord protected Gideon. The Lord instructed him to reduce his army to three hundred men, and, in a planned attack, they defeated the large army of Midianites.

My husband and I erred in forgetting his father's birthday. It was an unfortunate mistake but not a purposeful one. We were sorry for our mistake, asked for forgiveness, and became more attentive to the needs of my mother and father-in-law.

God was with us in difficult times, just as He was for Gideon. When life is good, there might be times when we forget about God, but He never forgets about us.

And that's *one good thing.*

Worksheet for My Daily Morsel #16

Personal Insight:

What do you think? Is it possible for people who have good intentions to turn their back on God? Your opinion: what might have caused the Israelites' "forgetting" to turn into a state of "completely forgotten?"

Reflection: My One Good Thing

Have you (or someone close to you) ever forgotten something of vital importance? If so, what happened? Was there resolve or forgiveness?

What *one good thing* came out of this experience?

Today's Serving: Instruction Through Remembrance and Kindness

The Israelites failed to remember the Lord their God and set up and worshiped idols. They also failed to show kindness to Gideon for all he had done for them. In today's story, a husband and wife forget about a father's birthday. Their forgetfulness was not a sin, but their failure to remember caused hurt feelings. In all times and eras, God's people have needed reminders to stay on track.

A Cupful of Reality:

Our feelings get hurt if someone forgets about us. God's immense love and compassion for us are hard to describe and sometimes hard to fully comprehend. However, as we are made in His image, it is plausible that the Lord would be affected when His people forget about Him.

A Taste of Spiritual Nourishment:

From today's verse in Judges comes a key word, *kindness*. It is one of the fruits of the spirit mentioned in Galatians 5:22–23. What kind words have had the most impact on your life?

_____

_____

_____

_____

The "Table of Optimism":

Hope resides at the Table of Optimism. What is your hope for today?

_____

_____

_____

_____

Prayer for Today:
Dear Lord,

I try my best, but sometimes I'm forgetful. Clarify my thoughts when worldly concerns intrude so I may keep You at the forefront of all I do. Increase my awareness of the needs of others and open my heart to greater compassion. Keep me humble when I make mistakes, bring peace to my heart when I err, and thank You for always thinking of me. In Jesus's name, amen.

Recipe

My Daily Morsel #17

Prep Time

Cook Time

Oven Temp

Serves

Topic: **Overstepping Boundaries**

Bible Verse for Study

"Therefore, do not give your daughters in marriage to their sons or take their daughters for your sons. Do not seek a treaty of friendship with them at any time, that you may be strong and eat the **good things** of the land and leave it to your children as an everlasting inheritance."

Ezra 9:12

A Dirt Road to Destruction and Salvation

The summer I was seventeen, a dirt road led to my downfall—and my salvation. It started innocently one June morning.

RaeAnne skipped out the door of her parent's cabin, and we headed down Pine Glen Road. She was glad to be away from her parents. Ditto for me. I was ecstatic when her parents purchased a mountain property just a mile from ours. Spending summer weekends with my best friend would be the nicest summer ever.

After walking about three miles down the road, we started to sweat and sought shade beneath a large pine tree.

Being in the mountains was a dream come true, and going for a walk gave us the opportunity for a heart-to-heart conversation. We talked about the things we wanted—but didn't have—like boyfriends. The problem was that RaeAnne wasn't allowed to date yet. She was only fifteen, even though she looked—and acted older. And as for me, I was shy and could hardly talk to guys. So, it was no wonder I'd never been asked out on a date, even though I was seventeen.

We felt peace sitting in the quietness of the forest around us; the only sounds were the occasional chirp of a bird or the whistling of the breeze through the pines. The tranquil moment was interrupted by the roar of two motorcyclists coming around the bend. As they approached, one engine sputtered. The riders—two guys—slowed down, then stopped across the road.

215

RaeAnne and I glanced at each other and giggled. The guys were about our age, maybe a little older. The tall one removed his helmet and flicked back a long, blond ponytail. I didn't care for guys with long hair, but this one had my attention. He wore a white tank, accentuating a deep tan and muscular chest and arms, and sported slim blue jeans and black motorcycle boots.

RaeAnne had her eyes on the younger guy with brown, wavy hair leaning over the motorcycle. The back pockets of his tan corduroy pants were torn. He wore a T-shirt with a big hole in the back and white tennis shoes caked with dirt.

Then the blonde guy saw us. I felt heat rise to my face as he strolled over, planting his tall form in front of us.

"Hey, girls." His voice was raspy and deep. "I'm Chris."

I clumsily shook his hand, noticing warm but rough skin.

"You girls new around here?"

I squeaked out a nervous "Yes." Chris was composed and made me feel at ease.

We talked about our families' properties; he pointed out his parents' home, four houses away.

Chris smiled a crooked grin, his green eyes momentarily locking with mine. My heart raced. I had to look away.

RaeAnne brushed back her red curls, smiling at the dark-eyed young guy.

"This is Jim, the *little* brother," Chris laughed, swatting at his brother's hat.

Jim swatted back, missing. He shyly acknowledged RaeAnne, then turned away to check on the bike. "Engine's cool," he called back.

"Good," Chris replied, turning to me with a wink. "See you girls around."

Before RaeAnne or I could respond, the guys had revved the engines and were speeding down the road. This was one time we didn't mind being left in the dust.

The following weekend, we hoped and prayed we'd run into the guys—and we did. From there, we met up with them on Saturdays. Over the next few weeks, we graduated to more extended conversations. However, we had to be careful because my parents would never accept a long-haired boy, and RaeAnne wasn't old enough to date.

Chris suggested we meet in the barn. He pointed to the faded red structure behind a stand of pines just a few lots away from their house. It had belonged to their grandfather but hadn't been used for a few years.

"What do you think?" Chris said with a crooked smile I couldn't resist.

I grappled for words. *Meet alone in a barn with two guys?* Would it be any worse meeting inside the barn than outside? *It's just one little doorway.*

RaeAnne raised her eyebrows in anticipation. I took in a deep breath.

"I guess it'll be okay," I replied.

Everyone looked happy. The plan was set.

We followed the guys to the barn. So far, they'd been very friendly each time we'd met. Chris unlatched the weathered door. The odor of old hay and dust permeated the air. A rusted tractor covered in cobwebs sat at the far corner. Splintered shelves along one wall housed dusty equipment. Small dingy windows, high up, provided light.

Chris lined up disintegrating bales of hay for us to sit on. My hands were sweating, and RaeAnne bit at her fingernails, but Chris's easy manner lightened the tension. Soon, we were talking, laughing, and having fun.

Two hours passed quickly. Our parents would expect us to be home soon. Filled with exhilaration, we felt like we were walking on clouds as we hiked back to RaeAnne's.

But that night, I didn't sleep. Guilt intruded as my father's routine lecture ran through my mind. "Make sure you're spending time with the right people," he'd say. I had a feeling Chris wouldn't fit that description according to my father's standards.

———

The following Saturday, Chris was quieter than usual. When the conversation came to a lull, he slipped his arm around my shoulder. Maybe it was wrong, but I gave in to the feeling and leaned close.

I glanced at RaeAnne. She smiled as Jim took her hand and scooted next to her.

A rumbling noise outside interrupted the tender moments. RaeAnne bolted upright.

"It's my father's truck," she said. "We gotta' go."

Before we reached the door, Chris wrapped his warm, muscular arms around me. I nervously reciprocated, sliding my arms around his broad shoulders. He gave me a gentle peck on the cheek—my first kiss. I didn't want the moment to end, but we had to go.

Chris smiled. "By the way," he said, "we're having a party next Saturday night. You in?"

I hesitated. He must have read my thoughts.

"Don't worry," he added. "My parents will be there."

RaeAnne shot me the "It's okay with me" glance.

"Okay, sure," I replied. "Sounds like fun."

"Great. Come over at dark. We'll have a campfire, food, drinks, music, the works."

On the way home, all we could talk about was the party. But there was one problem: we'd have to sneak out without our parents' knowledge.

———

We stewed about what to do, but luck turned our way. Rae-Anne's parents would take her younger brother to a scouting convention in Denver. It was a long drive, so they'd be there overnight.

RaeAnne begged to have me come for a sleepover at her house that night. Her parents—and mine—agreed if we followed their rules: "Don't leave the cabin, call us by ten o'clock at night, and don't invite others."

Saturday couldn't arrive soon enough. My father dropped me off at RaeAnne's at three o'clock in the afternoon. Her parents were loading the station wagon.

After a final lecture about the rules, we waved as RaeAnne's parents and brother pulled out of the driveway. We were free! We squealed like kids in a candy store.

We raced to the bathroom and spent two hours on our make-up and hair. After pizza for dinner, we changed into our clothes for the party. RaeAnne picked out her favorite jeans with fringed pockets, and I slipped on my best-fitting bell bottoms with embroidered flowers. We'd shopped for shirts, beaded necklaces, hoop earrings, and frosted lipstick.

We inspected our appearance in the mirror. We thought we looked cool.

The orange glow in the sky dimmed as RaeAnne locked the cabin. It got dark quickly as we walked down Pine Glen. There were no streetlights, only a bit of light from cabin porches and the light of a pale moon.

A campfire glowed in the distance toward Chris and Jim's place. It would be so romantic. We couldn't wait!

Usually, there was little traffic on this road, but tonight was different. The driveway was filled with cars, and vehicles lined the street as we approached the house. We had no idea there would be this many people at the party. Perhaps some of them were friends of Chris and Jim's parents.

RaeAnne and I zigzagged through the parked cars and onto the path toward the barn. Just beyond, there was a clearing where they'd started a campfire. People crammed around the fire pit. Rock music blared as people smoked, drank, and danced.

We didn't see Chris or Jim anywhere, so we decided to walk toward the house. Just as we passed by the barn, we saw the guys coming around the side of the building. They were laughing, joking, and drinking.

We called out to them as Chris, Jim, and a few of their friends stepped beneath the light pole in front of the barn. Now we could see their faces.

Chris came up to me. "What have we here?" he said with a crooked grin, tilting his head to take a drink from his beer bottle. "You look good, baby," he said, winking, then sucked in a puff of the cigarette.

Jim smiled slightly at RaeAnne between chugs of beer.

Chris told us there was food in the house. He smelled like alcohol and cigarettes. "Catch up with you girls later, okay?"

As the others walked away, Chris whispered, "Meet us at the barn at 10:00 p.m."

I nodded as he slipped away to catch up with his brother and friends.

As RaeAnne and I walked toward the house, we talked about the guys' behavior. We chalked it up to their drinking and hanging out with their friends. But at least Chris had invited us to see them later in the barn. He'd told other guests the barn was off-limits, a "parent rule," he'd said. But he was making an exception for us.

Once at the house, we waded our way through the crowd in the living room. The thick smoke caused both of us to gag, and the loud music hurt our ears. We grabbed leftover servings of food, then helped ourselves to the many choices of alcoholic beverages.

There was no place to sit in the living room, so we sat in the kitchen to sip our drinks. We poured a second round, then waded back through the crowd. A guy, about 30ish, emerged from a bedroom with a young girl. My rum was taking effect, but I still had my senses. *What kind of party is this, and where are Chris's parents?*

"Let's get out of here, RaeAnne," I said, grabbing her hand. We headed out the door. She tripped on a step but managed to salvage her drink.

Every inch of space was taken around the campfire, but RaeAnne and I found vacant seats at a picnic table. Two girls, one with a low-cut blouse and the other wearing short shorts, invited us to sit. They handed us beers. We sipped. They chugged.

We couldn't help but overhear their drunken conversation.

"*Tall boy* is asking for you, Monica," the girl in short shorts said, jutting out her chest.

"Don't I know it," Monica laughed, wiggling her hips.

"What about Jimmy?" another said.

"I have things to teach him, too," she smirked.

"Hey, *Moni*," someone yelled. "You know who is waiting for you."

"Ah, yes," she said, making a fish-shaped smooch with her bright red lips, then strutted away.

Probably heading to a room at the house.

RaeAnne reached for another beer, but I snatched it from her hand. "No more for you. We have to call your parents, remember? Then, we'll see the guys."

"*Which* guys?" the girl in short shorts asked.

"Chris and Jim," I replied.

"*Tall* Chris?" she asked.

I nodded.

"Ha," she smirked. "Don't you know he's a player, honey?"

I ignored her comment. *She couldn't be talking about my Chris. Besides, she's drunk.*

We decided to wait until we returned to the cabin to call

RaeAnne's parents. The only available phone was in the kitchen at Chris and Jim's house. That wasn't going to work. It was too noisy, with partying in the background.

At nine-thirty, we thought it wouldn't hurt to go to the barn a few minutes early. As we approached, the light on the pole outside had gone out, but a light flickered beneath the door.

I grasped the handle on the barn door and flung it open. We gasped as we came face to face with Chris and Monica sitting on dirty floorboards beside the tractor; Chris had a needle hanging out of his arm. We saw Jim hiding behind hay bales with a girl in a far corner.

I felt frozen with disbelief; RaeAnne's mouth hung open. Chris yelled, "Get out!" as it rang through the air. RaeAnne and I bolted out the door, stumbling as we stepped onto the path outside.

"What kind of guy gives their heart...then cheats," RaeAnne cried as we walked as quickly as possible in the darkness.

"I don't know," I sniffed, trying to control a sob as we reached the driveway crammed with vehicles and the silhouette of teens sitting in the back seat of a car.

It didn't make sense. How could they have lied to us? They'd seemed so kind and caring—we'd fallen in love with them.

Heartsick, dumped, and discouraged, we turned onto Pine Glen Road. A sliver of moonlight provided barely enough light to see where we were going. I hadn't thought about checking the time, either. We needed to get back to the cabin to call RaeAnne's parents.

Breaking the quietness like shattered glass, a police car suddenly sped by, its red and blue lights flashing in the darkness. Dust permeated our nostrils. We watched as it raced down the road.

"Looks like it pulled into Chris and Jim's place," I said. "Now, aren't you glad we left when we did, RaeAnne?"

"Yeah. Guess we better get moving before someone stops us,"

RaeAnne replied.

We turned and stepped up our pace to get away from the commotion down the road.

"I'm not surprised. I bet they're in big trouble. Someone must have called the cops," I said. "I'm glad we're not in troub..."

I didn't finish my sentence. Headlights from a vehicle behind us shined brightly as if purposely targeting us. RaeAnne and I scooted farther over to the shoulder of the road, but the vehicle lights followed us. It wasn't passing by.

"Heaven help us," I cried. The vehicle behind us slowed, then stopped.

"What the heck are they doing?"

"I don't know, RaeAnne. I can't see. The headlights are blinding."

Suddenly the headlights went off. RaeAnne and I spun around to look, but it was too dark to see much—until the driver turned on the interior light.

Grayish-white crewcut. Dark-rimmed glasses.

"Oh, no. It's my father, RaeAnne!"

The headlights flashed twice. I heard my father's voice. "I know it's you," he yelled. "Get in the truck—now!"

Paralyzed with fear, we approached my father's truck and reluctantly slid into the back seat. I didn't know what to say to my father. His usually sallow Scandinavian complexion had turned a shade of burgundy in the pale light. His piercing eyes darted in our direction as he started the ignition. He didn't say a word. His icy stare said it all.

—

Slumping onto the couch in RaeAnne's living room, our heads lowered, we passed the tissue box back and forth. We heard my father talking on the phone in the kitchen, telling RaeAnne's parents what we'd done.

We hadn't watched the time and didn't call by ten o'clock. We discovered my father had tried phoning the cabin numerous times with no answer. He drove to the house and was concerned when no one answered the door. He checked with a neighbor who told him she'd seen us leave the cabin a few hours earlier.

Irate, my father went looking for us and drove down Pine Glen Road, stopping where the commotion had taken place with the police cars and traffic. Looking for us but not finding us there, he drove back toward RaeAnne's cabin when he spotted us walking down the road.

What trouble I'd caused for us!

Because RaeAnne's parents were away for the night, the neighbor came over to stay with her. After my father finished his phone call to RaeAnne's parents, he waited for me in the Foyer. He was so mad he wouldn't look at me. RaeAnne glanced at me wistfully as I stepped out the door with my belongings.

"I'm so sorry," I whispered.

She looked at me tearfully. There wasn't much else to say.

—

My father was quiet on the drive home. He pulled into the dirt driveway, turned off the ignition, got out, shut the door with a bang, and stomped up the cabin steps. He didn't look back to see if I was coming. I didn't know what kind of punishment to expect, but so far, his silence was punishment enough.

I walked to the back of the cabin and dropped onto the hammock between the trees. It swung out of control, just like my emotions. As the futile sway slowed to a gentle rocking, I shivered as the temperature dropped and curled up into a ball in the hammock to stay warm.

My mother called from the porch. *No.* I didn't want to go inside to deal with my father's wrath. We hadn't been getting along. I'd overstepped my boundaries lately—and today was no exception.

It was another notch added to an already strained relationship.

I looked up at bright rays of moonlight sprinkled through the treetops. How could the world look so beautiful when I felt so tragic? I closed my eyes, trying to drift off to sleep, but jolted awake when someone called my name. It was my father. He stepped up to the hammock, his white hair taking on a silver appearance in the moonlight.

He steadied my slightly swaying hammock and sat next to me.

I was relieved he wanted to talk. I couldn't take any more of the silent treatment. In the beauty of the star-lit night, I swallowed my pride. I confessed everything. I was breaking my promise to RaeAnne that we wouldn't tell, but I couldn't lie to my father anymore. I cried. I told him I was sorry. He accepted my apology, but his eyes drooped with sadness.

At bedtime, I kneeled at my bed, poured out my heart to God, and asked for forgiveness.

Unfortunately, the crooked smile I adored reflected Chris's true character. He and Monica were arrested on drug charges, and Jim and other underage teens were reported and turned over to their parents.

Why had I been so infatuated with Chris? He was a liar—and a drug addict.

That summer, I'd overstepped my boundaries. A dirt road led to my destruction, but it also led to my salvation. My behavior broke my father's heart, but he forgave me, and my mother and I eventually mended our relationship.

Thanks be to my heavenly Father, who kept RaeAnne and me safe from danger and forgave our sins.

Life in Bible times differed from what we know today, but the human condition hasn't changed. In Ezra's time, people made the same kinds of mistakes in relationships as people make today. The Bible mentions they were warned they were entering a land filled with corruption.

Worst of all, the spiritual leaders—role models for the people—committed some of the greatest sins. Men took the liberty of marrying women not from their land or culture. This was not only a cultural taboo, for God had commanded the people not to engage with the wrong kind of men or women.

Ezra was upset about what the spiritual leaders had done, prayed about their behavior, and asked for forgiveness. God responded. Those who had sinned would be required to break off the unhealthy relationships, for these individuals would not make good husbands or wives.

Ezra 9:12 describes God's warning: fathers were not permitted to give their daughters in marriage to the wrong kind of men. Likewise, they were not to take the wrong type of girls for their sons. To do so would keep them from receiving the inheritance their children and future generations would receive.

Imagine their struggle in breaking off these relationships. Even if they hadn't chosen the "right kind of people," as my father would say, they would likely have had mixed emotions about leaving someone they loved. Choosing the wrong mate was a difficult lesson.

RaeAnne and I struggled emotionally with the breaking of our relationships with Chris and Jim. They'd led us on and were dishonest. Yet, we had fond memories of the fun time we'd spent with them—before things went downhill at the party. Fortunately, we found out their true character before it was too late.

The following summer, there was no roar of motorcycles, and Pine Glen Road was quiet. A rumor circulated about a local drug bust and arrests. We never knew what became of Chris and Jim. Later, we heard the family had moved away.

The summer I was seventeen, I learned a hard lesson. I'd

crossed the line and overstepped my boundaries. Fortunately, I had a father who loved and forgave me—and a heavenly Father who loved me enough to save me through the grace of His Son, Jesus Christ.

Thanks be to God who comes to our aid and teaches us His way, just as He did for Ezra's people—and as He did for RaeAnne and me.

And that's *one good thing*.

Worksheet for My Daily Morsel #17

Personal Insight:
Have you ever connected with the wrong kind of people and overstepped your boundaries? If so, what happened?

_____

_____

_____

_____

Reflection: My "One Good Thing":
About the question above, what "one good thing" came from your experience?

_____

_____

_____

Looking back on the situation, what advice might you have given your younger self to avoid making a wrong decision?

_____

_____

_____

Today's Serving: Goodness Through Obedience
In today's story, two girls learn an important lesson about resisting temptation, as did the people of Ezra. Without proper instruction, God's people can easily slip into unfavorable circumstances. Fortunately, by heeding His Word—and through forgiveness—we can find our way out of wrongful thinking and focus on the good things God desires for us.

A Cupful of Reality:
Describe an experience of God's forgiveness for a situation that invited temptation. What happened?

_____

_____

_____

_____

A Taste of Spiritual Nourishment:
From today's verse in Ezra comes a key word, *friendship*. Think of a special friend. What quality do you admire most about them?

_____

_____

_____

_____

What quality do you think they most admire about you?
It's not easy to find good friends, but a verse from Proverbs 18:24 reminds us of the friendship of Jesus: *"One who has unreliable friends soon comes to ruin, but there is a friend who sticks closer than a brother."*

The "Table of Optimism":
Hope resides at the Table of Optimism. What is your hope for today?

_____

_____

_____

Prayer for Today:
Dear Lord God,

You know me well and see every wrong path I take. When I stumble and fall, You pick me up. When I call out to You in distress, You hear my cry. When I go astray, You wait for me to return to You. Please help me make the right decisions about the people I choose to be in my life. Thank You for being my friend and loving me unconditionally. In Jesus's name, amen.

Recipe

My Daily Morsel #18

Prep Time _____

Cook Time _____

Oven Temp _____

Serves _____

Topic: **The Captivity of Sin**

_____

_____

_____

_____

_____

Bible Verse for Study

"But see, we are slaves today, slaves in the land you gave our ancestors so they could eat its fruit and the other **good things** it produces. Because of our sins, its abundant harvest goes to the kings you have placed over us. They rule over our bodies and our cattle as they please. We are in great distress."

Nehemiah 9:36–37

LOST IN FREEDOM

It was a perfectly beautiful afternoon, the sun finally making an entrance after days of clouds and rain. In Jean's little corner of the world, she'd struggled to gain greater personal freedom. She was determined today would be a day of change. She could do as she pleased with no appointments or immediate responsibilities looming with a day off work.

Jean pulled her Chevy Impala into the gravel parking lot facing the entrance to the model homes. Since her daughter and family would soon be moving back to town, Jean was anxious to get a head-start on house-hunting with them and looked forward to helping them get a new start. But she wanted to have a new beginning herself. After being a wife and mother all these years, as an empty nester, it was time to create a new life for herself.

Strolling past flowering plants to the real estate office entrance, she marveled at seeing a purple butterfly. Intrigued by the tiny creature, she watched it glide effortlessly from one bush to the next, its colorful, paper-thin wings shining in the sun. She envied the butterfly. If only she could float through life with such abandon. But maybe she could start to live that way?

Jean exchanged greetings with the real estate agent and walked through the model home's foyer. *It's so beautiful—why can't my life be like this?*

As if in a daydream, emotions swirled through Jean's mind. As she took in the aroma of the fresh new scent of furnishings, she noticed that crisp linen curtains lined windows from floor to ceiling, providing a view of a backyard garden oasis. Jean wondered if she lived in such a beautiful environment, would her life be better?

As she pushed back her graying bangs, she thought of the struggles her family experienced while she was growing up. Her family had been poor, and her father was sometimes unemployed. Yet, despite all they lacked, her mother would say, *"I don't know what I'd do without my faith."* These were words that had seemed important—*then*.

Jean skirted across the marbleized flooring's sleek grout lines, mesmerized by the tile's smooth appearance. Her mind drifted to the past. A loving wife, it was easy for her to be submissive. Her husband was intelligent and took pride in making decisions for his family. She was a good mother, too, of a grown son and daughter who now had their own families.

Robert was the primary wage earner, so Jean had only worked part-time while raising the children. She'd come to depend on him—maybe a little too much—since he'd always taken on the role of family decision-maker. But with grown children who move away, a mother and father's roles change. Jean's husband no longer had to be the chief decision maker—at least in Jean's thinking.

Decisions should be my own, Jean thought, lifting her chin. It was time for her to rediscover who she was. Already feeling more self-assured, her heart felt as light as the sun's streaming rays through the skylight.

Soft music swirled through the air as she walked up the stairs. With each step, she gained resilience. *I can make my own decisions.* And advice? A melody of thought glided through her mind as effortlessly as a butterfly. *I have lots of life experience. I can take my own advice.*

Jean entered the upstairs bathroom and stopped to look at her reflection in the mirror. The smile lines and wrinkles at the edge of each eye showed her age, as did the tufts of graying hair above each ear. She smiled slightly, trying to look her best in the soft pink blouse and pearl necklace she'd chosen to wear today. *I'm going to be okay,* she thought.

She looked down at the newly planted pecan trees on the island and the tile rooftops below the upstairs bedroom window. She wasn't accustomed to two-story homes but liked the feeling of looking down on the world below. She smiled. As of today, she was navigating on her own. It was nearly as exciting as the memory of the day she got her driver's license as a teen. She reveled in her new-found *freedom*.

Jean skipped down the stairs, her steps light yet strong. She would not need to ask anyone's opinion about decorating if she lived here. Her ideas were valuable, too.

To say no one noticed the change in her would be incorrect, for her husband had commented on the difference in her behavior. *It's just hormones, Robert*, she'd say. But she knew it was more than that.

Basking in a sunny room with tall green foliage, a sense of calm and joy came to her heart. She had great hopes for her daughter and family, who would start a new life in this area in a brand-new home. And she had great hopes for her own future, too, a future of self-reliance.

Soft music coming from the sound system pulled her into a dream.

"Oh!" Jean was startled as the realtor stepped around the corner. Jean didn't realize how late it had become. She was the last guest to step out of the model home.

The engine hummed as Jean got back onto the main road. An orange sunset spread across the sky, the brightness giving the distant low-lying mountains a purple hue. The peaceful moment was interrupted by one nagging thought. *This road doesn't look familiar.* When her children were small, this area was nothing more than cotton fields.

Stop worrying. You can figure this out.

New housing stretched for as far as she could see. Indeed, she'd see a familiar landmark.

As rush hour traffic slowed to a halt, Jean's patience waned. Maybe she should stop at a roadside business to ask for directions. But no. She could be confident like her husband. *Ask for directions? Never.*

When the traffic let up, Jean regained speed. While stopping at a red light, she saw a sign with the name of a familiar road: "Alma School." Great. Now, she'd make it home. But she didn't know which way to turn.

Passing a few more city blocks, she looked to the right and left. Sure, she'd recognized the road's name, but nothing looked familiar. Were her instincts wrong? She'd lived in the metro area for over thirty years. Why would she get lost now?

Upon seeing a vacant lot on the side of the road, Jean pulled over. She'd heard about an online map to help with directions but didn't know how to access it. So, she reluctantly reached for her flip phone to call her husband for directions. The screen lit up—for a split second—then went black. She pushed the "on" button again—and again. Oh, no. She'd remembered hearing a faint beeping while driving. *Low battery.* She hadn't paid attention. The phone was dead.

Jean rummaged through the glove compartment. No charger. As she closed the compartment, a small handwritten note slipped out. She picked it up. "*Embark on no venture you do not first submit to prayer.*" Advice she'd forgotten about. She used to have the note taped to the dash.

Jean stuffed the paper back into the glove compartment, then frantically searched the storage pockets in the door and looked under the front and back seats. Still no charger. It was probably at home—still plugged into the wall.

Jean scolded herself. *Why was I so negligent?* She'd been adamant about doing things independently, but today she'd failed.

She sucked in a deep breath, pulled out of the vacant lot, and turned onto the road. Not a store or gas station was in sight. Where was a payphone when you needed one? They'd become virtually extinct these days. What would she do now? Her husband would worry if she wasn't home soon.

I'll retrace my route, Jean thought, so she made a sharp U-turn, heading back the way she came. After leaving the housing development, she remembered the sparse landscape—but this wasn't it.

The peace and serenity she'd felt earlier in the day while touring the model home now felt like a distant memory. She was already tired, and it was getting dark. She'd turned onto every street near Alma School Road, but the streets didn't go through.

Jean passed the same vacant lot where she'd stopped and continued, even though she didn't know where it would lead. Dusk was setting in, so she turned on her headlights. She felt chilly now and hadn't thought to bring a sweater for the cool spring nights.

The silhouette of the mountains in the distance lined the horizon like an arc. It was too dark to see details, but Jean hoped it was the same backdrop she'd seen when leaving the housing development.

She pressed her foot onto the accelerator as the speed limit increased to 55 mph. As approaching headlights became fewer in number, a sinking feeling came over her. *I might be heading in the wrong direction.*

Streaks of twilight sky dimmed. Jean didn't want to admit it, but she was lost. Wiping tears with one hand, the car hit a pothole, jarring her steering as the car swerved from her lane. She straightened, blowing out a deep breath. This wasn't the well-maintained road she'd traveled earlier.

A smattering of lights flickered in the distance. Would this be the way? She didn't have a clue. If only she'd asked for directions when she had the chance! She felt utterly alone, having no way to contact her husband. She wasn't as independent as she thought.

Jean pressed her foot into the accelerator as if the increased speed would take away her frustration. Emotion welled behind her eyes as tears escaped. *Admit defeat. You're lost.*

Lost! Prickly heat coursed up her spine. She'd depended solely on herself, not asking for guidance or directions from anyone, including God.

"*Forgive me, Lord!*" she cried. Jean had turned down the wrong road—in more ways than one.

The headlights of the Impala were the only visible light in the blackness. Then, she saw a small white sign reflecting in her headlights. *Junction 6 miles ahead.* Would this lead her back to the city—or elsewhere? She didn't know.

Jean felt a glimmer of hope when a *Reduce Speed Ahead* sign appeared. The six-mile stretch to the Junction felt like the longest road she'd ever traveled. Emotionally, her uncertainty over the past few months rolled into a tangled ball inside her. Thorns of indecisiveness poked at her heart with each bump of the road.

Finally, out of the darkness, on the right side of the road, a green sign glowed in the beam of the headlights. *Phoenix, 20 miles.* An arrow pointed left. Navigation instructions! She let out a happy cry. "Thank you, God!"

With an answered prayer, she sighed as the muscles in her shoulders relaxed, and the tension in her hands softened. Turning left onto the highway—a major thoroughfare—would lead her home.

She felt comfort in the company of the glow of other taillights on the Interstate.

How she had strayed so far from home, she didn't know—or how she'd strayed from believing in herself—and God.

A band of midnight-blue peeked through the blackness across the skyline. She marveled at the expanse of the open desert sky as three words came to her heart. *"Freedom is vast."*

She thought about the happiness and freedom she'd felt earlier. A memory resurfaced from the day she was confirmed at her church as a teen. She recalled Pastor Anderson's words. *"You can choose to live as you please, or you can choose to follow God. It's up to you."*

There was a catch to free will. To make choices on her own was fine, but if she erred, she'd pay the price for her mistakes. The freedom she thought she had was not free. She'd chosen her own way, but in doing so, she made a detour away from prayer.

It was after eleven o'clock that night when Jean pulled into the driveway. She was relieved to be home. Safe. Secure. Her home was nothing like the model home she'd visited. It was old, in need of repair, and the décor was outdated. But right now, those things didn't matter.

"Robert!" Jean called out as she ran to the kitchen, wrapping her arms around her husband's neck. Worried, he'd waited up for her. She smoothed her finger over the marble cross he wore on a chain around his neck. *Who needs marble floors,* she thought? We have something better. She smiled as he wiped the tears from her cheek and asked what had happened.

As Jean lay in bed that night, she thought about the long, drawn-out day. Closing her eyes, she folded her hands. *"Thank you, God, for showing me true freedom—the freedom from being captive to my own desires."*

Jean's story isn't so different from Nehemiah's. His people acted in a similar way as Jean. They exercised free will to the extent that they became slaves to their own sins. Nehemiah 9:36–37 reads: *"...we are slaves today, slaves in the land you gave our ancestors..."*

Nehemiah's people wanted something better for themselves, just as Jean did. Each took control of their decision-making to get what they wanted. But in doing so, they became dependent on their own desires rather than depending on God. Like disobedi-ent children, they turned away when their heavenly Father called out to them, saying, "Listen!"

Nehemiah and the Israelites lived in a different time and era from Jean, but one thing hasn't changed since the beginning of time—human nature.

Despite warnings, the Israelites continued to disobey God. Their disobedience resulted in severe consequences. They fled from the refuge of their homes as the city of Jerusalem was de-stroyed. It was not a "model home" kind of day!

Nehemiah grieved over the people's sins and prayed God would forgive them. The Lord listened, and the people repented. Despite their previous behavior, good things would take place. Nehemiah and the Israelites would abandon the detour they'd taken in their faith. Their city was rebuilt in time, and life in Ju-dah was restored.

—

Jean picked up her Bible and came across Nehemiah's story. She realized the sin of past generations had trickled down to her own generation, landing right in her lap. *I behaved as badly as they did,* she thought to herself.

She could have avoided the trip into darkness if she'd first looked for guidance. When the window of opportunity was avail-able, she'd dismissed it. She thought she could do it alone, but she was wrong. She needed God's direction—His navigation—to get to safety, physically and spiritually.

Jean thought of the beautiful butterfly she saw among the flowering plants at the real estate office. For a time, the butterfly was merely a dormant caterpillar larva wrapped in the protective casing of its cocoon. When the time was right, it broke through the layers of the cocoon until it emerged as a beautiful, winged creature. Then, taking flight, it was free, no longer held captive.

God's only Son, Jesus Christ, was held captive on the cross, marked with the burden of the sins of mankind. Yet, a thousand-fold times more amazing than the emergence of a butterfly, His death and resurrection conquered darkness and gave light to the freedom of His salvation.

Jean knew the words coming into her heart were true: freedom was vast. She was no longer lost. Not physically. Not spiritually. She had hope for her future and her family, who planned to make their home in her community.

Like Jean, Nehemiah's people were no longer lost, either. Having repented, they renewed their faith in God.

And that's *one good thing.*

Worksheet for My Daily Morsel #18
Personal Insight:
Have you ever been lost, taken the wrong road, or felt lost spiritually? Explain.

_____
_____
_____

Did you look for—or find—help?

_____
_____
_____

Reflection: My "One Good Thing":
What is *one good thing* you learned from being lost?

_____
_____
_____

What is the greatest freedom you have known?

_____
_____
_____

Today's Serving: Instruction and Lessons of Free Will
Nehemiah's people exercised free will to the point of sinfulness—as did Jean. God didn't want to force them to do His will; however, the people of Nehemiah's day made poor decisions, causing them to sin. The same thing happened to Jean. Through the ages, human nature hasn't changed much.

A Cupful of Reality: In what way can you relate to Nehemiah's situation—or Jean's?

_____
_____
_____
_____

A Taste of Spiritual Nourishment:
In today's verse from Nehemiah comes a key word, *abundant*. God's love is abundant; it is infinite, without limits. So let your heart be glad today, for you are loved without measure!

The "Table of Optimism":
Hope resides at the Table of Optimism. What is your hope for today?

_____

_____

_____

Prayer for Today:
Dear Lord,

Thank You for giving me the freedom to make my own decisions. You guide me back to safety when, by my own fault, I step away. Thank You for your great love for me and the sacrifice You made to spare me from the captivity of sin. In Jesus' name, amen.

Recipe

My Daily Morsel #19

Prep Time

Cook Time

Oven Temp

Serves

Topic: **Greed/Provision**

_____

_____

_____

_____

_____

Bible Verse for Study

And he told them this parable: "The ground of a certain rich man yielded an abundant harvest. He thought to himself, '...I have no place to store my crops. This is what I'll do. I will tear down my barns and build bigger ones,...And I'll say to myself, "You have plenty of **good things** laid up for many years....Take life easy; eat, drink, and be merry." ' "But God said to him, 'You fool! This very night your life will be demanded from you. Then who will get what you have prepared for yourself?'..."   Luke 12:16-21 (NIV 1984)

WE HAD IT ALL

W e thought we had it all. Then everything changed.
I grabbed the stack of bills on the computer desk, sorted them, and made payments with the click of a button. One was left: the dreaded credit card statement. How had the balance increased so quickly—from manageable to out of control?

I heard my husband's footsteps in the hall.

I swiveled my desk chair around to see him standing in the doorway. He was wearing the same stained shirt and pants as the previous day. His unshaven skin made the tired look on his face even more apparent.

"I'm surprised you're up," I said. Lately, my husband wasn't getting up from the couch very often.

"Yeah, well...we need to talk," he said, his voice deadpan.

"All right. Hang on a minute." I turned to the computer, tapping quickly to finish a transaction, then logged out. I stuffed the credit card statement back in the envelope. It was time to pay off the card, but the balance had grown to a looming amount. It would have to wait—until how long, I didn't know.

I was surprised my husband hadn't returned to the comfort of the couch, which lately had been his place of refuge. Corporate management had taken its toll. This was the third time he'd taken short-term leave. He'd received help and was starting to feel better emotionally, but this morning was not one of those times.

I turned from the computer. My husband waited. With one shoulder slumped against the doorframe, he looked like a worn-out rag. His eyes matched his lackluster mood. Seeing someone who was usually so upbeat and energetic looking down-hearted, saddened me. He wasn't the same cheerful person I'd married many years ago. I felt like I was living with a stranger in my own home.

"What's going on?" I asked.

Without hesitation, he looked at me with glazed brown eyes. "I can't do this anymore," he said flatly.

"You can't do what?" I questioned. I feared what was coming, but denial kept my thoughts at a standstill.

"I'm not going back to work," he said.

His words dropped like a bomb. A surge of anger and confusion coursed through me. "You're not going to go back to work?" I said, my voice shaking. "Not at *all*?"

He shook his head definitively. "No."

I paused, firing a satirical reprimand. "So...what are you going to do?"

"I'm taking early retirement," he said, his mouth downturned.

My heart battled to keep peace, but my emotions declared war. Sharp words became my artillery. "You said we couldn't afford to do this!" I exclaimed.

He looked at me without expression. "I can't go back to this job anymore." He waited for my response.

Words wouldn't come. I was in denial. *How can you do this to us now?*

I didn't want to believe my husband had succumbed to anxiety and depression in such a short time. In retrospect, the signs had been there all along, but I didn't catch on. I should have noticed the little things that had changed over the past two years. My husband's frequent tiredness escalated to exhaustion. The nights he came home from work, going right to bed, not wanting dinner. And weekends of sleeping on the couch all day.

My husband was suffering, but I didn't know how bad it was

because he wouldn't discuss it. When I tried to interest him in getting out of the house on weekends to do something fun, he was too tired to go anywhere. At first, I thought he was just being lazy lying on the couch in front of the TV all day—and he'd fall asleep in front of the TV at night.

When he was too tired to go to our grandson's sixth birthday party, I knew something was wrong. My husband loved his grandson more than anything and had never missed one of his birthdays.

Depression changes things.

The first time my husband took a short-term leave from work, he felt distressed. He didn't say so, but I sensed his situation wouldn't be an easy fix. But then, noting his desperation, I asked him if early retirement would be an option.

"No," he responded adamantly. "We can't afford it."

Now, everything had changed. The banished idea became an ugly reality.

Sitting at my desk, I held my forehead with cupped hands as warm, salty tears slid past my lips. I withheld the sobs so my husband wouldn't hear me cry.

How would we meet monthly expenses, much less pay off the looming balance on our credit card? If only we had paid them off sooner. It was too late now. Soon, our income would decrease by more than two-thirds.

As a manager for a sizeable technological company, my husband had excelled in his thirty years of employment there. We lived in a spacious four-bedroom home with a two-car garage. We put our children through college, had the money for travel and vacations, and donated generously to church and charities. We had plenty to cover our expenses—until now.

I wondered what had happened to all the money we'd made. After paying our monthly mortgage and other expenses, we had funds left over. But, somehow, that money slipped right through our fingers. We spent most of it on little things—that added up.

Binging on gourmet coffee, jaunting off to restaurants on a whim, making impulse purchases for the kids, our family, or friends would be no more.

We'd never intended for money to be the focal point of our existence, but the "seed of greed" snuck up quietly, comfortably implanting itself into our fertile thinking, where it became deeply ingrained.

Like everyone else, we wanted a large home with a two-car garage and a spacious yard for our children and pets, surrounded by the proverbial white picket fence—the American dream. Our parents had achieved it, and we wanted the same.

I'd reflected on the past and my parents' stories about growing up during the Depression. Dispersed like too much salt and pepper on a favorite dish, my mother often reminded me of those struggles. On car trips out of town, she'd point to every roadside shack.

"Aren't you glad you don't live in a place like that?" she'd say. Naturally, my brother and I felt guilty. "When I was your age," she'd say, "I only had two dresses to wear to school."

We were passengers on guilt trips.

My father didn't have it easy, either. He quit school to help raise his younger siblings when his mother became ill. It was years later that he was able to finish his education.

Despite the overbearing nature of our parents, we knew they only wanted what was best for us. They bought us things we wanted to make up for all they had gone without. By an early age, the "seed of greed" took root. The more we got, the more we wanted.

Years later, when my husband and I had married and started our family, by the time our children were in upper elementary grades, my husband received several promotions at work and was making a good salary.

Cramped in a small house, we yearned for something more

substantial, so we sold our tiny home and moved into a large four-bedroom house. We wanted more space for ourselves—and for all the furnishings and household items we had—and desired to have.

When our daughters grew up and married, my husband and I realized we lived in a home overflowing with too much "stuff." Walk-in closets were not "walk-in," with boxes lining shelves and floors. The attic was crammed, and the garage was filled with so many boxes we had no room to park our cars.

The "seed of greed" had grown into something ugly.

Our lives had changed. Once, we had it all. Now, we'd have to scrape by from one month to the next. We collected a houseful of treasure—the wrong kind of treasure.

The words of Jesus in Luke 12:34 struck a chord: "For where your treasure is, there your heart will be also." Our treasure had filled our hearts with the wrong kind of longing instead of the treasure in heaven that does not wear out (see Luke 12:33).

We thought owning a lot of things would make our life better. Instead, it made it more complicated. Once, after tax season, I began to make a list of our possessions for insurance purposes. It became a monumental task I didn't think I would ever complete.

When we moved to a larger home, I thought "bigger would be better." But with all the extra space, you can imagine what happened—we filled it up with more things. It resulted in extra house cleaning, too. A few figurines would have been manageable, but with an overabundance of them, they became dust collectors. And I didn't like dusting!

—

The rich fool in the story of Luke 12:16–21 thought having more would be better, too. He built bigger barns and more immense storehouses to hold his extra crops, grains, and goods. That way, he was sure to have plenty of (good) things to last him for years, and he could sit back, relax, and take life easy. According to

Scripture, his motto was to eat, drink, and be merry. The rich, fool-ish man thought he could build a fortune by constructing bigger barns and storehouses for his possessions. He did not know the repercussions that would lay ahead for his greed. He trusted in his possessions instead of trusting in God. Then, as Scripture tells us in Luke 12:20, the Lord told the man, *"This very night your life will be demanded from you."* The man died—with the wrong kind of treasure—not the treasure he could have stored up in heaven through faith in Jesus Christ.

Jesus warns against excess in Luke 12:15: *"Watch out! Be on your guard against all kinds of greed; life does not consist in an abundance of possessions."*

The Lord does not speak of only one kind of greed but warns of "all kinds of greed." When we think of greed, we usually think of money or possessions, but there are other types of wants be-sides the desire to be rich. Some people want to have power or authority. Some want to have fame and social status. Some are gluttonous, and some covet, desiring what others have—or what doesn't belong to them.

That isn't all. We could add the following to the Bible's list of greed and gluttony: envy, arrogance, boastfulness, lust, immorali-ty, slander, or deceit. Even murder can result from greed.

Who would ever imagine gluttony could be so all-encompass-ing? Jesus's words show the truth: there are many kinds of greed.

Just as it takes accounting abilities (or an accountant) to track financial assets, God has His own "accounting system." He held the foolish rich man accountable for storing up wealth. The Lord warned the man; he would not live long enough to enjoy the things he'd put aside for himself to enjoy.

The rich, foolish man was rich in possessions but not rich to-ward God. He thought he had it all, and then everything changed.

God's "accounting system" is based on our richness toward Him. Fortunately, He is a loving Creator who understands man's sinfulness. If we watch out for all kinds of greed, as Jesus says, we can focus on the real treasure found in Him.

—●—

It took time to adjust to my husband's early retirement and the reduction in our income. I found full-time work to manage our monthly expenses. It wasn't easy, but we got through the additional five years I had to work.

I reflected on the years when my husband and I were first married. Each of us had very little in our bank accounts. My husband's possessions consisted of things that fit into the trunk of his 1976 Chevy Nova. I didn't own much, either, but I had some furniture my parents had given me for our apartment, and I collected books and papers. We didn't have a lot, but we were happy. We didn't know it then, but we had all we needed.

Although we faced financial hardship later, there were good things: we had our family, employment, and a roof over our heads. With my husband's early retirement, we had more time together, even though I was still working. We had to be frugal, but I was pleasantly surprised I didn't miss the extra money we'd made previously.

We had fewer dollars to spend, but our lives were richer with the time we had to spend together. We stayed home more often, made fewer trips to the store, and avoided impulse buying. We engaged in simple things that didn't involve spending money. We took walks, visited with neighbors, watched movies in the comfort of our own home. We enjoyed morning coffee on the patio rather than buying coffee from the local coffee shop. We played games and relished the time with our children and grandchildren.

After my husband retired, he started feeling good again and returned to his old self—only better. God had answered a vital prayer. It had nothing to do with finances; it had everything to do with the seed of faith that was planted. My husband turned his life over to Jesus Christ. I was beyond grateful. It was the best thing that could happen to him—and us.

We eventually cleared out the overabundance of items stored in our closets, attic, and garage. The excess not only weighed down the shelves in the house, but it weighed us down emotionally and spiritually. We felt happy once we were free from the weight of too many possessions.

Looking back, I was surprised at how fast our greed had grown. It had started as a tiny seed, the "seed of greed," as I call it.

When we rid ourselves of the wrong kind of treasure by disposing of excess, whether in our homes or the crevices in our hearts, it leaves room for the good things the Lord has in store—treasure that lasts for eternity.

May we trust in God—and not in greed.

Thanks be to God, who oversees our "all."

And that's *one good thing*.

—

Worksheet for My Daily Morsel #19
Personal Insight:
Has the "seed of greed" ever taken root in your life? If so, explain:

_____
_____
_____

Reflection: My "One Good Thing"
What "one good thing" has (or would) come into your life by focusing on the treasure of faith found through Jesus Christ?

_____
_____
_____

Today's Serving: Instruction—A Lesson in Overabundance
The rich man thought he had it all, and so did we. But the Lord showed the rich man—and He shows us—riches are not the things we hold in our hands. Instead, riches come from having Christ in our hearts and through believing in His Word.

A Cupful of Reality:
Did you ever "have it all," only to lose what you had? If so, explain:

_____

_____

_____

_____

A Taste of Spiritual Nourishment:
From our verse in Luke comes a key word, *rich*. Some have an abundance of wealth; some have little. Others are somewhere in the middle. In terms of faith, riches have little value unless used to serve others. To be spiritually rich is the greatest wealth of all. In what ways are you spiritually rich?

_____

_____

_____

_____

The "Table of Optimism":
Hope resides at the Table of Optimism. What is your hope for today?

_____

_____

_____

_____

Prayer for Today:
Dear Father in heaven,

I am sometimes swayed by earthly treasures and the "seed of greed." Free me from the desire to collect earthly things without lasting value. Instead, help me focus on the good things You have in store for me through the treasure found in You. In Jesus's name, amen.

Recipe

Prep Time

Cook Time

Oven Temp

Serves

Topic: **Obedience**

_____
_____
_____
_____
_____

Bible Verse for Study

"Then the servant left, taking with him ten of his master's camels loaded with all kinds of **good things** from his master. He set out for Aram Naharaim and made his way to the town of Nahor."

Genesis 24:10

_____
_____
_____

Seeing the Big Picture

The sun rises. A new day begins. We will visit three of God's people in different eras and parts of the world. They each present the same puzzling question: What will their day bring, and will they succeed in what they set out to do?

Jacob's excitement about starting school is almost more than he can stand. His mother hopes he will do well, but she is concerned. Will his impulsive tendencies hinder him from succeeding in kindergarten?

Sarah is elated. She's twelve years old now, and her parents allow her to shop at the mall by herself. She can decide how she wants to spend her own money. However, an unexpected situation challenges her moral standards. Will she succeed in doing what is right in God's eyes?

Eleazar, Abraham's chief servant, is required to take an oath. He must promise Abraham that he will carry out an important task. Will he succeed in living up to his master's standards? Will he be able to do what is required—or return to Abraham empty-handed?

Jacob, Sarah, and Eleazar's circumstances are different; however, as we shall see, their situations all have one thing in common.

Keeping the Puzzle Together: Jacob's Story
Outside the classroom door at the elementary school open house, Becca knelt at eye level to get her son's attention.

"Jake, we're going to go into the classroom to meet your teacher

253

and the other students. You will need to listen to your teacher. Okay?"

"Yes, Mommy." A sly grin erupted on his face.

The teacher welcomed Jake, his mother, the other children, and their parents into the classroom. When everyone was seated, the young brunette introduced herself. "I'm your teacher this year. My name is Miss Vita," she said, smiling.

"I'd like to tell you a story about this puzzle," she said, holding a small puzzle in her hand. She held it up for all to see. "Do you have your listening ears on?" she asked, watching for affirmative nods. "All right. Good. You will start the day at school with a puzzle like this every morning. But it's different from most puzzles," she said. "Can you see why?"

Jake popped his hand into the air enthusiastically. "Ye-e-e-s-s-s!" he responded in his biggest voice. "It's a *little* puzzle!"

"Right, Jacob. As you can see, it only has four pieces. It will be your job to keep the puzzle pieces together."

"Easy-peasy!" Jake bellowed. "I can do that!"

"Good!" the teacher replied. "It looks simple, doesn't it? If every student listens to me and follows my rules, you get to keep all four puzzle pieces at the end of the day. But, if you don't listen or talk out of turn, your puzzle piece will be taken away. You'll have to earn it back," she said.

Jacob's mother noticed the concerned look on his face.

The next day, Jacob came running in the front door after school. He could hardly contain his excitement. His face beamed. "I kept all my puzzle pieces, Mommy!" he exclaimed.

"Great, Honey! I'm so proud of you," his mother said, hugging him.

As the week progressed, classroom rules were in full force. The novelty of the first day of school wore off. Jake was impatient. He interrupted the teacher instead of raising his hand to wait his turn. Instead of being quiet when everyone did their paperwork, he made a clicking noise with his tongue and disrupted the class.

On Friday afternoon, Jacob dragged his feet up the sidewalk to his house. He frowned and lowered his head as his mother approached.

"Jake, what's wrong?"

"I lost two puzzle pieces today, Mommy."

"Oh?"

"I talked when it wasn't my turn."

"Can you do better tomorrow?" his mother asked.

He nodded. "I'll try," he said.

But the following day, the unthinkable happened. "I lost the whole puzzle, Mommy!" he cried, stomping his foot on the floor. He threw his short arms around his mother's waist and buried his face in her apron. "Now I don't have a puzzle, and I can't see the whole picture!"

"I'm sorry that happened, Honey," she said. "Why don't we sit at the table? You can have a snack, and we'll talk about your difficult day."

Jake agreed. They talked. Then his mother said, "How about a prayer?"

Jake and his mother folded their hands and bowed their heads. "I want to say the prayer, Mommy," he said. "Dear God. Please help me to do better. Amen."

The next day, to Jake's amazement, he only lost one puzzle piece. Miss Vita told him she was glad he was doing better. It brightened the day for Jacob's mom, too. She loved her son and was praying for him. *The road to obedience isn't easy for little boys with ADHD.*

There are many "Jacobs" in the world. It is an enormous challenge for children like Jake to do everything required of them. Even for the youngest, the pressure is tremendous. But as parents and teachers know, discipline is necessary for children to become responsible citizens.

As adults, we face similar challenges, but differently. Do we grumble when we must take direction or advice from our boss or those who have authority over us? It's not always easy for us to do what we are supposed to do, either!

Figuring out the Pieces: Sarah's Story
"We trust you, Sarah." These were golden words to Sarah's ears. Finally, in September of 1967, she'd turned twelve, and her parents told her she was old enough to shop at the mall by herself. A burst of joy welled inside her through her parents' acknowledging they didn't think she was a little girl anymore. She donned her favorite shirt with bell sleeves and Levi's, put her shoulder-length brown hair into a ponytail, and snapped on the bracelet Mom gave her for her birthday. She admired the deep burgundy letters embedded into the leather, "*WWJD.*" It was the latest thing. She knew what the initials stood for: "*What Would Jesus Do?*"

She felt free. *I can shop without Mom telling me to hurry up.* Within a few hours, she bought three new shirts and two pairs of brand-name jeans. Joy bubbled up inside her as she strolled the mall with her fancy shopping bags.

Intrigued by a shiny jewelry display in a merchant's window, Sarah stepped into the store. She approached the jewelry counter, set her heavy shopping bags on the floor, and reached for the shiny turtle earrings on the rack. She held them in one hand as she looked for other styles. But suddenly, one of the turtle earrings slipped off the cardboard backing. Where did it go? Had it dropped on the floor? She looked on the floor beneath the display but didn't see it.

A troublesome thought came to mind. Had the earring fallen into her open shopping bag? A nervous shiver ran up her neck as heat rushed to her face.

Sarah quickly returned the cardboard backing with the one

turtle earring onto the rack, placing it behind the others. Maybe no one would notice.

But what if the earring fell into her bag on the floor and security saw it?

The more she thought about it, the more she feared the earring had fallen into her shopping bag. Should she dig through the bag to find it? But would the store manager or clerk think she was stealing something if she did so?

Sarah debated. On the other hand, if the earring was in her bag and she didn't say anything, wouldn't it be the same thing as stealing?

What should she do? Sarah hadn't seen the earring fall into the bag but suspected it might be there. She took a deep breath. Picking up the bag, she nervously walked into the next aisle. She stalled for time, thinking about what she would do.

I won't feel guilty about the earring if I buy something. Sarah picked out a few toiletries and hesitated as she approached the check-out counter. Her hand shook as she pulled money from her wallet and paid for the toiletries. Her mind wrestled with her heart. Should she tell the clerk about the earring—or say nothing?

The discrepancy swirled in her thoughts. *I'm not going to say anything.*

After paying for the purchase, Sarah rushed out of the store. She glanced back. No one was watching. No one followed her. *Thank heavens.*

Relieved, she would continue shopping elsewhere, but worrying about the missing earring overshadowed this desire. She rationalized her decision. *I didn't do anything wrong. I didn't put the earring in the bag.* But it didn't make her feel any better.

Someone would eventually find the cardboard backing with the missing earring. *What's one earring? No big deal. Earrings get lost all the time.* She felt bad she hadn't said anything to the clerk, but at the same time, she didn't feel bad enough to do anything about it.

Sarah exited the double doors of the mall and walked to the bus stop. After boarding the bus, she opened the shopping bag, unfolding the clothing in her lap one piece at a time. As she pulled out the last shirt, her heart skipped a beat. The silver turtle earring was lying flat against the bottom of the bag. As she held the shirt in her hands, looking down at the earring, her bracelet slid down her arm, the embedded letters WWJD in plain view.

If the pieces of my life are a test, she surmised, *I just failed miserably.*

When Sarah got home, guilt consumed her. She spilled her story to her mom, along with a few tears. Lying awake that night, she knew what she had to do.

The following day, Sarah's stomach felt like it was doing flip-flops as she approached the check-out counter where she'd shopped. Her voice quivered as she told the clerk what had happened. The clerk summoned the manager.

Opening her wallet, Sarah unwrapped the silver turtle earring from a tissue paper. The manager, a tall, tight-lipped man with a dark mustache, approached. She felt like slinking beneath the counter. *Will he accuse me of stealing?*

As she relayed her story to the manager, he remained calm and was not accusatory. She was surprised when he held out his palm to shake her hand. "Thank you for being honest, young lady," he said. "Not everyone would have returned the earring."

Sarah nodded.

The manager reached into his vest pocket. "Because you were honest, I'd like to offer you this 50% off coupon. It's good for anything in the store."

"Thank you so much, sir!" Sarah tucked the coupon into her purse. As she passed through the exit, she twirled the "WWJD" bracelet on her arm. A feeling of peace washed over her. She'd made the right decision.

Finding the Edge: Eleazer's Story

Abraham had an essential task for Eleazer. It was time for Abraham's son, Isaac, to find a wife. But there was a condition: the wife for Abraham's son must be chosen from the people in his own country. Abraham was too old to make the journey, so he called upon Eleazer, his chief servant, to do this for him and asked him to take an oath. He must promise to make the journey to choose a wife for Abraham's son.

Eleazer agreed to do as Abraham requested and took the oath. He would choose a wife for Isaac from their own country, not from the Canaanites' daughters, among whom they were living. The choice would be an important one.

Eleazar dutifully obeyed but was concerned about completing this monumental task. Would he know where to go? When he arrived, would he know whom to look for and choose the right person to become Isaac's wife?

Scripture tells us Abraham provided well for Eleazar: *"...the servant left, taking with him ten of his master's camels loaded with all kinds of good things from his master"* (Genesis 24:10).

Eleazar may have felt overwhelmed; however, like Abraham, he was a man of God and trusted in the Lord. So, the chief servant bowed down and prayed to God to make his journey successful.

Arriving in the town of Nahor in the country of Abraham's family and ancestors, Eleazar led his camels to the well. There, Scripture tells us he prayed again to choose the right wife for his master's son.

A young woman named Rebecca came to the well to offer water to the servant's camels. From the guidance he'd been given through an answer to prayer, the servant knew she was the right one.

After finding Rebecca, Eleazar praised God:

"...and I bowed down and worshipped the LORD. I praised the LORD, the God of my master Abraham, who had led me on the right road to get

the granddaughter of my master's brother for his son" (Genesis 24:48).

Eleazar trusted Abraham, for he was a man of great faith. He looked to the Lord for guidance and found a wife for his master's son. He was a dutiful chief servant who listened to God and obeyed Him.

The whole picture came into play as it was supposed to: Abraham prayed to God and listened to Him for guidance. Likewise, Eleazar listened to Abraham, prayed to God, and followed His lead. Rebecca obeyed by returning with Eleazer to Abraham's town, where she became Isaac's wife. The puzzle pieces, so to speak, fell into place just as intended because each was obedient to God.

If you've ever put a jigsaw puzzle together, you know it can be frustrating to find all the right pieces. But once you finish the puzzle, you see the whole picture.

Sometimes, life feels like a puzzle with pieces that don't fit or are missing. Like Jacob, we want to see the whole picture. We may not always understand how things are supposed to go together, but God does. He can help us sort out the pieces and allow us to put things together. It's a good feeling when we see the "big picture."

Jacob, Sarah, Abraham, and Eleazer present portraits of different lives and different eras, but they have a common thread: obedience.

To keep his puzzle pieces together, Jacob has to obey his teacher. Sarah's puzzling experience with the missing earring reminds her to do what is right—how Jesus would do. Eleazar prays to God for help and follows His lead, resulting in a successful journey and a wife for Isaac.

If Jacob's, Sarah's, or Eleazer's decisions had been different, negative consequences would have ensued. And negative consequences can lead one to sinful actions.

In today's verse from Genesis 24:10, Abraham counts on Eleazer to find a wife for his son from the right kind of people. The choice is important, as future generations would come from the union of Rebecca and Isaac.

God provides good things for His people. He helps us keep the pieces of our lives in order so we can see the big picture He has in store for us.

And that's *one good thing*.

Worksheet for My Daily Morsel #20

Personal Insight:

When have you struggled to do the right thing? What decision did you make, and what happened because of your decision?

_____

_____

_____

_____

What would have happened if you had made a different choice?

_____

_____

_____

_____

Reflection:My "One Good Thing"

What "one good thing" has come from your obedience to God?

_____

_____

_____

_____

Today's Serving: Instruction Through Listening

Obedience comes from listening and from heeding what one is asked to do. Jacob, Sarah, and Eleazar first have to listen to instructions to obey. Likewise, we can do the same.

A Cupful of Reality:

What might happen if Eleazar does not make the right choice for a wife for Isaac?

_____

_____

_____

_____

What might happen if Jacob or Sarah make wrong choices?

_____

_____

_____

_____

A Taste of Spiritual Nourishment:
From our verse in Genesis comes a key word, *kneel*. The camels kneel at the well. When a camel kneels, it enables its master to pack or unpack the load on its back. Some people prefer to kneel when they pray to show reverence; some people bow their heads. The important thing, of course, is the intent of the one who prays. Sometimes, we can feel as heavy as a camel with packs on its back. But through prayer, the Lord comes to lighten our load and set us free from burdens.

The "Table of Optimism":
Hope resides at the Table of Optimism. What is your hope for today?

_____

_____

_____

Prayer for Today:
Dear Father in heaven:

Open my ears to Your Word so I may follow Your will instead of mine. I pray for wisdom to make good choices and look forward to being a better listener as I look to Your Word as my guidebook. In Jesus's name, amen.

Recipe

My Daily Morsel #21

Prep Time

Cook Time

Oven Temp

Serves

Topic: **God's Commandments**

Bible Verse for Study

"Just then a man came up to Jesus and asked, 'Teacher, what **good thing** must I do to get eternal life?' 'Why do you ask me about what is good?' Jesus replied. 'There is only One who is good. If you want to enter life, keep the commandments.'"

Matthew 19:16–17

KNOWING IT ALL

Arizona. Late April on a Friday afternoon. I looked at the thermometer outside my kitchen window: ninety-five degrees—shade temperature. Having just moved from Colorado, I expected warm weather, but not this warm.

I opened the door and windows in my apartment, but there was no breeze—only hot air. I grumbled as I shut the door and windows and turned on the air conditioning. I dreaded the high utility bills my Arizona friend told me about.

Speaking of my friend, there she was. I was expecting her.

"Hey, Dani!" I grinned as she stepped inside. "I'd hug you, but I'm all sweaty."

"Yuck. You sure are. Why is it so hot in here?" All four-foot-eleven-inches of Dani looked at me with raised eyebrows, her white-framed glasses sliding down her nose. She fanned herself with one hand.

"I know it's hot. I'm sorry," I replied. I handed her an iced tea as she sat at my small, wobbly kitchen table. "I didn't think I'd have to use the air conditioning so soon. I just turned it on before you came in."

"Whew. Well, it will take a while before it cools off in here," Dani exclaimed.

"Want to go outside instead?" I asked.

"No, are you kidding?"

"Dumb thing to ask. Guess I'm an Arizona newbie."

"You sure are," Dani chuckled.

"Is it always this hot in April?" I asked.

"Yep," Dani responded, sipping her tea. "Welcome to spring in Arizona, my friend."

"Yeah, some welcome," I said, snickering.

"Just wait until summer," Dani replied dryly.

I wasn't sure what to think. I'd never spent a summer in Arizona. I was happy to move here for a change of scenery. I'd just graduated from college, landed a job at the university, and settled into my apartment.

It was good to see Dani again. We'd gone to junior high together until her family moved to Arizona. I hadn't seen her for years, so I was glad to rekindle our friendship now.

Dani and her family were kind. They often invited me to their house for dinner and included me in their weekend plans—church included.

One afternoon, while leaving work on campus, I saw an ad for a community hiking and desert survival class. Intrigued, I told Dani about it, and we immediately signed up. Tomorrow would be our first hike with the class.

Dani set down a small bag on the table.

"Homemade trail mix and granola bars for tomorrow," she said.

"Great. Thanks," I replied.

"All right," Dani said, reaching for my newspaper. "Let's check the forecast."

The high for tomorrow would be ninety-three degrees. "Warm for a hike," she said, "but we'll be in the high desert, so it might be a few degrees cooler there."

"We never had summer temperatures like that at home," I remarked.

"Arizona is a different kind of place," Dani said, pushing up her glasses. She changed the subject. "Did you read the instructions for the hike?"

"Uh, no," I replied. "I think they're in my notebook," I said. I hadn't looked at the instructions. I didn't think they'd be a big deal.

"Never mind. I have a copy," Dani said, reading the first page out loud. "Do you have the following basic items? Canteen, hiking boots, knapsack, sunscreen..."

"Dani," I interrupted. "You're talking to a *Colorado* girl here." I flicked my palm in the air to make a point. "I've done a lot of hiking. So, the answer to your question is, 'Yes, I have all those things.'"

"All right," she said, "but what about the rest of the things on the list?"

"*Tsk.*" I gave her the same smirk my mother used to give me.

"Sorry," she said, looking down. "I forgot you're experienced."

"It's all right. I appreciate your concern, but I have all I need."

I didn't admit to her that I hadn't hiked since late October—cold weather set in early. I was also preoccupied with university classes, graduation preparation, and employment. A few months away from the trails wouldn't matter. *Anyway, what could be so different about hiking in Arizona?*

Dani left to go home. We'd have to be up early in the morning. I unpacked a box in my closet containing my hiking equipment: one pair of faded brown hiking boots with scuffed toes. Worn, but comfortable. One neon-orange knapsack with enough room for trail mix, granola bars, dried fruit, a bandana, sunscreen, a first-aid kit, an extra pair of socks, and my camera. I packed a lunch, filled my two-quart canteen with water, and set aside a hiking shirt, shorts, sunglasses, and a wide-brimmed hat. *There. What else could I possibly need?*

I set my alarm for early the following day. We'd need an hour and a half to drive to the trailhead to arrive by seven. Our instructor wanted us to be early so we'd be done with the hike by the time it got hot in the afternoon.

Barnhardt Trail. I looked at the map for directions—Highway 87. *Turn off before the Gisela exit.* Take a left on Barnhardt Road to the Trailhead—a round-trip hike of 10.2 miles. Reading further, I noted the elevation of 7,900 feet. *Much lower than most peaks in Colorado.*

Twenty minutes before seven, we reached the end of the five-mile gravel road leading to the Trailhead. Dani pulled the Corolla into a spacious, dirt parking lot. Our instructor and a few classmates had gathered near the trailhead. Soon, all fourteen of our class had arrived. Our instructor, Bill, was the fifteenth person.

Bill didn't waste time. He repeated what he'd already told us— start early; get off the mountain before it gets too hot. He held up the instruction sheet. "Does everybody have everything on this list?" He had a way of emphasizing words in a gruff voice.

The group responded affirmatively. I'd heard this before, so I wasn't listening. Hiking wasn't new to me, as it was to some in the class. The only difference is that this was my first hike in Arizona.

I looked beyond the trailhead at the sparse vegetation. High desert, they call it. The scrub brush seemed vastly different from the grassy meadows of Colorado.

Dani and I donned lightweight jackets to cut the chill of the brisk morning air. It seemed odd to wear a jacket in the desert. Later, we'd trade the long sleeves for short ones and slather on sunscreen.

As we stepped onto the trail, I watched with interest as tiny wrens flitted back and forth between scrub brush plants. Dani pointed out Juniper and, in the near distance, Piñon pines.

The peak ahead appeared to be a gradual climb. "It doesn't look bad at all," I told Dani.

She raised her eyebrows. "I hope you're right. I haven't been on this trail before. You're experienced. You should know better than me."

So far, Dani was keeping up with me.

The couple behind us, who looked to be in their fifties, expressed concern about the climb.

I shook my head. "Seven thousand nine hundred feet is nothing," I replied. "You should see the mountains where I'm from," I boasted. I had statistics to prove it, too.

We pressed on. An hour into the hike, the trail became steep and rocky. As the sun emerged from behind the clouds, we ditched the jackets and put them in our packs.

Dani complained her feet were cramping. "And how are you doing?" she asked.

"I'm fine," I said, pausing to catch my breath. I was getting winded but didn't want to admit my weakness. I'd reached for my canteen more often than I thought, too.

A half-hour later, Bill's voice rang out from the front of the line. "Break time!"

"Thank heavens," Dani shouted.

I just smiled but was glad for the break, too.

Dani and I sat on a rock and munched on the trail mix she'd made. I kept the canteen in my lap. I knew it was best only to take small sips of water, but my mouth was so dry I took large gulps.

After ten or fifteen minutes, we were back on the trail. It quickly became rugged. We were no longer walking but climbing over large rocks and boulders. Then, the switchbacks appeared. None of this had been evident from the view at the Trailhead.

Dani and I had initially chatted through much of the hike, but now I felt too winded to keep up a conversation. I felt the sting of discomfort in my calf and thigh muscles. I expected that. What I didn't expect was the heat. As the sun beat down, I took more frequent sips of water. About an hour before we reached the summit, I ran out of water.

My cheeks felt burning hot, even though I wore a wide-brimmed hat. Did I dare mention my mistake? I could make an excuse, but what good would it do? I sheepishly admitted to Dani that I was out of water. She looked surprised but didn't question me. She slid the strap over her head and handed me her canteen.

The midday sun was at full intensity when we reached the summit. My mouth felt like cotton; my skin was hot, and I felt lightheaded. My feet sweltered in the hiking boots. Wool socks hadn't been the best choice for this climate.

Dani was right about Arizona being different. Unfortunately, I found out the hard way I wasn't experienced in hiking in this type of terrain—at least not in hot weather.

Fortunately, reaching the summit meant we could break for lunch. Others complained about being tired, including Dani, but no one seemed to be in as bad a shape as I was. I felt overheated and exhausted.

A few pines dotted the hillside. I stumbled over to one and sat. I didn't care that I'd landed in sticky pine needles. I leaned forward, resting my head and arms on my knees. Dani knelt next to me. "You don't look good. Your face is flushed. Are you okay?"

"Yeah," I replied, cradling my head in my hands. "I think so. I just need to rest."

I think Dani was worried because she went to get Bill. The thud of his heavy footsteps approached. I squinted, opening my eyes. Bill looked at me and pulled out a water container from his backpack. He handed it to me as I lifted it to my parched lips. He asked a barrage of questions. Yes, I felt dizzy and had a headache. No, I wasn't nauseated, and my vision hadn't changed.

"Stay in the shade and keep hydrated," Bill ordered. "Keep an eye on her, will you, Dani?" he said. "I'll be back in a few minutes."

I closed my eyes, hoping the dizziness would subside. I overheard Bill and Dani's conversation as they stood within view. "Is that all the water she brought?" he whispered.

"Yes," Dani replied. "Surprised me, too. I thought she had more than one canteen."

"I thought you said she had experience," Bill exclaimed.

"She does—in Colorado," Dani replied.

I saw Bill look over at me, shaking his head.

After resting in the shade for a while, the dizziness began to subside, and I felt better.

"Your face is less red," Dani said. She handed me a sandwich. "Here. Eat something."

She was right. I needed something in my stomach. I didn't feel very hungry but nibbled on the sandwich.

"I'm glad you're feeling better," Dani said. "I was starting to worry about you. You never know what to expect in the desert."

I had to agree with her about that.

As we ate lunch beneath the pine tree, I heard the rumors and rumblings from people in the class about me getting overheated. I felt embarrassed—and ashamed. I boasted about my hiking expertise and didn't heed Bill's instructions. *Now, look at me.* I thought I had all the answers. I was wrong.

I apologized to Bill and Dani. I should have listened. I knew enough to get by while hiking in Colorado, but as Dani said, Arizona is a different kind of place. My meager two-quart canteen was a testament that I didn't have enough water to hike in the desert.

How foolish I felt! Dani could have criticized me as some of the people in the class, but she didn't. She was kind, caring, compassionate—and forgiving.

Because of me, our whole group was delayed in getting down the mountain that afternoon. By the time we reached the parking lot, I felt awful. I'd been given plenty of water, but the damage of being overheated was already done. I'd exhausted any remaining energy I had.

Back at the parking lot, Dani and I headed toward the highway and met up with the rest of our class in a tiny café in the small town of Rye.

We sat at the counter and placed our orders. I craved ice-cold Dr. Pepper. Dani and other classmates told me I should be drinking water, but I couldn't pass up the thought of soda. I downed two Dr. Pepper's. Before we left, I'd ordered two more.

On the drive home, the dizziness returned, and I felt hot. I lay down in the back seat of the car. My stomach was upset, too. With the combination of being in the heat, dehydration, and ingesting too much sugar, I was done. Traffic on the way home was slow, and Dani's air conditioning in her car wasn't very cool.

I learned a harsh lesson about heat exhaustion and didn't feel good for the next few days.

I thought I had all the answers, but I didn't. I'd ignored Bill's handout. He was the authority on hiking and desert survival. He knew best, but I paid the consequences when I failed to follow his advice. Likewise, I hadn't listened to Dani or my classmates when we went to the café.

I was fortunate not to have landed in the hospital.

—

The young man in today's study of Matthew 19:16–17 didn't follow the advice he had been given, either. He had approached Jesus with a critical question: "Teacher, what *good thing* must I do to get eternal life?"

The Bible doesn't reveal the man's age but shows he was young. As was common in those days, large crowds gathered to hear Jesus speak. He left Galilee to go into Judea, where he went to the other side of the Jordan River.

The young man may have had to travel far to where Jesus was preaching. We don't know where he came from, but he probably walked along dirt paths, roads, fields, rocks, and hills to reach his destination. Even though he was rich, some places could have been unsuitable even for the most agile donkey to cross.

We do not know what obstacles this man might have faced on this journey; however, an obstacle would surface after he arrived.

The young man reached an area near the Jordan where the crowd gathered to see Jesus. He may likely have had to wait quite a while. But finally, the moment he had been waiting for arrived. He approached Jesus.

Imagine Jesus's dark, piercing eyes welcoming the young man. This man may have been drawn to the Rabbi in a way he couldn't explain. Seconds may have felt like an eternity as the young man raced to organize his thoughts.

Then, in the presence of the Holy One, we wonder whether he felt peace and strength instead of nervousness or fear.

The young man's question would be simple. Indeed, the Master Teacher would provide him with the answers he desired, wouldn't He? Then, the young man asked the question that had probably been burning in his soul:

"Teacher, what good thing must I do to get eternal life?" he asked.

Imagine Jesus surveying the young man's soul. His gaze locks in with that of the young man. Then, with authority in His voice, Jesus says (paraphrasing), "Why do you ask me about what is good? Only God is good. But to answer your question, you can receive eternal life if you keep the commandments."

Keep the commandments. The words must have echoed through the young man's mind. He questioned which of the commandments he should obey. When Jesus answered, he realizes the Lord had only focused on the commandments specifically applying to him.

When Jesus asked if he had obeyed the commandments, the man said, "All these I have kept."

However, something stood in his way. He had obeyed the commandments, but something was missing. So, he questioned Jesus, saying, "What do I still lack?" (v. 20).

Jesus answers in the next verse, "If you want to be perfect, go, sell your possessions and give to the poor, and you will have treasure in heaven. Then come, follow me."

The young man was filled with tremendous grief and sadness when he heard this. The answer to his question was not what he expected. He left sad, knowing he could not give up his riches to follow Jesus.

The young man did not take the advice of Jesus, the Authority on all of heaven and salvation. He thought he was doing everything right, but he was wrong.

In our story for today, I was the one who didn't listen to the directions given by my instructor, the authority on hiking and desert survival. I thought I knew what I was doing, but I didn't. Because I disregarded the rules, I suffered the consequences of heat exhaustion.

The young man thought he knew what was best, too, and told Jesus he had followed every commandment. But he didn't follow the advice Jesus gave him. He walked away sad, knowing he could not give up his wealth.

Authority. It's part of what we must revere in this earthly life. As for our salvation, we are asked to revere the authority given to Jesus by our Father in heaven. We would do well to listen to the One who knows all.

And that's *one good thing.*

Worksheet for My Daily Morsel #21

Personal Insight:
The young man in today's story learned that his wealth posed an obstacle in following Jesus. Is there any obstacle that has—or could—stand in your way as you follow Jesus?

Reflection: My "One Good Thing"
What is one good thing you can do to remedy an obstacle to your salvation?

Like the young man in the story, have you ever had a burning question you wanted to ask Jesus? If so, what would you ask Him?

Today's Serving: Instruction Through God's Word
The young, rich man wanted to know the truth from Jesus, but he didn't like the answer he received. He knew he wouldn't live up to Jesus' request. In today's story, the hiker also thought she knew what was best. Sometimes, it's easy to be overconfident. Has overconfident thinking ever gotten you into a precarious situation? If so, what happened?

A Cupful of Reality:
A point to ponder: How can the habit of listening in secular life be applied to listening in one's spiritual life? (There is no right or wrong answer.)

A Taste of Spiritual Nourishment:
In Matthew 19:16 comes a key word, *eternal*. When I was seventeen, I thought I was invincible and would live forever. Perhaps you felt the same way. Christians can claim eternity as the truth, for we believe Jesus died for our sins on the cross. When it is time for us to leave this earth, God promises us eternal life in heaven—a spiritually nourishing thought, isn't it?

The "Table of Optimism":
Hope resides at the Table of Optimism. What is your hope for today?

Prayer for Today:
Dear Father in heaven,

You sent Your precious Son, Jesus, so I might learn to obey Your Word and Commandments. Free me from the urge to control my own life. Free me from the desire to boast unless I boast of You. Be with me as I encounter obstacles that hinder my Christian walk, and give me the courage to face them. Thank You, Father, for Your supreme power, love, and authority over all creation. In Jesus's name, amen.

Part Three: God as Master Teacher

Recap of Morsels #15-#21

Congratulations! You have just completed the first twenty-one Morsels—Parts One, Two, and Three, and showing God's influence through His instruction in Part Three. Now that you have read the stories, completed the worksheets, and your One Good Thing journal entries, the following questions will help you assess your progress:

1. What insight have you gained from the stories?

_____

_____

_____

_____

2. In what way(s) have you been encouraged to be optimistic?

_____

_____

_____

_____

3. How have the Bible verses about "good things" applied to you? Give an example.

_____

_____

_____

_____

4. Which stories did you appreciate the most, and why?

_____

_____

_____

_____

5. How are you doing with your daily "One Good Thing" journal entries? If you've kept up, good job! If you've missed a few, don't worry. You're putting "good things" to work and making progress! Fill in missed en-

tries if you can. Otherwise, go on to the next day. Do your best to be consistent and save time by keeping your entries short.

6. Using the following scale, how would you rate your optimism now? (zero = none; ten = 100%)

0   1   2   3   4   5   6   7   8   9   1 0

7. How has your outlook changed from when you began this book?

_____

_____

_____

_____

8. Have you noticed a difference in your ability to avert negative thoughts? If so, how? (If not, are you recording your daily journal entries? They will help you develop the habit of thinking positively.)

_____

_____

_____

_____

9. Looking back at your previous Table of Optimism responses, which desire for hope is most important to you now?

_____

_____

_____

_____

10. If you need encouragement to finish the stories, worksheets, or journal pages, what goal can you set to complete them before you begin the last section of this book?

_____

_____

_____

11. Consider a goal to keep; in mind when you finish this book.

Wherever you are in your journey toward spiritual optimism, be kind to yourself, for you are making an effort. Prayerfully consider how God can help you reach your goals.

PART FOUR
GOD AS MASTER COUNSELOR

GOD AS MASTER TEACHER

Counselors serve in many capacities as advisers, mentors, guides, and advocates in our schools, hospitals, and communities. In addition, some serve as Christian counselors for clients who wish to work through issues using a faith-based approach.

Following are Bible verses that describe God's counsel:

"Plans fail for lack of counsel, but with many advisers, they succeed." — Proverbs 15:22

"For lack of guidance a nation falls, but victory is won through many advisers." — Proverbs 11:14

"I will instruct you and teach you in the way you should go; I will counsel you with my loving eye on you." — Psalm 32:8

The following scriptures show the counsel of the Holy Spirit:

"But when he, the Spirit of truth, comes, he will guide you into all the truth. He will not speak on his own; he will speak only what he hears, and he will tell you what is yet to come." — John 16:13

"But the Advocate, the Holy Spirit, whom the Father will send in my name, will teach you all things and will remind you of everything I have said to you." — John 14:26

As you read the stories, notice how God brings *good things* to those who need His guidance.

Recipe

My Daily Morsel #22

Prep Time

Cook Time

Oven Temp

Serves

Topic: **Sharing Faith**

Bible Verse for Study

"I pray that your partnership with us in the faith may be effective in deepening your understanding of every **good thing** we share for the sake of Christ."

Philemon 1:6

Lonnie—Nice Enough

Lonnie seemed nice enough to the older couple. The young blond man smiled, eager to undertake the bed and bath remodeling project.

"Got a good referral, Georgia," Harold whispered into his wife's ear. "Remember my old friend Ray? Lonnie is his nephew."

Georgia smiled. She was excited about the updating of their old home.

Within a few days, Lonnie removed the broken fixtures and cabinetry in the bathroom. It had taken him all morning. There was still more work to do. New counters and fixtures would be delivered later in the day.

Harold came in to see how things were going but noticed Lonnie was on the phone, so he stepped out.

When Lonnie finished removing the old cabinets, he called out to Harold. "Look at this," Lonnie pointed with the toe of his work boot to a corner behind the commode where the linoleum had lifted.

"I can get you a great deal on tile, Harold," he said, grabbing a pen and notepad. Biting his lip, he wrote down some figures and handed the quote to Harold.

Lonnie cleared his throat. "You won't beat these prices."

Harold pushed up his glasses, inspecting the paper. He pursed his lips together in thought. He and Georgia were retired and lived on a fixed income, so he debated whether to risk spending the extra money.

Georgia poked her head in the door. "What's this I hear about *tile*? Her voice bubbled over with excitement.

Harold thought about the rough time she'd had during the past year with the cancer diagnosis and chemotherapy treatments. Harold looked over at Georgia lovingly. *I can't disappoint her if this is what it takes to make her happy.* He raised his eyebrows. "All right, Love. We'll do the tile."

Georgia grinned and gave a thumbs-up as she headed for the kitchen.

"All right, Lonnie. We'll go for the tile."

Lonnie brushed at the sweat beading up on his forehead. "Got it," he said as he grabbed a screw and drilled a cabinet hinge in place.

Harold noticed the redness in his face.

"Are you okay, Lonnie? Can I get you some water?"

Lonnie shook his head. "No...no thanks," he replied, his eyes fixed on the cabinet.

Harold went to the bank since Lonnie told him he'd need cash to buy the tile. He handed the twelve crisp one-hundred-dollar bills to Georgia when he got home. She went to her desk in the other room, put the money in an envelope, and gave it to Lonnie.

A short time later, Georgia noticed Lonnie putting his tools away in a rush. Sawdust and packaging materials littered the floor. She looked perplexed.

"Something came up," Lonnie quipped, stuffing his cell phone into a back pocket. He tossed the tools into a canvas tote with a clang, swung the bag over his shoulder, and raced out the front door. He nearly collided with Harold as he ran down the front steps.

"You're leaving already?" Harold called out.

"Yeah—Georgia knows." Lonnie's voice trailed off as he climbed into his truck.

"He said something came up, Harold."

"Did he say what happened?" Harold asked as Lonnie revved the engine, tires squealing as he sped down the road.

"No, he didn't," Georgia replied. "I hope everything is okay."

"Me, too," Harold responded as the truck disappeared down the street.

"He said the sawdust and trash will have to wait until tomorrow," Georgia said. "I think he had a lot on his mind."

"I think you're right, honey," Harold said, squeezing Georgia's hand. Don't worry. He's young and probably has a lot on his plate." He couldn't wait to see her face when the remodeling project was complete.

Georgia put the coffee pot on the stove and looked at the kitchen clock. Before Lonnie's abrupt departure yesterday, he'd told Georgia he'd be back at seven in the morning. She'd have an hour to bake the sausage and egg casserole. *A growing young man like Lonnie would probably enjoy a nice hot breakfast before he starts to work.*

Harold cleaned the front patio, stocked the refrigerator with bottled water and soda, then opened the front screen door to let the warm spring breeze blow into the living room. He pulled up the old metal chair on the small patio, sipped his coffee, and read the morning newspaper.

He glanced at his watch. Six fifty-five. Lonnie would arrive soon. So far, the street had been quiet, except for the sputtering engine of a neighbor's VW backing out of their driveway. He'd nearly finished his coffee when the screen door squeaked. Georgia poked her head out the door. "Isn't Lonnie coming? It's twenty minutes after seven."

Preoccupied with a news story, Harold hadn't noticed. "Oh. Well, he has to pick up the tile this morning. Probably running behind," he said, returning to reading.

Georgia reached for Harold's coffee cup. "I'll make another pot of coffee."

Harold nodded, engrossed in the article.

Georgia returned to the porch every few minutes.

"Stop worrying, dear!" Harold pleaded. "I'm sure he'll be here."

It wasn't long before forty-five minutes had passed, then an hour. Georgia came unglued.

"All right, I'll call Lonnie right now," Harold assured her. "We'll see what's going on."

Harold dialed the number, but there was no answer except for a beep to leave a voicemail. Perturbed, he left a message and then walked outside. Standing on the sidewalk, he looked up and down the street. There was no sign of Lonnie's white pick-up truck.

It was already nine o'clock. Harold and Georgia didn't know whether to feel worried—or mad.

Feeling irritated, Harold dialed his friend's number. "Ray? It's Harold. Have you heard from Lonnie today?"

"No." There was a pause. "I thought he was going to your place."

"He was supposed to be here over two hours ago."

"I don't know anything about it. Good luck."

The receiver clicked. Harold expected a little more help than that from Ray. Wouldn't an uncle know what his nephew was doing?

As the day grew long, Harold and Georgia's patience wore thin. Repeated calls to Lonnie had returned no response. When they sat down to dinner, the phone rang. Harold raced to answer it, ready to give Lonnie a piece of his mind. *He'd better have a good explanation for not showing up.*

But it wasn't Lonnie. It was Ray's ex-wife, Starla. Georgia noticed the look of disappointment on her husband's face.

"Harold, the news about Lonnie leaving you high and dry is all over town. I haven't seen him, but when I came home from work a few minutes ago, I noticed that some of his belongings are missing—and the credit card I keep in my jewelry box is gone."

The phone connection started to break up. Harold heard Starla mention something about Ray and her grandmother's diamond ring. He couldn't make out the rest of the conversation.

What did it matter now? He'd heard enough. For whatever reason, Lonnie was gone—and so was Harold and Georgia's money.

Further attempts to contact Ray weren't successful either. Something strange was going on, and he would have to get to the bottom of it.

The next few days were unsettling. Harold and Georgia had filed a police report and contacted the sheriff, but there was no word about Lonnie—or Ray. Rumors spread throughout the small town. "That boy's a thief," Edward Smithers said, citing construction materials taken from his garage. Beatrice and Suzette, two ladies who worked at the laundry, were sure Lonnie was using drugs.

Lonnie was a thief, all right. Harold could barely contain his anger. All the money he and Georgia had saved for house repairs was gone.

Georgia became depressed and cried a lot. Harold tried to console her, but it was hard to do because he was filled with anger.

"He took our money and our dignity," Harold told the news reporter the following day. "We trusted him with our home, possessions, and investment," Harold snapped. "I will never forgive such insolence."

Did I let those words slip? Georgia always said he was one of the most forgiving people she'd ever met. He felt embarrassed and ashamed, but he couldn't help it. His anger ran deep.

The police and sheriff's department conducted a thorough search, but neither Lonnie—nor Harold and Georgia's money— could be located.

A rumor circulated that Lonnie had fled out of state, but no one knew. And no one had seen Ray, either. Harold had stopped by Ray's house several times, but there was no answer at the door, and the neighbors hadn't seen him.

Over the next year, Harold and Georgia scrimped to rebuild their savings. Lonnie had left them in a mess. It would take months to save what they'd lost.

Harold had always been trusting, but now he was cautious in business dealings. It wouldn't be easy to discern who might be reputable—or who might deceive him.

One afternoon, the doorbell rang. Harold opened the door but remained behind the locked screen. It was hard to see clearly through the tinted screen, but he could tell the man was shabbily dressed and unshaven.

"Mr. Spencer?"

Harold paused, confused. *Who is this man, and why does he know my name?* Harold squinted to see through the screen. The man looked like a bum. Probably just looking for handouts. Harold was ready to shut the door in the man's face, but something kept him from doing so. There was something familiar about the sound of the man's voice. Harold knew who it was as he pressed his face onto the screen. *Lonnie.*

Harold felt his face turn hot. His first inclination was to slam the door and call the police. But instead, he stood there, dumbfounded, gaping at the unkempt young man who kept his gaze downward.

"Don't you know...who I am?" the shaky voice asked.

Harold cleared his throat. "Yes," he quipped. "I remember, all right!" he shouted.

"I'm...I'm sorry. I came here to...apologize. I want to tell you I truly regret..."

Harold shook his head. "You stole..." His words faded as he gazed at Lonnie's torn shirt, ratty trousers, and boots with a hole in the toe.

"Why? Why did you do it?"

Lonnie looked down as he began to weep. Harold opened the screen door. "Come in," he said.

"Okay," Lonnie replied with a ragged breath as he stepped into the entry.

Harold's gaze met Lonnie's sad eyes. He looked like a lost boy.

"I want to tell you what happened, Mr. Spencer. I got caught up with some bad people. Got trapped in the dirty business of drug deals and money laundering," he said, his voice quivering. "I'm so sorry."

Harold vacillated between sympathy and anger. "We didn't know what was going on," he began gently. "At first, we were worried something had happened," Harold said, his voice rising. "Then we got angry when you didn't show up and never returned our phone calls. Starla said you'd left, and Ray didn't know where you were, and then Ray disappeared. And so did our money," he said, fuming. "What happened to our *money*?" Harold said, lashing out.

"They took it," Lonnie responded grimly. "Things got worse. I was thrown in jail in Mexico. Thought I'd never get out..." Lonnie's voice broke.

Harold's anger dissipated as he realized other factors contributed to Lonnie's disappearance. He offered Lonnie a seat in the living room.

Then, Georgia appeared from around the corner in the kitchen. She took small steps with her walker to reach the living room. The chemotherapy made her weak and tired.

"I thought I heard some emotional words of apology coming from here," Georgia said softly. She shook her head and looked at the scraggly man sitting in their living room chair.

"Hello, Mrs. Spencer."

Georgia adjusted her glasses. "Lonnie?"

"Yeah...it's *me*."

Georgia's lip twisted as she lowered her eyes.

"I'm so ashamed," Lonnie cried as he knelt on the floor before Georgia.

"I'm sorry. Please forgive me." Tears streamed down his face.

Georgia leaned forward, brushing back the stringy, sand-colored hair that fell into Lonnie's eyes.

"It's okay, Lonnie," she said. "Please sit down."

Lonnie sat down as Harold brought him a glass of water. He took a sip, then sucked in a deep breath.

"Harold, I know you thought my Uncle Ray was a friend," Lonnie began.

Harold felt puzzled.

"I'm sorry, but he wasn't. He was lying. It was a set-up," Lonnie explained. "Ray called me after I began working on your house that morning. He threatened to...hurt my mom...if I didn't lie about the tile and take the money...and...Lonnie's voice broke. "I never wanted to...*steal*...from anyone. I had to leave your house because of him."

Harold cupped his hand over his mouth in thought. "That explains why I never heard back from you—or Ray."

Lonnie nodded. "You wouldn't believe the schemes he had planned in this town. And Georgia," he stammered. "I want to thank you for the envelope..."

"The *envelope*?" Harold interjected. "My *money*?"

"No. I'm not talking about the money. I'm talking about...."

"The metal token," Georgia said with a smile.

"What metal token?" Harold asked.

"Let me explain, Mr. Spencer," Lonnie said. "Ray had it all figured out. He threatened Mom and me, then forced me to drive him to Mexico. He made me turn over the money to him. I removed the bills from the envelope so he could count them, then stuffed the empty envelope into my back pocket.

"A group of men were waiting for him when we crossed the border. They took my wallet and my truck, then punched me. I blacked out. When I woke up, I was lying on the cement floor of a jail cell.

"A guard searched me. There was nothing in my pockets except the crumpled-up envelope. The guard threw it on the floor of my cell. When he left, I picked it up. That's when I noticed the small token inside."

Georgia nodded.

"It's a small, thin piece of brass with a symbol of a cross on one side. On the other side," he said, choking up, it says, 'Jesus Saves.' " Lonnie's voice broke. "It's true. Jesus saved me."

Georgia's eyes moistened.

Harold's mouth dropped open.

"I couldn't be caught with an object, so I buried it in a crack in the floor. I thought about the words on the token. I repeated them every morning and every night, down on my knees on the cold cement floor. *Jesus saves. Jesus saves.* All those months, I didn't think I'd make it out of there. Then, one morning, the guard released me." Lonnie looked down. "I know it was because of..."

"Jesus," Harold replied, as he tried to swallow his emotion.

Georgia grasped Lonnie's hand. "I'm sorry, Lonnie. We had no idea what you went through," she said softly.

Lonnie looked up. "Thank you for sharing your faith with me, Mrs. Spencer," he said. "I can't tell you how much it meant. But there is something I need from you and Mr. Spencer. Forgiveness."

Harold recalled the sadness in Lonnie's eyes when he'd opened the screen door. Now, that sadness was replaced with a look of hope.

Georgia spoke without hesitation. "Of course, Lonnie, we forgive you."

Lonnie took in a ragged breath and clasped Georgia in a tight hug. "Thank you," he cried.

Harold recalled how he'd insisted earlier that he'd never

forgive this man. But everything had changed now. Harold summoned up the courage to get the words out. It wasn't as difficult as he had imagined. "I forgive you, too, Lonnie," he said, noting the tension easing in Lonnie's face. What a feeling. It was as if a weight had been lifted from his shoulders.

He turned to Georgia. "So, you put the token in the envelope?"

"Yes, dear. You never know when you'll need to share your faith," she said, winking at Lonnie. "I'm going to heat the dinner. Will you join us, Lonnie?"

"Sure, Mrs. Spencer. I'd like that." Lonnie cleared his throat. "But I have a request," he said quietly. "I'd like to pray before the meal if you don't mind."

"Yes, Lonnie. We'd be glad to have you say the prayer," Harold remarked.

After Georgia set the food out, they took their places at the table. "I have something to say. Lonnie," Georgia said, catching his gaze. "Will you forgive Harold and me for misjudging you?"

"Of course," Lonnie responded with a nod.

Then, they bowed their heads in prayer.

—

Harold and Georgia had blamed Lonnie for stealing their money and their dignity, but not knowing the truth, they'd judged him wrongly. He'd returned asking for their forgiveness, but now, it was their turn to ask for *his* forgiveness.

Sometimes, things aren't as they appear.

—

To everyone's relief, Ray was convicted and arrested. When the police investigation was complete, the money was recovered and returned. As initially planned, Lonnie would take care of Georgia and Harold's renovations after all.

A simple act of faith can go a long way. When Georgia placed the metal token in the envelope, she never knew what a blessing it would be for Lonnie. In a desperate situation, he'd found hope.

We open the door to good things when we share our belief in Christ. By sharing, we give of ourselves, and by giving, we also receive.

Good things come from sharing God's Word. We never know when something we do or say might make a big difference in someone's life, just as it did for Lonnie.

Our verse for study today is from the Book of Philemon, the sixth chapter. These writings stemmed from Paul's letter to Colossian church leader, Philemon. Paul thanks Philemon for his faith in Jesus Christ and for his love. He also tells him that he keeps him in prayer (Philemon 1:6), saying, "*I pray that your partnership with us in the faith may be effective...*"

In verse seven, Paul thanks Philemon for his love, stating that it gave him "*great joy and encouragement,*" for he had "*refreshed the hearts of the Lord's people.*"

In verse ten, Paul appealed to Philemon to forgive and free his slave, Onesimus, who had become a Christian. Through his release, Onesimus would be able to practice his faith freely. Paul had confidence in Philemon and trusted that he would accept his advice.

Paul not only gave thanks to Philemon, but he prayed for him and shared his beliefs with him. In turn, Philemon acted on behalf of Onesimus. He forgave and set him free, allowing Onesimus to practice and share his faith with others.

Instead of being enslaved, Onesimus was treated as a brother in Christ.

By forgiving Onesimus, Philemon showed he trusted him. They shared something in common: their faith in Jesus Christ.

Sharing is an action, an act of giving. As Paul says in today's verse from Philemon 1:6, this type of sharing will result in a "deepening [of] your understanding of every good thing we share for the sake of Christ."

In a sense, Lonnie was enslaved, too—by the deception of sin. If it hadn't been for Georgia sharing her faith when she placed the token in the envelope, Lonnie might never have known about Jesus' saving grace and the good things He provides for those who believe in Him.

And that's *one good thing*.

Worksheet for My Daily Morsel #22

Personal Insight:
Have you shared—or will you share—your faith with someone? Explain.

_____

_____

_____

_____

If so, what *good things* came from the sharing—for them—and you?

_____

_____

_____

_____

Reflection: My "One Good Thing"
Referring to today's verse from Philemon 1:6, what *good thing* comes to mind when you think about Christ's presence in your life?

_____

_____

_____

Everyone is blessed with individual talents or abilities. Lonnie had expertise in carpentry. In what way has God blessed you with skills or abilities? How might you share your faith using your talents?

_____

_____

_____

Today's Serving: God's Counsel Through Sharing Faith

Paul spent time counseling Philemon and sharing his faith with him. In turn, Philemon shared his faith with his slave, Onesimus. Georgia didn't have the opportunity to meet with Lonnie to speak about faith; however, when she placed the token in the envelope, she hoped it would benefit him. Then, when Lonnie sought forgiveness, she further counseled him as a new believer in Christ.

A Cupful of Reality:

Some people learn lessons the hard way. How might you deal with a "Lonnie" in your life? What would you do to influence them to believe in Christ?

_____

_____

_____

_____

A Taste of Spiritual Nourishment:

In today's verse from Philemon comes a key word, *active*. Faith is an essential component of our belief. We can have faith on the inside, but we need to *exercise* faith to put it to work. God didn't create us to be idle, but instead to act. We have hands to serve, feet to take us where we need to go, ears to hear and listen, eyes to see ahead and look to Christ, and a heart to hold love and compassion as we serve others.

What is one thing you can actively do to express your faith?

_____

_____

_____

_____

The "Table of Optimism":

Hope resides at the Table of Optimism. What is your hope for today?

Prayer for Today:

Dear Father in heaven,

Like Georgia, I would like to be confident in professing Your Word. Please give me the courage to share my faith with the Lonnies of the world. Using the gifts You have given me, help me to be aware of those who are in need of hearing the good news of the Gospel. In Jesus's name, amen.

Recipe

My Daily Morsel #23

Prep Time _____   Cook Time _____

Oven Temp _____   Serves _____

Topic: **Sharing in the Community**

_____
_____
_____
_____
_____
_____

Bible Verse for Study

"If you come with us, we will share with you whatever **good things** the LORD gives us."

Numbers 10:32

_____
_____
_____
_____

GIVE ME SHELTER

I couldn't help but grin as I pulled the car away from the curb. Freedom! Mom wouldn't be squirming in the passenger seat, saying, "Eek!" every time I made a left turn into traffic. And no more of Dad's broken-record sermons about pumping the brakes in the rain. Now that I had my driver's license, I could drive without their comments and criticism.

The Fairlane hummed—until I hit a pothole on the neighboring street. I should have been watching where I was going. At least it was just a bump. I hadn't run into anything. When I reached the intersection at 30th Street and Baseline, I was relieved to turn left without waiting for oncoming traffic.

I pressed my foot down on the accelerator and watched the speedometer rise, feeling confident as I kept up with the fifty-five mile-per-hour speed limit. Ha! What a feeling—driving on my own!

It was a sunny May afternoon. The vinyl seats began to warm up, so I rolled the window down. *Yeah.* Just in time to hear the chorus of a Rolling Stones' hit. I let my voice ring out, right along with Mick. That was something I could never do with my parents in the car.

The times were changing. Even our quiet university town was not immune from the social unrest fueled by the Vietnam War. Boulder had become a mecca for hippies, vagrants, and transients. They flocked in by the hundreds to "The Hill," a popular university shopping district, which became a gathering place for these sorts.

299

Dad's stern words echoed in my mind. "Stay away from The Hill." He wasn't kidding.

I'd never gotten into serious trouble. I was a good student, attended church and youth group, and was active in Camp Fire Girls. I listened to my parents most of the time. But Dad knew I was impressionable, and he was concerned I might be swayed by the Hippie culture that had invaded our community. I'd just turned seventeen.

Energized by the music, I cranked up the radio while cruising 30th Street. Such a feeling of freedom! My parents agreed with me taking the car to the mall and the library.

Unleashed happiness burst through me as a smile erupted. I shopped at the mall, happily purchasing the clothing of the time: a tie-dye shirt, bell-bottom jeans, and a fringed leather bag. My parents probably would disapprove of my purchases, but I was old enough to make my own choices, especially since I was paying for these items with my own money.

After purchasing the items, I hurried to the restroom to change into my new "threads" and switched my old purse for the new fringe bag.

I felt rather sly as I maneuvered the Fairlane onto 13th Street. My car radio blared, the melody mixing with other vehicle radios and the rhythms of curb-side guitarists, tambourine-shakers, and Hare Krishna chanters. The sidewalk teemed with people, colors, and sounds. The heart of the hippie community was a feast for the eyes and ears.

Traffic inched along the Hill. *Ka-plunk*. The Fairlane jerked as I struggled to switch my foot between the clutch and the gas pedal.

"Hey, baby," a guy on the curb shouted. "Want me 'ta drive that thing for ya'?" My face turned warm. I pretended I didn't hear what he said and was relieved when the Fairlane reached the top of the hill.

I searched for a parking place. None were available in front of the merchant shops, but I found a spot in a residential area two blocks away.

Removing items from my shopping bag, I put on the beaded headband I'd bought, adjusting it in the rearview mirror. The colors blended with my blue, pink, and purple tie-dye shirt. *I'll fit in with the crowd now.*

I felt a smile break loose, but guilt stepped in. Dad's lecture— *Don't go near The Hill.* I shook my head. I was seventeen now— not a kid. I'd been sheltered long enough, but now I was holding the car key. *Ha.* With a clang, I threw them into my purse and rechecked my image in the mirror. *Cool.*

Walking the tree-lined sidewalk toward the shops, I sensed the faint aroma of incense. Everybody was burning that stuff these days. There was another odor, too, sweet and musky. I guessed it was marijuana.

As I reached the main street where the crowds gathered, I was surprised that the hippies looked older than I'd thought. Most were in their late twenties or thirties—or older. They gathered in groups on the sidewalks and on the street corners. Many had long, stringy hair and wore dirty clothing. These people weren't just hippies—they were vagrants—street people. Maybe even homeless.

The stench of body odor made my stomach turn. Incense wafting through the air only partly disguised the disgusting smell.

I'd expected to see people about my age, plus the college crowd, milling around The Hill and frequenting the merchant shops. But the vagrants were different. One shirtless man with long gray hair pranced on the sidewalk before me, arms waving about, talking to himself. Weird. I stepped off the curb to get around him.

Approaching an intersection to cross the street, I tried not to stare at the long-haired bikers wearing jackets with the letters "S.T.P." I'd heard of a drug by that name. A shiver coursed down my back as a wiry, gray-bearded man stared at me with glazed eyes. His ankles were as skinny as my wrists, and his face weathered and wrinkled. I quickly looked away and picked up my pace as I crossed the street.

The colorful sights and sounds of the crowded city block permeated my senses. A guru wearing an orange Madras shirt chanted words I didn't understand. A transient sat on a blanket, strumming a guitar beside him while a young girl in skimpy clothing swiveled her hips as he played. A woman dressed in a free-flowing gypsy skirt caressed a lamp pole as she danced around it. A wolf whistle sounded out as a crowd of admirers watched. I felt uneasy and quickened my pace.

The end of the block was less crowded and not as intimidating. I stopped to look at beaded jewelry in a store window. Walking into the shop, something caught on my pant leg. As I looked down, it wasn't some*thing* but some*one*.

"Gotcha, girly!" A toothless man laughed, crouched down on the entryway floor; he'd grasped the cuff of my bell-bottom pants in his hands.

"Let go!" I jerked my leg away. Laughter hissed between his missing teeth. *Crazy man.*

I hurried through the entrance and turned into a store aisle, Crazy Man's cackling voice behind me. My pulse raced. I stepped into an aisle to compose myself and then walked to the checkout, but there was a line of people waiting to pay. Music blared from the speakers behind the counter. I tried to get the cashier's attention.

"That man over there is..."

"You need to get in line," the cashier snapped.

"You don't understand," I began. But she wasn't listening. "He's bothering people!" I said in a raised voice. No one seemed to notice.

I stalled for time, looking at the merchandise in each aisle. I felt like leaving the store, but Crazy Man was still sitting next to the door, so I continued shopping. After perusing each aisle of the store, other undesirables gathered out front. *Oh, great.* I wasn't going to leave now.

I browsed the aisles I'd already been through but couldn't focus on shopping. It didn't seem important now. All I could think about was not feeling safe in this place.

The commotion of people gathering outside created a low roar of conversation that filtered through the store. Minutes later, the store became strangely quiet. People suddenly dispersed, including the undesirables out front. Something wasn't right.

Then, the loud crack of a gunshot rang out. Panic coursed through me as I ran to the back of the store and ducked behind a display. I got down on the floor, shaking. *Dear God, help! Someone has a gun!*

I tried to breathe without making a noise. My heart pounded. Dad had warned me to stay away, but I didn't listen. If there was any time I needed the safety of my parents' shelter, it was now.

A single deep voice came from the front of the store. I couldn't make out the words. I heard scuffling. A woman's timid voice. Then silence.

I peeked out of the side of the display. Then, footsteps came my way. *God, help me!*

A man with dark hair in a yellow vest approached. He was an employee. I let out an audible sigh.

He knelt next to me. "Are you okay?"

I looked up. "Yes," I replied. "Just shaken up." My voice quivered. "Was the loud noise a gunshot?"

The clerk nodded. "Yep. We got robbed," he said solemnly. "But don't worry," he motioned, lifting a hand. "He took off, but we called the police. They're on their way. It's safe for you to come out now."

The clerk helped me to my feet. My knees ached from hunching down. "Where did he shoot the gun?" I asked.

"Into the wall. Fortunately, it didn't hit anyone. I think it was a scare tactic."

I blew out a deep breath. "Whew. I'm glad no one was hurt."

"Yeah."

I thanked him for his help as I headed for the exit.

"Wait, miss!" he said, walking toward me.

I turned to face him.

"The police will have questions. I need you to stay."

I felt numb as I followed the employee to the front counter. My heart raced. I'd never been questioned by the police before.

I hadn't regretted my actions earlier when I'd changed into *this* clothing and donned the beaded headband and accessories. But now, I felt ashamed. I should never have come here. My father was right.

A husky officer with sandy hair questioned the clerks and then approached me. I trembled as I looked up at the officer to answer his questions. *No.* I didn't see the man who fired the shot, and I didn't see him rob the store. *No.* I didn't have anything to do with the crowd that had gathered in the street. I could only describe Crazy Man and the sudden quietness I'd noticed before hearing the gunshot.

When the officer asked what I was doing on The Hill, I felt like slinking to the floor. He asked my name, where I was from, and if I was a student. I nervously nodded, "Yes." He assumed I was a college student. I was relieved he didn't prod further, and I was free to go.

I passed by the front checkout. The cashier, who hadn't listened to me earlier, looked somber. "I'm sorry," she said.

"Yeah. Me, too," I responded quietly. I crossed the threshold of the store entrance. There were no more vagrants—and no Crazy Man hanging around the store, but I felt nervous and afraid. The store manager made sure I made it back to my car safely. He felt badly that the cashier hadn't paid attention to me. I didn't know for sure, but I wondered if Crazy Man was a set-up for what would occur later in the day.

I should have been happy that I wasn't approached by the thief wielding the gun, but fear gnawed at me. Tonight's incident would surely end up in tomorrow's newspaper. I couldn't sleep that night. The policeman had asked for my name and phone number. What if he had other questions and called our house? What if my father learned I'd disobeyed and gone to The Hill? I couldn't imagine the consequences—and him finding out I was in the store when the robbery occurred.

The Hill proved to be a harsh lesson. Sin interfered with the good things my parents wanted for me—and what God wanted for me. To be safe. To be sheltered. Because of my wrongdoing, I'd stepped away from safety and into a place I didn't belong.

Lured by worldly things, I'd ingested the bait of the deceiver, wrongly believing I could disregard the rules of the establishment.

I thought I needed freedom to escape the shelter of my overprotective parents. Instead, I found myself in a place that offered little protection. I thought the hippie community would be a peace-loving group, but it wasn't what I thought it would be.

My footsteps of free choice led me away from my parents' sheltering love—and God's.

Growing up, other than being in a few power-depleting rainstorms, I had never needed food, clothing, or "a roof over my head," as Mom would say. Instead, I was fortunate to have been raised in a loving, God-centered home. But instead of appreciating what I had, I'd dismissed my shelter and protection—an extension of God's love for me.

In the tenth chapter of the Book of Numbers, Moses and the Israelites set out from the Desert of Sinai. The Lord's presence was hidden in a mysterious cloud as they traveled with the Ark of the Covenant. Imagine what the people must have thought as the cloud followed them.

According to Scripture, the cloud would set down when it was time for Moses and the people to set camp for the night. Then, when it was time to break camp, the cloud lifted, and the people resumed travel.

Then, Moses ran into an issue. He said to Hobab (who was either Moses's brother in law or father in law), "*We are setting out for the place about which the Lord said, 'I will give it to you.' Come with us and we will treat you well, for the Lord has promised good things to Israel*" (Numbers 10:29).

But Hobab didn't want to go. He wanted to do things his way, returning to his own land and people. Moses begged him not to leave, saying, "*You know where we should camp in the desert, and you can be our eyes*" (Numbers 10:31).

When Moses told him about the good things the Lord had in store that they would share, Hobab changed his mind and accompanied them. If he had gone his own way, the Israelites might have ended up without proper direction in a place that didn't provide the shelter they needed in a harsh environment.

The Lord desires good things for His people but wants His people to follow willingly. He didn't want us to behave like robots. Instead, He offers us free will to follow Him—or not.

Just as Moses tried to convince Hobab to do the right thing, my father lectured me in similar fashion. For me, The Hill was not the appropriate place to go, but like Hobab, I wanted to do things my way. I thought my decision would provide me with what I wanted, so I ignored his advice—even though he was knowledgeable about many things.

Children are taught to listen to their parents, trust them, and follow their directions. This is not unlike our heavenly Father, who expects us to do the same. In return for our obedience, He provides us with His sheltering love. God's love—what an incredible shelter that is!

It has been many years since the incident on The Hill. Occasionally, I see the old photos of the Ford Fairlane. The car is long gone, but the pleasant—and unpleasant memories surface. I was ungrateful when my parents punished me by taking away good things—the privilege of driving the car, or Dad imposing on my free time by making me do my math homework, or when Mom kept me from going places with people I considered to be "friends."

But one good thing they never took away was the shelter of their love for me.

What I wanted—personal freedom away from my parents—turned out to be a wrong turn, not just in the Fairlane. I thought I knew what was best, but I was wrong.

When leaving shelter, one is exposed to the elements. On The Hill, I was exposed to many undesirable people and things that were not good for me.

I thought of the rock song I used to listen to on the radio, "Gimme Shelter." Maybe the Stones knew something about seeking shelter that I didn't know.

As I got older, I realized the shelter my parents provided would only last a while. But *God's* love, the greatest refuge of all, would always be with me.

Following the Lord's guidance, I did my best to avoid the things that were not good for me—such as The Hill. I steered away from potholes and avoided wrong turns. I learned to follow God's Way—and all the good things He had in store for me.

And that's *one good thing.*

Worksheet for My Daily Morsel #23

Personal Insight:
Think of a time when you chose to do something your way instead of
how you were asked. What happened, and was there a consequence for
your decision?

_____

_____

_____

_____

Regarding the experience above, what would you do differently if faced
with the same situation now?

_____

_____

_____

_____

Reflection: My "One Good Thing"
Who has provided for you—sheltered you? How did they provide for
you?

_____

_____

_____

_____

What is *one good thing* that God's sheltering offers for you spiritually?

_____

_____

_____

_____

Today's Serving: God's Counsel through the Sharing of Shelter
Moses and his people had God's protection and shelter as they traveled
through the wilderness. As a young student, I had shelter, too, but didn't
realize how good I had it until I ran into a difficult situation.

Moses, the Israelites, and I had something good to be thankful for. Events
could have continued to be harmful if certain people had not been put

in place to intervene. For Moses, that intervention was the help he received from Hobab. For me, it was the realization that shelter came from my parents and God's love for me.

A Cupful of Reality:
If you were to look back on your teenage years, what advice would you give your younger self about making good choices?

_____

_____

_____

_____

A Taste of Spiritual Nourishment:
In today's verse from the Book of Numbers comes a key word, *share*. Think of the things that you—or others—share. It's a warm feeling to know there is *goodness* in this world!

The "Table of Optimism":
Hope resides at the Table of Optimism. What is your hope for today?

_____

_____

_____

_____

Prayer for Today:
Dear Father in heaven,

Open my ears and my heart to be fully receptive to You. Please guide me to make the right decisions and look to You to keep my heart sheltered from worldly influences. Thank You for sheltering me with Your love. In Jesus's name, amen.

Recipe

<u>My Daily Morsel #24</u>

Prep Time _____

Cook Time _____

Oven Temp _____

Serves _____

Topic: **Sharing in the Word** _____
_____
_____
_____
_____
_____
_____

Bible Verse for Study

"Nevertheless, the one who receives instruction in the word should share all **good things** with their instructor."

Galatians 6:6

_____
_____
_____
_____

CLASSROOM JITTERS: DAY ONE

Marcia nervously readied herself for her first day of teaching. She'd set her alarm early, already picking out her dress, shoes, and jewelry. Sliding on a favorite bracelet, she took one long last look in the mirror. Her sandy blonde hair curled at her shoulders, and her new tan pumps matched nicely with her light brown corduroy skirt and almond-colored blouse. She was ready on the outside, but was she prepared on the inside?

She gripped her hands on the steering wheel as she started the car. *Please help me get through this day, Lord.*

There would be no assistant today, no expert standing beside her to turn to for guidance. She looked at her watch, sucked in a deep breath, and prepared to greet her class.

The morning was off to a good start with student introductions. However, as Marcia delved into the lesson, she found her plan to "share and impart knowledge" wasn't working. The boy in the second row with fuzzy hair repeatedly got out of his seat. A girl with freckles and curly pigtails refused to answer questions. Two boys in the back of the classroom made disruptive noises even though Marcia asked them to stop. The contagion spread quickly. Kids talked out of turn and fidgeted in their seats. One pupil launched a paper airplane from the back of the room, nearly hitting her in the face.

Marcia's usually calm demeanor took a stand of defense, as a surge of heat rose to her cheeks. Thoughts raced through her mind. How could she teach a lesson to children who wouldn't listen?

At recess, after she'd dismissed the children to the care of the playground supervisor, Marcia retreated to a quiet corner of the classroom. She flipped off the light, plopped into a chair, and bowed her head. She felt desperate and hoped God would hear her prayers.

But the afternoon didn't go much better. By the end of the day, Marcia could barely contain herself. As the last student exited the classroom, she dashed to the restroom to dab cold water on her puffy eyes. As she entered the hallway, she saw a familiar face. It was Beverly, the experienced teacher from down the hall.

Beverly stopped, her chin-length espresso bob tilting, as she met Marcia's gaze with compassionate brown eyes. "Are you all right?"

Marcia swallowed. "No," she said, wiping moisture from her cheek.

"Can I help?"

Marcia nodded.

Beverly led her to a vacant meeting room with comfortable seating. "We can chat privately here, Marcia."

"Thank you," Marcia responded, taking a seat.

"Tell me what happened," Beverly said gently.

"All the training I had...maybe I'm not meant to teach," Marcia said, looking down as tears dripped onto her new leather pumps.

Beverly handed her a tissue. "It's only your first day, isn't it?"

Marcia nodded.

"I'm not surprised if you feel overwhelmed. I felt that way the first day I taught."

"Good....I mean, not good, but at least I'm not alone in my feelings," Marcia responded as she wiped her nose with a tissue.

"Let me take one guess," Beverly remarked. "Did you have an issue with discipline?"

"I sure did," Marcia said, wiping perspiration from her brow.

"Discipline is challenging whether you are a new or experienced teacher," Beverly added. "It's an age-old problem, but it gets easier as time passes."

"I hope so," Marcia said, raising her palms. "I don't understand what happened. The day started just fine, but everything went downhill after the first lesson." She closed her eyes momentarily and supported her forehead with one hand. "I knew what I was supposed to do, but the children wouldn't listen."

"Knowing what you're supposed to do is only half of it," Beverly replied, adjusting her tortoise-framed eyeglasses. Marcia looked up. Beverly's soft eyes glistened. "You'll see, Marcia," she said. "Come with me," she motioned.

Marcia followed Beverly into the corridor, their footsteps echoing in the quietness. Beverly unlocked the door to her classroom. "Notice the wording of my poster above the chalkboard."

"Okay." Marcia looked up, noting the colorful title, "Student Rules and Responsibilities." She read each rule aloud: "(1) Listen the first time, (2) Pay attention to the teacher and your classmates, (3) Be respectful of others and yourself."

Bev lifted a hand. "The *responsibilities* are the other half I was talking about."

"Oh," Marcia responded. "Now I understand. I'd put so much pressure on myself to succeed in teaching the lesson that I forgot to tell the students what I expected."

"Teaching is a huge responsibility. It can feel like the whole world is on your shoulders," Beverly said. "And you're right—the students need to know what you expect from them."

"I'll be doing that. Bright and early tomorrow morning," Marcia exclaimed. She let out a sigh and thanked her new mentor.

"You're going to do fine," Beverly assured her. "Remember that teaching is a two-way street. I know. I've been there," she said. "Besides," she added, "If something *good* hadn't come from my experience in the classroom, I would have chosen another career."

Marcia went home that afternoon with a renewed sense of hope. Her tears belonged to a day that had passed away. Tomorrow would be a new start, and she knew what to do.

Her bracelet sparkled, as bright rays of the setting sun passed through the car window. It sparked a memory from Sunday School years before. The teacher gave shiny bracelets to the girls, the kind that formed a solid circle. The boys received leather bands. She remembered the teacher saying the solid circle was like their relationship with God—continuous and never-ending. Yes. It represents a reciprocal relationship: God as the Master Teacher and His children—the students.

Marcia hoped to have that kind of giving-and-receiving relationship with her students. She felt certain it was like the relationship God desired for her, too. As Marcia got ready for her second day in the classroom, she donned her favorite bracelet. With prayer and patience, she'd encourage her students to be responsible. She'd share her instruction with them—the way Beverly had shared with her.

—

The Bible has many references to teaching. One example is Paul's teaching in his letter to the churches of Galatia. He said to them, "*Nevertheless, the one who receives instruction in the word should share all good things with their instructor*" (Galatians 6:6).

When we communicate what we learn, it reinforces the material. This was true for the Christ-followers in the churches of Galatia. If they could share what they had learned from Paul, they would probably have a good understanding of what they'd been taught.

To share all good things with one's teacher is to reciprocate, communicate, impart, and relay knowledge back to the person who is teaching. Paul tells the Galatian churches to do good and carry each other's burdens (Galatians 6:2). In doing this, they would be fulfilling the law of Christ.

It was a confusing time for the Galatians and a frustrating time for Paul. He did his best to teach them to live by the New Covenant of Jesus Christ—the gospel—versus abiding by Old Testament law.

People from Judea came to Antioch and told the new Christians they had to be circumcised *"according to the custom taught by Moses,"* (Acts 15:1) or not be saved. This caused Paul to become angry with them, for this teaching was contrary to Christian beliefs. We can imagine how frustrated Paul must have been, trying to get them to understand they were no longer slaves of the law but had been freed by the truth of the Gospel of Jesus Christ. Paul must have been a patient man; anyone who teaches knows how frustrating it is to try to teach people who won't listen. Even Jesus's disciples challenged Him, saying His teachings were difficult to believe. For example, in the synagogue at Capernaum, Jesus taught the disciples about the symbolic partaking of His body and blood—our modern-day communion for the redemption of sin. Some of the disciples were not receptive to His teaching because they did not understand it. Jesus explained the teachings, but some of the disciples still did not comprehend them and didn't want to follow Him.

As their Master and Rabbi (teacher), Jesus wanted to impart and share the knowledge His heavenly Father gave him. Jesus expected the disciples to listen to Him, reveal what they had learned, and share it with others.

Throughout the Old and New Testaments, God called upon His people to listen and obey. Because of His love for them, He gave them a choice to believe or not to believe. Jesus did the same, according to the will of His Father. He gave the disciples a choice to follow Him.

Paul's teaching was confined to prison walls as he instructed the churches of Galatia through his letters. Jesus traveled by foot to many towns and communities to share the good news.

Now, thousands of years later, you and I—and others—have benefitted from those who shared their teachings with others.

Marcia wanted her students to benefit, and the Lord answered her prayers through Beverly's help and wisdom. As a result, Marcia gained renewed confidence in herself, and in time, her students learned to share what they had learned with her and others.

Good things come from sharing God's Word!

And that's *one good thing*!

Worksheet for My Daily Morsel #24

Personal Insight:
When have you felt inspired by what you learned? How did this impact you, and how did you use what you learned to better yourself—or others?

_____

_____

_____

_____

Reflection: My "One Good Thing"
Think of a time when you received instruction in God's Word, whether through a sermon, Bible study, Sunday School, or other classroom teaching. What is one thing you would share with your instructor?

_____

_____

_____

_____

Today's Serving: God's Counsel through Sharing in the Word
Paul instructed the Galatians to share what they had learned, and Jesus traveled to many towns, villages, and hillsides to teach. That was then. But even now, teachers know that if students share what they have learned, they understand what they have been taught.

Marcia's mentor, Beverly, was instrumental in helping her. Marcia related to Beverly what she had learned, thus facilitating the instruction of her students.

A Cupful of Reality:
Teachers have a responsibility to teach, but students are responsible for learning. As a teacher—or student—what obstacle have you overcome in teaching or learning, and what *good thing* came from it?

_____

_____

_____

_____

A Taste of Spiritual Nourishment:
From today's verse in Galatians comes a key word, *instruction*. When I was young, my favorite part of going to the buffet at Furr's Cafeteria was choosing from the vast selection of desserts. I couldn't get my eyes off the cake with detailed piping, puddings with soft swirls of whipped cream, and intricately decorated cookies. The instruction we receive from God's Word can be detailed, too, but it is richer than a dessert and filled with nutritional value for our souls!

The "Table of Optimism":
Hope resides at the Table of Optimism. What is your hope for today?

_____

_____

_____

_____

Prayer for Today:

Dear Father in heaven:

I prayerfully request that You facilitate my ability to communicate with others and realize the importance and significance of these relationships. Enable me to give of my heart to encourage and help others openly. Sustain me in Your love and compassion. Keep my heart ready, waiting, and willing to dwell richly in Your Word so that I may share what I learn with others. In Jesus's name, amen.

Recipe

My Daily Morsel #25

Prep Time

Cook Time

Oven Temp

Serves

Topic: **Nothing without God**

Bible Verse for Study

"I say to the LORD, 'You are my Lord; apart from you I have no **good thing**.'"

Psalm 16:2

BECCA'S CONNECTION

Becca's bright blonde hair framed her wide blue eyes, and when she smiled, her toothless grin brightened the pink color of her freckled cheeks. Our five-year-old daughter had a curious nature. She wanted to know how the world worked.

One afternoon, we were in the back yard. Becca ran up to my husband, bubbling with excitement. She was full of questions, and today was no exception.

"What are you doing, Daddy?"

"I'm tilling the garden, Sweetie."

"What does that mean?" she asked, wrinkling her nose. She did this when she wasn't sure about something.

"It means I'm digging in the soil to prepare it for planting the seeds. All trees, plants, and flowers on the earth need soil to grow."

My husband noticed the puzzled look on Becca's face. She was thinking hard about something.

"Daddy," she paused, "the earth must be the biggest thing in the whole world!"

I noticed the expression of surprise on my husband's face. An eloquent speaker, he was stumped for words.

"I think you're right, Sweetie. The earth is the biggest thing in the whole world."

Our little girl had just touched on a significant connection about our existence. Her statement caught my husband off-guard.

Later, we talked about Becca's comment. "She's so little," my husband said, shaking his head. "How could she possibly perceive the size of the world?"

"Good question," I shrugged.

Our daughter was intrigued by nature. She loved spending time in the back yard and developed a passion for the vegetable garden. It became her favorite subject, and she couldn't stop talking about it—and she talked a lot.

My husband bought a child-sized rake and let her help. When it was time to plant vegetables, Becca held out her tiny hand, eager to receive the seeds he placed in her palm.

"This is how you make the indentation in the soil," he said, pressing his index finger into the moist dirt. He took a few seeds and placed them in the spot he'd made in the soil, then let Becca make the holes in the dirt for the rest of the seeds.

These seeds would produce a garden, sprouting corn, green onions, beans, peas, zucchini, tomatoes, and small watermelons.

Every evening after dinner, Becca couldn't wait to race to the backyard to check on the plants in the garden. My husband would hand her the sprayer, and she'd happily water the garden—and partly shower herself in the process.

Days later, one afternoon before my husband got home from work, Becca yelled from the backyard. "Mommy! Come quick!"

I dashed outside, thinking something was wrong. To my relief, Becca was hopping up and down excitedly.

"Look, Mommy!" she squealed. "My plants are growing!"

I bent down. Sure enough, the seedlings she planted had developed tiny green tendrils. She could hardly contain her excitement.

The next evening, while my husband was on a business call, I stepped into the garden. Becca skipped over to me, then stopped.

"Mommy?" she said, looking up.

"Yes?"

"God gives us water to grow plants, doesn't He?"

"Yes, He does."

"And He made the dirt, Mommy?"

"Yes. You're right about that."

It was a short conversation. She ran off to play. Then, a few minutes later, she heard the faint chirping of baby birds in our Eucalyptus tree.

"Mommy!" she called. "There's a birdie up there with babies!"

She wanted to see into the nest. I explained that the mommy bird built the nest high in the tree to keep the babies safe. The mama bird was probably glad it was safe from us, too.

Although Becca didn't yet understand all the intricate workings of the web of life, she understood basic things that went together: plants needed water and soil to grow; birds needed nests in safe places for protection, and children had mommies, daddies, or others to love and care for them.

Becca's curiosity didn't end there. She wanted to know more about things that go together. At the breakfast table, she pressed her lips together in thought.

"Mommy," she said, with a serious expression. "Does the whole world go together with God?"

Now, it was my turn to be caught off-guard. Her bright blue eyes locked with mine. She was waiting for my answer.

I hesitated. "Yes, honey. ...The whole world goes together with God, but,..." my voice trailed off. Satisfied with my answer, Becca asked to be excused from the table.

I couldn't stop thinking about her question and the answer I meant to provide: *The whole world belongs to God, but not everyone wants to belong to Him.*

But, if I had explained this, would she understand why some people didn't believe in God as we did? I wasn't sure; however, she could think outside the box when she concluded the earth was the "biggest thing in the world" and assumed the whole world "goes together with God." Those were big thoughts for a child.

That night, Becca knelt by her bed to pray. She had big prayers, too. She thanked God for Daddy, me, her sister, her grandmas and grandpas, uncles, aunts, cousins, teachers, friends, and our three parakeets. Becca's world was near-perfect, where everyone connected to God, no one was left out, and no one was unloved. If only the real world could be like her perceived one!

Becca tried hard to understand our connection to God and how everyone fit into the big scheme of things. It was the beginning of a quest for knowledge for her that would continue. Admittedly, I was still trying to figure it out, too.

It's vital in understanding our verse for today from Psalm 16:2. Applied to our relationship with God, it's like finding the sweet spot where your cell phone has reception without interruption in service and you have instant access to communication. It's that way with God. He's available for us 24/7.

God responds to our wants, needs, and desires by answering our prayers. It's a beautiful two-way connection, a reciprocal relationship. His phone line is always open, but as in any relationship, we must be willing to be "on receive" and willing to listen.

Our five-year-old had a purely innocent understanding of the relationship we should have with God. She trusted He would care for her, our family, her friends, and our pets. She had no doubts that the doorway to God was always open. Such is the faith of a child. If only the world could be so trusting!

A connection intervenes and acts to join something together. Such it is with our relationship with God, as our hearts are united with Him, and nothing can separate us from His love. No matter what happens, we belong to Him. He will never leave us, and He loves us unconditionally.

Many verses in the Bible point to the connection we should have with God. Following are a few of those verses from the Book of Isaiah:

"I, even I, am the LORD, and apart from me there is no savior" (Isaiah 43:11).

"I am the first and I am the last; apart from me there is no God"

(Isaiah 44:6).

A third scripture entry addresses the earth in its entirety:

"Turn to me and be saved, all you ends of the earth; for I am God, and there is no other" (Isaiah 45:22).

God's Word is clear: He is the only one we are to follow.

I thought about our little girl's question about the whole world. With a pure heart and unquestioning faith, she believed everyone belonged to God.

I wished I could believe as she did. I searched my heart, for there were times I had questioned my faith. But truthfully, there is nothing wrong with asking questions, for it is one way we learn and gain understanding. However, there is a difference between questioning and questioning to the point of doubting to cause one's beliefs to disintegrate.

Also, my little girl's faith wasn't hindered by negative thoughts, as mine was at times. Becca's connection—and optimistic outlook—was one I needed to embrace.

Today's verse from Psalm 16:2 brings to light David's great faith in God and his connection with Him. However, for a period, he compromised that connection due to sin. Fortunately, he righted himself, renewed his faith, and reconnected to God.

David's words from the Psalm ring true. Apart from God, with a frayed or broken connection, we also step away from receiving the things that are good for us spiritually.

We are fortunate. To be in a relationship with our Creator and to be in contact with Him, we don't need a fancy WiFi connection or a premium cellular service. A way to think of this is that God is already "downloaded" into our hearts. He's always there, always available for us, 24/7.

I am continually amazed at God's creation and all He provides for us. My five-year-old understood this. She knew certain things go together: God and us.

My daughter devised a slogan combining her interest in gardening and her faith. With a huge grin on her face, while we were talking about God's creation and gardening, she said, "Mommy and Daddy, let's 'Plant God!' "

To plant the seed of God was David's quest, too—as it was ours. May we spread the good news of Jesus Christ so that, according to Becca, "the whole world goes together with God."

And that's *one good thing*.

Worksheet for My Daily Morsel #25

Personal Insight:
Name one way you feel connected to God. What good thing has resulted from your connection with Him?

_____

_____

_____

Reflection: My "One Good Thing"
No one else on earth is exactly like you (even twins have differences). Your Father in heaven created you to be unique. What *good thing* (or things) make you unique?

_____

_____

_____

Today's Serving: God's Counsel through Connection
In her own way, a little child understood we should have a connection to God. David understood this, too. Through our communication with Him, we maintain that connection. But we must watch for doubt or sin to interfere. To trust God is to have spiritual optimism because *good things* come from our relationship with Him.

A Cupful of Reality:
Doubt negatively interrupts our connection with God. Is there a time when you doubted God? Explain. Did you overcome your doubt?

_____

_____

_____

A Taste of Spiritual Nourishment:
In today's verse from the Psalms comes a key word, *apart*. Years ago, we had a navel orange tree in our backyard. I was in the backyard with our younger daughter, Beverly, when she picked up a round, shriveled object from beneath the tree. "This is yucky, Mommy. What is it?"

"It's an orange that fell off the tree."

"Why did it fall off the tree?"

"It was probably overripe and fell off."

"Why is it yucky looking?"

"Because when it fell off the tree, it couldn't get nourishment from the tree branch. That's how it gets fed."

"And that's why it got all yucky?"

"Yes, Honey. The orange couldn't survive. It turned rotten when it fell off the tree."

"Ew, I'm glad I didn't get rotted, Mommy," Beverly exclaimed.

"Yes, I'm glad of that, too, Sweetie," I said.

"Poor orange," she said, shaking her head.

I hugged my little girl. It was a perfect teaching moment: Jesus is the vine; we are the branches. What a beautiful truth, for we are nourished through Him.

The "Table of Optimism:"
Hope resides at the Table of Optimism. What is your hope for today?

_____

_____

_____

_____

Prayer for Today:
Dear Father in heaven:

Thank You for making me Your child and filling my life with *good things*. Sometimes, I need to be reminded that I am part of Your grand design and that You created me with a unique purpose. I am grateful for connections with family and friends and the opportunity to cross paths with others with whom I may provide help—or receive support. I am eternally thankful to be connected to You, my Lord, Savior, Counselor, Helper, and Redeemer. In Jesus's name, amen.

Recipe

My Daily Morsel #26

Prep Time

Cook Time

Oven Temp

Serves

Topic: **Trust and Affirmation**

Bible Verse for Study

"Sovereign LORD, you are God! Your covenant is trustworthy, and you have promised these **good things** to your servant."

2 Samuel 7:28

PERSONALITY SURVEY

Take a step back in time. Remember teen magazines? If so, you might have also encountered the "personality quizzes" in them, sporting topics such as "What is your love quotient?" "How likable are you?" or "What are your chances for success?" (And much more).

Long before the invention of the personal computer or cell phones, teen magazines were the rage. If you wanted to "discover who you were," all you had to do was turn to the latest personality quiz.

When I was thirteen, I became addicted to these surveys. What would it say about me? How did I fit into the world? I wanted to know.

One day in Home Economics, a classmate, Debbie, sat beside me and said, "If you'd speak up, you'd be popular." Debbie was outgoing, popular, and talkative, unlike me. I was shy and had a hard time speaking in front of people. I would never be like her—or the others.

By the end of seventh grade, we were expected to meet with our counselor to plan for high school. I'd come across a personality survey about occupational choices that matched my interest in teaching and nursing.

Nervous and shy, I met with my counselor and told him about my interests. Instead of receiving an encouraging word, he stared at me and replied, "Oh, come on, be realistic." He didn't think I had what it would take, which caused me to question everything

I believed about myself.

My mother did her best to console me. "Have faith," she said. I *did* have faith in God, but that wasn't the problem. I needed confidence.

I turned to personality surveys for moral support, looking for positive affirmations. I hoped to find something "good" about myself each time I completed one. Then, I would retake the survey two or three times to get better results.

By the time I got to high school, I thought I'd have myself figured out. But I didn't. In college, I reflected on the time I'd spent on the surveys. Finally, I concluded that I was looking for affirmation in all the wrong places. I was looking outward. Instead, I should have been looking *upward*—to God. As I later learned, I'd need to say goodbye to my inadequacies and hand them to the Lord.

I was determined to find what I needed by studying the Bible. And as I did so, I became very interested in the people who lived in those times. I was especially intrigued by shepherd, servant, harp-playing King David. He wasn't exactly perfect. And neither was I.

David's prayer from 2 Samuel 7:18 begins, *"Who am I, Sovereign LORD, and what is my family, that you have brought me this far?"* The words stuck. I felt a kinship with David. He wasn't a show-off kind of guy. He was humble and subservient despite holding the title of king.

The verse provides a glimpse of who David was and indicates the characteristics of his faith. Putting these things together describes what I like to call David's *"faith personality."*

A *faith* personality. Has anyone heard of such a thing? I hadn't— and I was a self-professed queen of personality surveys.

So, what do we know about David? We can only assume the color of his eyes or hair, the appearance of his clothing, or the sound of his voice as he sang praise to God on his harp. But, as we look closely at the words of his prayer in 2 Samuel 7:28, we get a glimpse of his "faith personality." He wrote, "*Sovereign LORD, you are God! Your covenant is trustworthy, and you have promised these good things to your servant.*"

From this prayer, seven attributes of David's faith become apparent. We'll call these:

Seven Faith Personality Characteristics of David

1) David Acknowledged God
In the first sentence of the prayer from 2 Samuel 7:28, David said, "*Sovereign Lord, you are God!*" He acknowledged God's sovereignty, power, supreme rule, and authority.

2) David Had Confidence in God
In the same verse, David didn't say he *thought* the Lord was God but adamantly exclaimed, "You are God!" He had no doubts about this. His words reveal this certainty as "God-confidence."

3) David Depended on God
David looked to God's leadership for guidance. As a result, he frequently communicated with the Lord through prayer and heartfelt supplication.

Early on, David proved God was steadfast. Whatever task the Lord provided for him, whether shepherding flocks of sheep, soothing the frayed nerves of King Saul on the harp, or ruling over the land of Israel, David knew he could rely on the Almighty for guidance.

4) David Trusted God
David believed the words of the Lord were true (2 Samuel 7:28), when he wrote, "*Your covenant is trustworthy.*" He was also aware of God's provision, saying, "*...you have promised these good things to your servant.*" He was confident God would provide him with good things through his faithful service.

5) David Praised God
In 2 Samuel 7:28, David glorifies God through prayer. Such

exultations appear in many of his writings.

6) David Sought Forgiveness

David had first-hand experience with sin and forgiveness. He had intended to be honorable, obedient, and subservient to God, but temptation struck.

Instead of doing things God's way, David took things into his own hands. His misdeeds got him into a lot of trouble. Afterward, gravely sorry for his sin, he begged for forgiveness. God listened to his plea and forgave him.

7) David Was a Humble Servant

David was not outwardly arrogant or boastful. On the contrary, his humble nature was evident throughout his servanthood. His integrity, humility, and compassion made him great in God's eyes.

We are well-acquainted with the word *servant*. In worldly fashion, one might think of a maid or butler. However, through the eyes of faith, a servant is part of a ministry, where one actively performs a deed or task unselfishly to help others.

To serve God requires obedience but also includes praise and worship. David's acts of serving included both. He was obedient (most of the time), and he routinely worshiped God.

When we look at *serving* in this manner, we note that David served God first. This equiped him to serve others according to God's will.

David dutifully carried out what was expected of him, whether as a shepherd boy, harpist, composer of psalms, or king. Obedience and worship were an integral part of his "faith personality."

After considering David's faith personality, I applied the concept to myself. (You already know I love personality surveys.) But truthfully, God had the answers I needed. I no longer had to rely on the world's definition for my identity. Instead, I "surveyed" the status of my faith. You can do the same.

The "Faith Personality Survey" is available on the following pages. It is based on the attributes of David's faith characteristics found in today's Bible verse from 2 Samuel 7:28.

The Faith Personality Survey:

Do I acknowledge God?

Do I have confidence in God?

Do I depend on God?

Do I trust God?

Do I praise God?

Do I seek God's forgiveness?

Do I strive to be a humble servant?

(This survey is combined with the personal reflection questions below.)

Worksheet for My Daily Morsel #26

Personal Insight:

Before reading today's lesson, how would you have defined "to serve"?

_____

_____

_____

_____

How would you describe your role as a servant?

_____

_____

_____

_____

Reflection: My "One Good Thing"

Just as we gleaned faith personality characteristics of David's, think of four characteristics that describe your Faith Personality. They could be like David's—or different. List in order of relevance (#1 being the most prominent):

1_____   3_____

2_____   4_____

What is your strongest faith personality characteristic? What is *one good thing* that comes from this, and how have you/will you use it to serve God?

_____

_____

_____

_____

A Snapshot of Your Faith:
Imagine a picture of your faith in action. What does it look like?

_____

_____

_____

_____

_____

How satisfied are you with your faith picture? Is there anything you would change or add?

_____

_____

_____

_____

This completes the survey. May you be encouraged in your faith as you walk the path God has set for you! The remainder of the worksheet questions for this chapter follow:

Today's Serving: God's Counsel Through Trust and Affirmation
By trusting in God, we affirm His promises for the good things He desires for us. David found this to be accurate, as did the author of today's story. We don't need worldly affirmations, as they may not be true. But we can always rely on God as our source of assurance about "who we are." I can imagine Him adding, "You are mine!"

A Cupful of Reality:
Young people can be especially vulnerable while they test the waters to discover who they are. Thinking back to your younger years, how might you have counseled your former self?

A Taste of Spiritual Nourishment:
From today's verse in 2 Samuel comes a key word, *sovereign*. It's a reminder that God is in control and supreme in authority over heaven and earth. For all that takes place in your world today, may your heart and spirit be comforted, knowing God's love for you will never fail. He is ever-present.

The "Table of Optimism":
Hope resides at the Table of Optimism. What is your hope for today?

Prayer for Today:

Dear God,

Help me to discern my own "Faith Personality" characteristics. You know me better than anyone. I am so glad Your love for me is unconditional, even when I make mistakes. Thank You for giving me talents and abilities which I may share with others. May I learn to be a humble servant like David. In Jesus's name, amen.

Recipe

My Daily Morsel #27

Prep Time _____   Cook Time _____

Oven Temp _____   Serves _____

Topic: **Rejoicing**

_____

_____

_____

_____

_____

Bible Verse for Study

"Then you and the Levites and the foreigners residing among you shall rejoice in all the **good things** the LORD your God has given to you and your household."

Deuteronomy 26:11

_____

_____

_____

Mommy's Terrible, Wonderful Day

I propped my pillow against the headboard. Once. Twice. Three times. *Frustrating.* As much as I tried, I couldn't sleep. It was a day I would like to have deleted. I'd grumbled and complained and wasn't proud of my behavior. I'd been a poor example of a Christian for our two daughters.

Scenes from the day flashed in my mind. My seven and four-year-old wouldn't quit fighting, so I yelled awful things. The look on their faces made my heart sink. It was too late to take back the words. Later, the neighbor boy kicked in our screen door and broke the hood ornament on our car. If that wasn't enough, the door on the birdcage was left open, and the finches were flying all over the house.

We shooed the birds into the kitchen and back into the laundry room. Once in the laundry room, my oldest daughter retrieved her butterfly net from the closet. She, her sister, and I finally captured the poor, overexcited creatures into the net and got them back into their cage.

The doorbell rang. It was the dishwasher repairman. (My advice: never put sink detergent in your dishwasher if you run out of dishwasher detergent, especially if the dishwasher isn't working correctly.) When the repairman entered the kitchen, suds spewed from the top of the washer and all over the floor. My face turned beet red as the repairman shook his head.

After the repairman left, the girls yelled and fought over a toy. I sent them to their rooms. Frazzled by the events of the day, I

335

turned on the radio. A song with a great beat caught my attention. Then came the words: *"Don't worry...be happy."* Such timing. I wasn't in the mood to hear that. I punched the "off" button. Don't worry? Be happy? *Yeah, right.*

My husband got home late from work. Dinner was lukewarm (this was before we owned a microwave). We said grace, but I hardly felt thankful.

My seven-year-old looked up at me with piercing sea-blue eyes. "Why do you look sad, Mommy?"

Tears welled up. Before I could say anything, my daughter, in her infinite childlike wisdom, said, "Mommy, don't think about being sad. Change your mind."

I grabbed a napkin to wipe at the tears that were beginning to escape. "Oh, Honey, I know. I'll do my best." I tried to smile.

My daughter was right. I had no real reason to be sad and could change my mind. But lately, instead of being grateful, I grumbled and complained. The kids weren't the only ones who had misbehaved—add this mom to the list. I hardly felt like the mom that Jesus would want me to be.

By midnight, unable to sleep, I sat up in bed, switched on the reading light, and retrieved my Bible from the nightstand. I closed my eyes and prayed. *Please, God, help me to be a better mother. Please show me what to do.* I clutched the Bible in my hands. The Holy Spirit must have known the right moment for me to open my eyes to wherever my fingers landed on a page.

I squinted as I opened my eyes, my hand beneath a verse from Deuteronomy 26:11. Right there in black and white were the words I needed to see:

"...you shall rejoice in all the good things the LORD your God has given to you and your household."

How wrong I'd been! I'm sorry, Lord. I've neglected to be happy for the good things. I hadn't rejoiced—especially today.

I re-read the beginning of the verse, the part about rejoicing. It made me think. What had the people done—or did not do—that prompted the Lord to tell them to rejoice? Did their lives resemble mine, even though they lived in different times?

Then, I thought about human nature. Would it change over time? That was the clincher. The answer would most likely be "No."

So, the quest began. How might life in the Old Testament relate to my life today? Would there be a connection? I wasn't sure, but I wanted to know.

I laid my head on the pillow and closed my eyes. I drifted off into a surreal dreamscape where my family and I embarked on a journey into Old Testament life and times, joining Levites and foreigners in travel across a vast, harsh desert.

Would I grumble and complain—or follow God's guidance? Would I be the woman of faith that God expected me to be—and be accepting of life each day?

How bad could things be?

The virtual journey began.

—

"Come quickly!" a man in a dusty cloak called out. "Put on these linen robes, then strap on those sandals. Hurry. Then follow me!"

"Wait!" I stammered. We dressed quickly.

"You must catch up!" the bearded man replied.

We gathered as a family, dressed in similar natural fiber robes and leather sandals.

We got in line, following behind Levite men, women, and children as we climbed a rocky path.

"Watch where you place your feet," a man with long brown hair called as those in front of us stopped abruptly. "Stay back! Be quiet!" He picked up a large stick. That's when we heard the *hiss*.

I heard myself scream along with the other women and girls as the thick, dark form rose only a stone's throw from where we

JUST ONE GOOD THING

stood on the path. The snake coiled and then raised its head in our direction. The girls scattered behind me. Instinct told me to freeze in place—a moving target could provoke a strike.

We dared not move. My husband suddenly appeared. He pushed us away from the snake's striking distance with solid, swift arms. The hissing got louder. Then, we saw the blurred movement of the snake's strike within a split second. *Snap.*

The bearded man shielded us from the snake with the large stick, hurling it at just the right moment to deter the viper. He struck the snake in the head as my husband led us from danger.

My husband dripped with sweat. I wanted to offer him a cloth to wipe off with, but he said there was no time to stop now. I grasped my daughters by the hand, detouring around the dead snake's habitat and following the others up the rocky incline.

Thank you, God! I was grateful for the bearded man who saved everyone from the snake. I wanted to thank him but didn't see him in the crowd ahead.

We moved forward in the late-day sun. I adjusted my scarf, wiping the moisture from my forehead. Conflicting emotions coursed through me. I was grateful for the man who saved us from the snake. Simultaneously, I shuddered at the thought of bedding down for the night. Even in a tent, what other treachery might befall us? I was mainly concerned for our children.

After our daughters went to sleep, I lay awake. My husband whispered, "I'm going outside to talk to the other men." As he stepped out of the tent, I heard the deep voice of the man who had fended off the snake. Someone called out, "Moses!"

Moses? Was this him? The great man of faith, the leader of the Israelites? I was in awe, but at the same time, I worried. If he was in charge, how could he keep everyone safe? How could he provide for our needs or problems? There I was, grumbling and complaining again.

My husband returned to the tent. He noticed I was still awake.

"You are overthinking, aren't you, and becoming fearful."

"Yes," I said.

"I thought you were a woman of faith, are you not, my dear?"

"Y-yes," I said hesitantly. "I think so."

"You know," he said as he lay next to me, "some people doubt—and some doubt Moses."

"Oh?"

"Yes." He paused. "They are the people who are grumbling and complaining."

I felt heat rise to my cheeks. I hadn't doubted Moses but knew my guilt.

After our first few days of travel, I understood why some people doubted. I'd heard the complaints about the conditions and done some of it myself.

Travel was difficult. Not everyone had equal stamina, especially us women and the children. Most of us had blisters on our feet by dusk, and even then, our work was not done.

In no time, the seed of doubt spread throughout the camp like a burning ember. "Moses knows not what he is doing," some argued. Another said, "Look at us! We are nothing more than nomads wandering through a wasteland!" The people blamed Moses for everything that went wrong.

My husband frequently reminded me of the hardships we'd already been through. "We must be grateful," he said, "for the Lord God set us free from enslavement by the Egyptians."

Yes, God had been good to us, but still, I struggled with the weariness of travel. After a day-long journey to set up camp, I felt ready to collapse from exhaustion, but there was work to do after my husband set up the tent. Obtain water. Fix the meal. Clean up. Tend to the children. Prepare the bedding.

The girls had little time to play and bickered. As a family, we gathered in our tent upon waking and at bedtime for prayer. We needed to be grateful for what we had but were exhausted and downhearted. Would this incessant travel ever end? We were always on the move. It was hard to recuperate when we constantly moved from one camp to another.

How long was this going to go on? How much more could we bear?

Then, I squinted, barely opening my eyes to the morning light. Bewildered, I looked about to get my bearings. Pillows were propped behind me, and blankets warmed me. I was safe. I wasn't lying on a makeshift mat on the floor. I was *home*—in my own bed. I let out an audible sigh. Thank heavens the scenario was only a dream—but, oh, such a real one.

I gathered a smile. *Thank you, God. You showed me what I needed to see.*

The sun peeked through the curtains. Today would be a new day. Quick. Get up. There is much to do. Make sure the girls are getting ready for school. Fix breakfast—pack lunches. Pull clothes out of the dryer. Load the dishwasher (with the correct detergent).

It was a typical morning as we hurried to prepare for work and school. But today, I looked at my life from a new perspective. I rounded up the family long enough for a quick breakfast at the table—instead of each eating on the run.

"I know you're in a hurry," I said, "but we need to pray and sit at the table together, even if just for a few minutes."

We sat at the table and bowed our heads.

"Thank you, God. We are indebted to you for your guidance and rejoice in this new day. Amen."

My husband looked over at me with a sly smile.

"No more grumbling?"

I raised my eyebrows.

"No more grumbling," I smiled.

My seven-year-old had the last word.

"See, Mommy? I was right. You *can* be happy! A grin erupted from her pink, freckled cheeks.

The four-year-old giggled, jam spread across her lips.

It was going to be a *good* day. I made up my mind to rejoice and not worry. In part, I had the Israelites to thank for that.

And that's *one good thing*.

Worksheet for My Daily Morsel #27

Personal Insight:
Think of a situation when you grumbled, complained, doubted, or looked for a "self-help" solution instead of looking to God for direction. What happened, and what were the results?

_____

_____

_____

_____

_____

Reflection: My "One Good Thing"
Looking at God's instruction in Deuteronomy 26:11 to rejoice in the good things He provides, how do you rejoice for what God has given you?

_____

_____

_____

_____

_____

Today's Serving: From Grumbling to Rejoicing
Anyone who cares for children knows that some days can be challenging. It's easy to whine or complain. In today's fictionalized incident, the author and her family grumbled, just as many Israelites did. Yet, God reminded His people to rejoice, and He wants us to do the same.

A Cupful of Reality:
If you are a caretaker of children or someone who oversees others, how do you think God's instruction might turn "grumbling" into a positive learning experience on a difficult day?

_____

_____

_____

_____

_____

_____

_____

A Taste of Spiritual Nourishment:

From today's verse in Deuteronomy comes a key word, *rejoice*. Remember the lollipops that came out years ago that were so large you thought they'd last forever? We felt such excitement to receive that sugar-laden treat. When our hearts are grateful to God, we have the kind of joy that doesn't run out like a day-long lollipop!

The "Table of Optimism":

Hope resides at the Table of Optimism. What is your hope for today?

_____

_____

_____

_____

_____

Prayer for Today:

Dear heavenly Father,

Remind me that You are in charge when I try to control my own destiny. When my journey is rough, and doubts creep in, assure me You are at my side. Sometimes, my prayer requests aren't answered how I expect them to be. But I know that what You desire for me will always be good. In Jesus's name, amen.

Recipe

My Daily Morsel #28

Prep Time

Cook Time

Oven Temp

Serves

Topic: **Seeking God**

_____

_____

_____

_____

_____

Bible Verse for Study

"The lions may grow weak and hungry, but those who seek
the LORD lack no **good thing**."

Psalm 34:10

THE LION CALLS

My daughter peered through the iron gate. "I can't see the lion, Mommy!"

I lifted her tiny body just enough so that she could see over the heavily barred retaining wall. The lion came out of its cave, pacing across a rocky ledge. It stopped abruptly, then turned in our direction with an icy stare. My daughter's eyes widened with nervous excitement as the lion stepped off the ledge and walked toward us.

"Mommy! The lion's coming!" My daughter wriggled out of my arms and hid behind me, gripping my pant leg.

"It's okay, Honey. Don't be afraid." I reached back and stroked her sandy hair. "You're safe with me. The iron bars protect us. See?" I tapped my fist against the iron-clad wall. "It's solid and firm. It keeps the lion from escaping, and it protects the lion's home, too."

My inquisitive three-year-old was not convinced as she crouched behind me.

A crowd gathered.

"The lion looks mean, Mommy!" My daughter made a growling sound as if to offer a defense against the mighty beast. She pulled at my hand. She'd had enough.

"No more lion, Mommy!"

I grabbed her hand as we stepped away from the exhibit. At such a young age, she was already acquainted with fear. Her reaction to the lion was instinctive but also partly learned. Children's books, stories, and movies portrayed the lion as a scary beast, dominating other animals in its environment.

My daughter's fearful reaction incited me to reflect on my own fears. As an adult, I admit the lion also evoked a fear response in me. I'd had experience with those emotions, but these feelings were new for my daughter.

I could protect my daughter from the lion, but how could I protect her from fear? Or could I? She was afraid of the lion but was scared of other things, too: the dark, monsters, spiders, ghosts, and shadows in her room at night. Her life was just beginning. Would she fall prey to fear as I had? Would it become an obstacle that would keep her from fulfilling her dreams, as it had done to me? I prayed this would not be the case.

Fear—the very word has the propensity to keep our thoughts chained, to keep our minds imprisoned, like a caged lion, unable to escape. Would my daughter find the saving grace that would protect her from such things? I didn't want her fears to imprison her like my own fears had imprisoned me.

My daughter couldn't get the lion out of her mind all day. "Will it get out and come after me?" she worried. I reassured her it couldn't escape through the heavy iron bars, but she wasn't convinced.

I prayed she would outgrow her fear. But, as a mom who tended to be a worrywart, would she be able to keep the "lions" at bay later in life? Would she learn that "lions" didn't have to cloud her thinking as they had mine? It was a battle I'd personally fought most of my life.

But God's message tells us not to fear. Many Bible verses serve as a reminder not to be afraid. (If you look up "Fear" in a Bible concordance, you will see numerous verses.)

Here are a few verses about not fearing:

"The LORD is my light and my salvation—whom shall I fear? The LORD is the stronghold of my life—of whom shall I be afraid?" (Psalm 27:1–2)

"So do not fear, for I am with you; do not be dismayed, for I am your God." (Isaiah 41:10)

"There is no fear in love. But perfect love drives out fear, because fear has to do with punishment. The one who fears is not made perfect in love." (1 John 4:18)

God's message is straightforward. He doesn't suggest that we not fear but commands us not to fear (see Isaiah 41:10).

I thought about the advice I gave my daughter: "Don't be afraid" and "I'm right here!" My wisdom was not enough consolation for her. She had difficulty going to sleep, so I laid beside her, stroked her hair, and sang to her until she closed her sleepy eyes and drifted off.

Fear of the unknown had gripped my own life. My challenge was to trust God enough to erase doubt from my vocabulary. After all, if I let fear linger inside me, how could I expect my daughter to do differently?

Lions had clouded my thinking for a long time, trying to crowd out the place where the Lamb of God resided within me. I'd neglected to trust God fully. How long would I continue to let the lions call?

Oh, those *lions*! I'd have to hold on tight to the iron gate of faith. It would hold me up to see over the lions that prowled to occupy a space within.

I knew what I needed to do, and I wanted to teach my daughter to do the same. It was time to put up our stronghold—the iron bars of faith.

Lions. David knew them well. He had his own story about fighting "lions." He succeeded in taking down Goliath with a simple stone as a slingshot. He killed a bear and a lion to rescue sheep being attacked. David declared the Lord delivered him from the lion's paw and the bear, and He'd delivered him from Goliath, the

Philistine giant.

David faced other "lions," too. King Saul became jealous of David and sought to kill him. Fearing for his life, David ran away to the City of Gath, where King Abimelech reigned. When he discovered this king did not have his best interest in mind, he knew his life was in danger. So, he pretended to be insane to avoid harm.

Noticing David's strange behavior, King Abimelech sent him away. David fled to a cave where refugees gathered. Times in Judah were difficult, not only for David but also for others who feared for their lives.

Fear drove David to act differently. It can affect us in this way, too, although hopefully not to the extent it affected David.

In Psalm 34:10, David writes about lions, saying, "*The lions may grow weak and hungry, but those who seek the LORD lack no good thing.*"

Yet, whoever hears of a weak lion? It's not what comes to mind when we think of the powerfully dominant animal that presides over God's other creatures. But, whether human or animal, no living being is immune to weakness, including the lion.

It's easy to visualize a hungry lion on the prowl, awaiting its next unwary victim. But a *weak* lion is the opposite of what we are taught to believe. So, our curiosity piques. Why did David refer to a weak and hungry lion? Was it because he realized that trusting God would dispel his fear of the "lions" in his life and render these lions as weak compared to God?

The lions also refer to the enemy. In David's day, Goliath, Saul, and King Abimelech tried to kill him. They may have been strong and mighty, but they were not immune to weakness. Using a simple slingshot, David took down the Philistine giant, Goliath.

David's method of dealing with the "lions" came from his faith, trust, and dependence on God. The Lord delivered and protected him from a real-life lion and other tumultuous, fear-inducing situations.

In the first ten verses of Psalm 34, David prayed when his life was threatened. "*I sought the* LORD, *and he answered me; he delivered me from all my fears*" (Psalm 34:4).

There is much we can learn from David. First, he wanted our attention (Psalm 34:11) when he wrote, "*Come, my children, listen to me; I will teach you the fear of the* LORD." As one with authority, David wanted to show that we are to "fear" the Lord; that is, to revere God above all else by praising Him, glorifying Him, trusting Him, and obeying Him.

Other verses penned by David in the Psalms show comfort through faith:

Psalm 34:7: "*The angel of the* LORD *encamps around those who fear him, and he delivers them.*" And Psalm 34:20: "*he protects all his bones, not one of them will be broken.*"

David's ironclad faith protected him from the "lions" in his life. If he were with us today, I am confident he would want to remind us of the *good things* in store for those who seek the Lord.

My little girl eventually conquered her fear of the lion at the zoo. As she grew up, she dispelled the fear of the other "lions" that came to prey upon her and put her trust in God.

Whenever the lions roar, I think of God's instruction—not to be afraid. I'd said those words to my daughter that fateful day at the zoo. Just as she had looked up to me for protection, God desires for us to look to Him for help. He wants us to know He is there for us.

And that's *one good thing*.

Worksheet for My Daily Morsel #28

Personal Insight:
What "lions" have come to call in your life because of fear?

_____

_____

_____

_____

Were you able to resolve your fears, and if so, how?

_____

_____

_____

_____

Reflection: My "One Good Thing"
Think of one fear you have conquered. What is "one good thing" you learned from it?

_____

_____

_____

_____

_____

How has God helped you grow through a concerning or worrisome situation?

_____

_____

_____

_____

Today's Serving: God's Counsel Through Seeking Him
"Lions" cloud our thinking. The little girl in today's story feared the lion would escape its cage and come after her. Oh, those lions! David fought them off both physically and figuratively. Psalm 34:4 shows that he sought God's help and was delivered from his fears. *Lions*. We all have them—but we also have a God who is more powerful than any beast that crosses our path.

A Cupful of Reality:
We desire to live a life of goodness; unfortunately, negative influences, such as fear, can interrupt our intention to focus on good things.

What positive things could you do to avert a negative thought or influence?

_____

_____

_____

A Taste of Spiritual Nourishment:
From today's verse in Psalms comes a key word, *seek*.

"Help me find the onion soup mix, will you?" my husband asked. We had just restocked a new pantry. It took time to find everything.

To look for something is different than seeking something. If we look for a food item in the cupboard and can't find it, we add it to the shopping list or go to the store to buy it.

To *seek* is an earnest desire to find something, such as seeking peace, forgiveness, or an answer to prayer.

Thanks be to God—for when we seek Him, He is already in our midst! What is one thing you have been seeking?

_____

_____

_____

The "Table of Optimism":
Hope resides at the Table of Optimism. What is your hope for today?

_____

_____

_____

Prayer for Today:
Dear Father in heaven:

You know my limitations. Sometimes, I am burdened by fear and worry, even when I do my best to trust in You. I pray for strength, Lord, and courage like David did when facing the lions that crossed his path. When I call out for help, You hear my prayers. Thank You for being the Lord of my life, my Savior, Helper, and Redeemer. In Jesus's name, amen.

Part Four: God as Master Counselor

Recap of Morsels #22-#28

Congratulations! You have just completed the Daily Morsels in Part Four—God as Master Counselor—and the final pages of this book! Now that you have read the stories, completed the worksheets, and your *One Good Thing* journal entries, take a few moments to answer the following questions to evaluate your progress through Part Four:

1. What insight did you gain from the stories?

_____

_____

_____

_____

2. In what way(s) have you been encouraged to be optimistic?

_____

_____

_____

3. How have the Bible verses about "good things" applied to you? Give an example.

_____

_____

_____

_____

4. Which stories did you favor, and why?

_____

_____

_____

_____

5. How did you do with your "One Good Thing" journal entries? If you kept up, good job! If you've missed a few, you know not to worry, for you have put "good things" to work and made progress! Fill in missed entries if possible.

Now that you have finished this book, you have the option to continue using the journal pages. It may have become a habit; if so, that's a *good thing*! The entries will create a record of many *good things* for you to look back on in the future.

6. Using the following scale, how would you rate your spiritual optimism now?

(zero = none; ten = 100%)

> 0   1   2   3   4   5   6   7   8   9   1 0

7. Compare your results: Look at your scores from Chapter Two and each recap and record them in the spaces below:

Chapter Two: ___

Recap One: ___

Recap Two: ___

Recap Three: ___

Recap Four: ___

What do you think about your results?

Is there anything you would have changed?

----

8. Now that you have finished the book, how do you feel about your ability to avert negative thoughts and focus on positive ones?

----

9. How did you do with the goals you set? Were you able to meet them, or would you do something differently?

_____
_____
_____
_____

10. What have you learned on your journey through *Just One Good Thing (A Faith-Inspired Recipe for Optimism)*?

_____
_____
_____
_____

11. Check any of the following which were most helpful to you in building spiritual optimism:

Daily Morsel Stories ___

Worksheets ___

Bible Verses ___

Prayers ___

"One Good Thing" Journal ___

Your thoughts:
12. Which stories in the book were most helpful—or inspirational—for you?

_____
_____
_____
_____

13. If you consistently kept up with the *"One Good Thing"* Journal, did the journaling help you to develop a habit of thinking positively?

_____
_____
_____
_____

14. Do you foresee continuing to use the journal daily or as needed?

_____

_____

_____

_____

15. What one thing stands out for you after reading this book?

_____

_____

_____

_____

16. Visualize sitting at God's Table of Optimism. How has God's goodness and Word led you to experience the *good things* He wants for you, such as joy, peace, or hope?

_____

_____

_____

_____

Standing in God's proverbial "kitchen," you put the Master's Recipe for living to use as you sought a faith-inspired answer to optimism. Congratulations on becoming a "Purveyor of God's Goodness!"

A Final Note

Dear Reader,

Congratulations to you on completing this book! Thank you for choosing *Just One Good Thing (A Faith-Inspired Recipe for Optimism)*. I pray you gained insight into the *good things* our Lord, the *Good Shepherd*, has in store for you. My hope is that you discovered—and will continue to discover—a renewed faith outlook each day.

I would love to hear about your journey using this book. Feel free to leave comments on my contact page at OneGoodThingGod. com.

May you always know the *good things* God desires for you!
In Christ,

Nancy Pelander Johnson

"One Good Thing" - Journal Page

Week: _____

Monday:

Tuesday:

Wednesday:

Thursday:

Friday:

Saturday:

_____

_____

_____

_____

Sunday:

_____

_____

_____

_____

Index to "My Daily Morsel" Bible Verses

My Daily Morsel	Bible Verses	Topic
1. Grandmother Olafsson's Gift	Ecclesiastes 7:11	Wisdom
2. Let Me Count the Ways	Isaiah 63:7	God's Compassion/ Kindness
3. Mayhem for Thanksgiving	1 Chronicles 17:26	God's Promises
4. The Perilous Wallow Fire	Lamentations 3:38	God Rules
5. Oh, No, Not Edna!	Luke 6:45	God's Goodness
6. Your Shadow— A Glimpse of You	Hebrews 10:1	God's Sacrifice
7. Disaster in Aisle Five	Psalm 84:11	God's Favor
8. A Diet Unintended	Psalm 107:9	Spiritual Thirst/ Hunger
9. DJ's Rescue	Exodus 18:9	God's Rescue
10. The Worst Best Christmas Ever	Psalm 103:1–5	Fulfillment and Renewal
11. An Unforgettable Vacation	Proverbs 12:14	Goodness and Renewal
12. Joy Ride	2 Chronicles 7:10	Joy and Kindness
13. "Way to Go, Jerry!"	Jeremiah 33:9	Peace, Prosperity, Provision
14. Taking the Right Path	Psalm 104:28	Having a Great Need

My Daily Morsel	Bible Verses	Topic
15. For Rent Only	Deuteronomy 6:10–12	Do Not Forget the Lord
16. An Honest Mistake	Judges 8:33–35	Staying Close to God
17. A Dirt Road to Destruction—and Salvation	Ezra 9:12	Overstepping Boundaries
18. Lost in Freedom	Nehemiah 9:36–37	The Captivity of Sin
19. We Had It All	Luke 12:16–21	Greed, Provision
20. Seeing the Big Picture	Genesis 24:10	Obedience
21. Knowing It All	Matthew 19:16–17	Keeping God's Commandments
22. Lonnie—Nice Enough	Philemon 1:6	Sharing Faith
23. Give Me Shelter	Numbers 10:32	Sharing in the Community
24. Classroom Jitters: Day One	Galatians 6:6	Sharing in the Word
25. Becca's Connection	Psalm 16:2	Nothing without God
26. Personality Survey	2 Samuel 7:28	Trust and Affirmation
27. Mommy's Terrible, Wonderful Day	Deuteronomy 26:11	Rejoicing
28. The Lion Calls	Psalm 34:10	Seeking God

WALKING HAND IN HAND AS CHRIST'S LOVE
transforms lives

MEETING THE
DEEPEST NEEDS

WE BELIEVE THE GOSPEL IS TRANSFORMATIVE
And you can change the world one child at a time.

Thousands of children in the world are born into a cycle of poverty that has been around for generations, leaving them without hope for a safe and secure future. For a little more than $1 a day you can provide the tools a child needs to break the cycle in the name of Jesus.

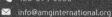

Made in the USA
Monee, IL
26 April 2024

57450711R00215